Phineas Stowe

Ocean Melodies, and Seamen's Companion

A collection of hymns and music: for the use of Bethels, chaplains of the Navy, and

private devotion of mariners. Twelfth Edition

Phineas Stowe

Ocean Melodies, and Seamen's Companion
A collection of hymns and music: for the use of Bethels, chaplains of the Navy, and private devotion of mariners. Twelfth Edition

ISBN/EAN: 9783337318123

Printed in Europe, USA, Canada, Australia, Japan

Cover: Foto ©Thomas Meinert / pixelio.de

More available books at **www.hansebooks.com**

OCEAN MELODIES,

AND

SEAMEN'S COMPANION

A COLLECTION OF

HYMNS AND MUSIC;

FOR THE USE OF BETHELS, CHAPLAINS OF THE NAVY,

AND PRIVATE DEVOTION OF MARINERS.

By PHINEAS STOWE,
PASTOR OF THE FIRST BAPTIST BETHEL CHURCH.

"While mighty ocean
Rolled the wild, profound, eternal bass
In nature's anthem, and made music,
Such as pleased the ear of God."—POLLOK.

TWELFTH EDITION.

BOSTON:
PUBLISHED BY PHINEAS STOWE,
NO. 8 BALDWIN PLACE
1866.

PREFACE.

The design of the Melodies is two-fold:—To counteract the demorolizing tendency of productions claiming to be poetry and music, and to furnish such as will interest the mariner and awaken the better feelings of his nature. Of the influence of that which has already been scattered broadcast upon our wharves, or in our forecastles, there can be but little doubt, in the minds of such as have observed carefully the results. No one, it is presumed, can question the utility of anything which will eject such pernicious *trash* from our vessels, and substitute a collection which will call up remembrances of home, and such as will lead seamen to recognize God's power, and hear his voice when tempests rage and thunders roar.

It affords us much pleasure and satisfaction in supplying seamen and their friends, with a large collection of original hymns and familiar tunes, from those who are desirous of promoting the temporal and spiritual welfare of the sailor. A number of descriptive pieces of poetry have been introduced in the Melodies, and it is presumed they will not give offence, but be read with interest.

We are fully persuaded that every generous-minded person will pardon all blemishes, and appreciate whatever is truly valuable in this humble effort to provide melody for the long neglected sailor. As there are no competitors in this vast ocean-field, we anticipate a favorable reception for the first book of the kind ever published, with so large a number of hymns and familiar tunes.

The significant appellation of "Jack" and "Tar," so frequently but inappropriately and injuriously applied to sailors, with other common nautical expressions, are excluded from the Melodies, as they are *very offensive* to *all* intelligent mariners, whenever employed in prose or poetry. A Burial Service has been introduced, and is regarded as a very important accompaniment of the Melodies.

Confident are we that all evangelical denominations and all who love the worthy mariner, will rejoice at the appearance of the Melodies; but especially those who have friends on the "great and wide sea."

Entered according to Act of Congress, in the year 1849, by PHINEAS STOWE, in the Clerk's Office of the District Court, for the District of Mass.

INDEX OF FIRST LINES.

First Line	Page
A bright unfading crown	23
A cheering ray of hope	184
A cry fills all the air	160
Again thou leav'st thy	203
A hardy mariner	100
All kinds of beasts and	137
Amazing sight! the	146
Am I a soldier of the	96
A mother's yearning heart	205
And didst thou Jesus	97
And is thy lovely shadow	138
And will the Judge	91
And wilt thou stoop great	139
Another day is past	40
A poor wayfaring man	15
Appear for my defence	130
Are there tidings in yon	58
As flows the rapid river	45
Asleep in Jesus! Oh how	109
As onward speeds the	25
Author of the mighty	161
A wail comes o'er the breeze	180
A wail comes o'er the wave	30
Awake, my soul, stretch	107
Band of soldiers of	177
Bear, oh bear the gospel	36
Behold, behold the lamb	155
Behold that stately ship	91
Behold the spirit from	108
Behold the throne of	134
Behold upon the raging	23
Benighted on the troublous	9
Beset with snares on	125
Blessed be that voice	113
Blessed Saviour! we adore	74
Blessed Saviour! we will	204
Blest are the sons of	135
Blest be the tie that binds	167
Blest is the man who	166
Borne o'er the ocean's	107
Bow down my spirit and	89
Bright was the guiding	107
Broad is the road that	149
Buried in shadows of	149
Burn the ships, I'm	177
Bury me, bury me quick	206
But as they sailed	37
Change comes with	139
Child of the sea! hast	17
Christian heralds like	119
Cling to the Mighty One	181
Closer, nearer, brother	157
Come, blessed Spirit	146
Come, brothers, launch	209
Come, gracious Spirit	146
Come, Holy Spirit	147
Come, let us now forget	129
Come, Lord, and warm	113
Come, sailor, come with	95
Come, sailor, fly to Jesus	169
Come, saith Jesus' sacred	77
Come, sinner, at our	132
Come, sinner, to the gospel	150
Come, thou Fount of	72
Come, thou soul transforming	75
Come, weary souls with	150
Come, we that love the	33
Come, ye who love the	139
Dark and fearful clouds	43
Dear Saviour, hear our	128
Dear Saviour, teach our	81
Dear to me the sacred hour	179
Death cannot make our	138
Death has been here,	129
Deathless spirit, now	76
Deceitful is the breeze	164
Deep are the wounds	133
Deep, fiery clouds o'ercast	22
Deep in the watery	163
Delay not, delay not	153
Did Christ o'er sinners	135
Do we not know that	151
Down to the sacred	152
Down to unfathomed	143
Earth glorious wakes	13
Earthly pleasures what	169
Earth sleeps with all her	13
Eternal Spirit, we confess	147
Faith is a precious grace,	101
Faith is a spy-glass for	84
Far, far from childhood's	100
Father of mercies, in thy	145
Father, the storm is loud	31
Father, 'tis right, I clasped	139
Fearful lightnings break	77
Fear was in the tossing	188
Fierce was the storm that	67
Flag of the pure and	115
Float gently on, thou	11
From every stormy wind	149
From many a noble	56
From whence doth this	128
Full flowed Bethesda's	186
Give me the wings of faith	106
Give thanks to God most	71
Glory be to God the Father,	179
God gave the gift to man	41
God is love, his mercy	72
God is my strong salvation	79
God is the seaman's friend	35
God moves in a mysterious	99
God of Creation, Lord of	82
God of heaven, earth	74
God of mercy, hear the	170
God of my life, through	137
God of the boundless	176
God of the boundless rolling	206
God of the earth and	99
God of the ever rolling	25
God of the land and	27
God of the mariner	201
God of the mighty rolling	211
God of the seas, thy	14
God's moral lights, his	94
God's voice is heard	95
Go speak of Jesus' dying	145
Go speak to that poor	45
Go when the morning	78
Go, ye messengers of God	111
Grace, 'tis a charming sound	69
Gracious Saviour, we	152
Great God, at thy command	68
Great God, Eternal King	32
Great God! in safety keep	179
Great God! may seamen	109
Great God! we will thy name	65
Great Universal Lord	24

INDEX OF FIRST LINES.

Hail, everlasting Spring!	70
Hail to the precious Sabbath	87
Hardy seamen, listen	119
Hark! hark! the notes of	79
Hark! that shout of	111
Hark! the bell! the hour of	110
Hark! the notes of angels	156
Hark! upon the midnight	87
Haste, O sinner! now be	105
Hear! dwellers on the	92
Hear, O sinner! mercy	145
Hear what the voice from	144
Here in this lonely, humble	24
He dies! the friend of	10
He tempts once more the	27
He that in vent'rous barks	20
Ho! every one that thirsteth	11
Holy Bible, blessed treasure	119
Holy source of consolation	73
Home for the wanderer	204
How are thy servants blest	67
How beautiful the setting	39
How blest the righteous	85
How changed the vision	96
How happy is the child	120
How long shall virtue	41
How oft have sin and	95
How softly on the bruised	189
How sweet is that home	123
How sweet on thy bosom	128
How sweet the songs of	19
How swift, alas! the	93
How vain is all beneath	133
Humble souls, who seek	141
If on a quiet sea	90
If Paul in Cæsar's court	86
I heard a voice from	31
I love my Bible,—precious	67
I love thy kingdom, Lord,	33
I love the sparkling sea	204
I'm a pilgrim, and I'm	171
I'm bound upon the sea	29
I'm weary of sighing	172
In evil long I took delight	155
Inscribed upon the cross	103
In the cross of Christ I	151
In the furnace God doth	175
In the tempest of life	55
I send the joys of earth	85
Is this the kind return?	134
I think of thee, mother,	60
It is not in the parting hour	208
It was a fearful night!	202
I've launched upon the sea	17
I would not live alway;	172
Jesus, and shall it ever be!	132
Jesus, at thy command,	125
Jesus! delightful, charming	106
Jesus demands this heart	136
Jesus, I look to thee alone	210
Jesus, I love thy charming	126
Jesus is gone above the	140
Jesus, our anchor firm,	165
Jesus, refuge of my soul,	195
Jesus, thy boundless love	132
Just as thou art—without	154
Just launched upon the	45
Kindred, and friends, and	174
Laborers of Christ, arise,	53
Land ahead! its fruits are	152
Launched on blue ocean's	193
Let all the heathen writers	148
Let me go; my soul is	43
Let our united voices rise,	13
Let party names no more	40
Let us awake our joys;	81
Let worldly men, from	148
Light, love and joy are	207
Like Israel, Lord am I;	131
Like morning, when her	109
Like sunlight playing on	168
Lo! he comes, with clouds	75
Lonely wand'rer on the	73
Look toward the sea, where	156
Look, ye saints; the sight	159
Lord, when the mists of	11
Lord, with a grieved and	137
Love is a bright and burning	12
May the grace of Christ,	51
Men vow to Him who rules	83
Merrily the temperance horn	181
Morn wakes and waves	12
Mother, mother, I must	50
My faith looks up to thee	81
My father's house on high	141
My mother! many a year	83
My soul has fixed her	129
My years roll on; the tide	94
Native land! in summer	174
Night cometh o'er the sea	29
No one on earth now cares	136
No peace! no peace! Jeho	115
Not all the outward forms	148
Not in the churchyard	116
Not yet! the flowers are in	144
Now is th' accepted time;	101
O blessed day of holy rest	66
O cease, my wandering soul,	69
O chief of all the heavenly	128
O! cold is the night wind,	207
O for a breeze of heavenly	126
O for a faith that will not	107
O for the death of those	29
O God of sailors, hear,	35
O God! thy name they	89
O honored saint! O glorious	26
O how divine! how sweet	131
O how I love thy name, my	114
O let each soul now praise	169
O Lord, our heavenly king,	90
O Lord, when billows o'er	181
O Lord, to thee we bow,	71
O place me not in sordid	87
O pray for hardy sailors,	66
O pray for the sailor now	55
O think on the sailor toss'd	121
O thou of little faith,	69
O thou, my soul, forget no	140
O thou! the high and lofty	139
O thou whose matchless	18
O when shall I see	197
O where shall rest be	135
O who can tell, that	26
O worship the King,	124
O'er raging waves, thou	187
Of old did Jesus	97
Oh! Pilot, 'tis a fearful	194
On Jordan's stormy	113
On that great, that	105
Onward, onward, men	175
Our blest Redeemer, ere	147
Our God we bow before	138
Our little bark, on	126
Our Saviour bowed	151
Out on an ocean all	196
Out on the crested surge	168
Palms of glory, raiment	110
Praise to Heaven! peace to	77
Praise to the grace which	63
Praise ye Jehovah's name	81
Praise ye the Lord! on every	88
*Prayer is the breath of	131
Prayer is the soul's sincere	131
Prayer may be sweet in	65
Pray for the sailor—pray	130
Remember me, my Saviour	116
Remember thee, redeeming	141
Rise, my soul, and stretch	127
Roll on, thou mighty ocean	47
Ruler of the earth and	37
Sailing on the boisterous	28
Sailor, enter not life's	118
Sailor, lift up thy voice,	54
Sailor, on the trackless	118
Sailor, speed thee o'er the	11
Sailor, is it well with thee?	104
Sailor, we need thee, to	85
Saints of the living God	190
Saviour, blessed should	166
Saviour, inspire us now	205
Saviour, o'er the restless	162
Saviour, on the mighty	183
Saviour, on the raging	170
Say to the storms, exhaust	21

INDEX OF FIRST LINES.

First Line	Page
Seamen, there's noble work	126
Seamen who love the	99
See daylight is fading o'er	121
See the sailor just embarking	73
Shed not a tear o'er your.	52
Shine, mighty God, on	174
Show pity, Lord; O Lord,	150
Sing, seamen, sing to God	83
Sing to the Lord most	71
Sinners, hear the mighty	119
Sinners, will you scorn	145
Sinner, what has earth	105
Sleep on, sleep on, above	143
Softly now the light of	77
Son of the ocean! stop and	27
Sow in the morn thy seed;	101
Speed, speed the temperance	41
Spirit of love and light	161
Star of peace, to wanderers	154
Star of the East, the	9
Stay, father, stay, the night	181
Stay, thou insulted Spirit,	146
Still on, still on, still on, we	142
Sweet bow of promise, thy	199
Sweet land of song, thy	202
Sweet, on the mourning	23
Tell me not in mournful	39
The bard of Israel swept	21
The Bethel is the place for	95
The Bible is a polar star	102
The billows foam: the ocean	64
The billows swell; the winds	102
The blessed Spirit, like the	147
The boundless power of God	68
The Christian sailor fears	166
The Christian voyager	82
The Cross is my anchor,	123
The Father will protect and	26
The glorious gospel now	115
The glorious morning dawns	28
The gospel ship along is	167
The gospel ship's a gallant	142
The heavens declare thy	9
The Light-ship! how welcome	54
The Lord is our shepherd,	122
The Lord our God is clothed	86
The man is ever blest	134
The morning light is	127
The night was dark and	48
The noble ship glides	200
The pity of the Lord	91
The purple gems forever	143
The rolling waves of Ocean's	7
The sailor boy, how hard	103
The sailor's home is on	87
The seraphs bright are	46
The Spirit, in our hearts	101
The storm is on the deep,	31
The truths of the Bible	120
The wicked labor much	160
There is a faith, the gift of	64
There is a fountain filled	151
There is a Friend who's	95
There is a hope, a blessed	99
There is a land immortal	164
There is a land mine	133
There is a land of pure	141
There is an hour of hallowed	117
There is an hour of peaceful	154
There is a place of sacred	19
There is a pure and	109
There is a time, we know	117
There is a world of perfect	113
There is joy for our sorrows	63
There's magic power in a	198
There's not a star whose	93
They roam where danger	165
They that toil upon the	104
Though hard the winds	44
Though to the wanderer	108
Thou'rt sounding on, thou	16
Time is wafting us along	170
'Tis finished! so the Saviour	132
'Tis midnight, and on Olive's	10
Toil-worn sailor, come and	43
Tossed on the stormy sea,	80
Tossed upon life's raging	42
Tossing on a stormy sea,	37
To thee be praise forever	127
To thee, O blessed Saviour,	79
To thee. O God, whose awful	89
To thee, O God, whose just	88
'Twas on that dark, that	140
'Twas when the seas with	138
Thy kingdom come! Almighty	183
Thy neighbor? It is he whom	21
Thy works of glory, mighty	93
Upon a hill there stands a	97
Upon the waters, glorious	98
Upon the waters, glorious	114
Up to the fields where	137
Wanderer from God,	65
Wanderers o'er a stormy	73
Watchman, tell us of the	111
We are but young, yet	129
We are scattered — we are	47
We are those who wandered	209
We, cold water girls and boys	181
We come. O Lord, before	87
Weeping sinners, dry	148
We kindle here a beacon	84
Welcome, delightful morn;	71
Welcome, stranger, to the	178
We live as pilgrims and	197
We praise Thee, glorious	205
We praise Thee, matchless	211
We seek a rest beyond	112
We're travelling home to	173
We sing the Saviour's love,	91
We thank thee, Father, for	40
We trust forevermore	163
We were crowded in the	203
What fearful cry, so wild	103
What glory gilds the sacred	130
What heavenly music do I	39
What if the little rain	117
What sinners value I	153
What's this that steals,	144
When floating o'er life's	98
When I can read my	192
When I survey the	149
When launched upon	182
When marshalled on the	8
When o'er the mighty deep	21
When o'er the restless deep	69
When on the ocean's	19
When power divine in	149
When sailing on the ocean	79
When shall we all meet	173
When shall we meet	171
When thickly beat the	85
When through the torn	156
When thy trembling	178
When we pass through	153
When will rebellious	163
Where are those we	168
Where is thy home? I	24
Which is the happiest	25
While life prolongs its	136
While o'er life's troubled	112
While o'er the Adriatic	165
While o'er the angry	115
While on the swelling	92
While others on the	201
While some in folly's	109
While thee I seek,	158
Whither goest thou	43
Who can forbear to sing,	135
Will you, trembling sinner	170
With glowing heart, blest	207
With glowing hearts, great	40
With reverence let the	97
Would you behold the	24
Vital spark of heavenly	157
Ye angels, who stand	152
Ye brave sons of the main,	158
Ye chosen few of Christ	175
Ye Christian seamen, praise	130
Ye servants of God, your	125
Yes, Lord, my grateful	65
Yes! thou art gone from	25
Yes! we trust the day is	75
Your harps, ye trembling	29

INDEX OF TUNES.

America	80	Laban	28	Sailor Boy's Farewell	50
Are there Tidings	58	Lenox	34	Sailor Boy's Grave	52
Balerma	96	Lyons	124	Shirland	68
Bavaria	38	Majesty	188	Siberia	26
Bethel	46	Marlow	98	Sicily	72
Bounding Billows	42	Medfield	66	Silver Street	32
Boylston	90	Mellow Horn	186	Sorrow on the Deep	30
Cheerful Hope	44	Missionary Chant	84	St. Martin's	88
Christ in the Garden	54	Missionary Hymn	78	St. Thomas	100
Coronation	18	Morning Light	56	Sweet Home	60
Dedham	86	Newman	70	Uxbridge	94
Devizes	106	Nichols	16	Ward	10
Devotion	182	Northfield	22	Watcher	48
Duke Street	82	Nuremburg	76	Way-faring Man	14
Effingham	102	Old Hundred	7	Wells	114
Eltham	110	Peterborough	20	When I can read my	192
Greenville	118	Pilot on the Deep	194	When marshalled on	6
Hamburg	108	Pleyel's Hymn	104	Woodland	112
Hebron	12	Portugal	64	Woodstock	116
Hinton	122	Portuguese Hymn	120	Zion	74
Homeward Bound	196	Red Sea Passed	190		
Hosanna	184	Rochester	92		

OCEAN MELODIES.

THE OCEAN SPEAKS. L. M.
(*Old Hundred.*)

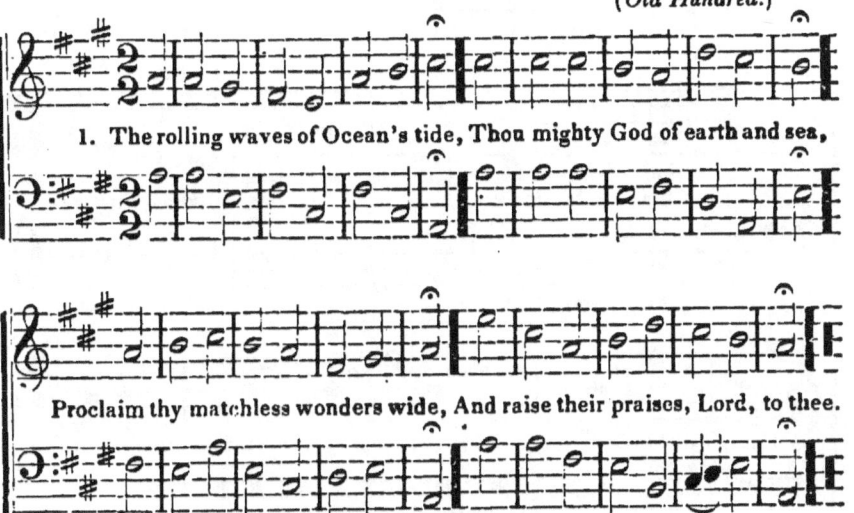

1. The rolling waves of Ocean's tide, Thou mighty God of earth and sea, Proclaim thy matchless wonders wide, And raise their praises, Lord, to thee.

Thy voice is heard in thunder's roar,—
In lightning's glare thy glories shine;
The heaving billows, towering, soar,
And ever heed thy Word divine.

8. When marshal'd on the raging main. L. M.

1. When marshal'd on the raging main, The star alone of all the train, Can fix the sailor's wandering eye, one alone, the Saviour speaks, It is the star of Beth-le-hem. Hark! hark! to God the chorus breaks, From every host, from eve-ry gem; But glittering hosts be-stud the sky, One wandering eye.

Once on the raging seas I rode,
The storm was loud, the night was dark,
The ocean yawn'd, and rudely blow'd,
The wind that toss'd my foundering bark.
Deep horror then my vitals froze;
Death-struck, I ceased the tide to stem;
When suddenly a star arose,
It was the Star of Bethlehem.

It was my guide, my light, my all,
It bade my dark foreboding cease,
And thro' the storm and danger's thrall
It led me to the port of peace.
Now safely moor'd—my perils o'er
I'll sing first in night's diadem,
Forever and forevermore,
The Star—the Star of Bethlehem

OCEAN MELODIES.

The Morning Star. L. M.
BY WM. B. TAPPAN.

Benighted on the troublous main,
　While stormy terrors clothe the sky,
The trembling voyager strives in vain,
　And nought but stern despair is nigh.
When lo! a gem of peerless light,
　With radiant splendor, shines afar;
And through the clouds of darkest night,
　Appears the Bright and Morning Star!

With joy he greets the cheering ray,
　That beams on Ocean's weary breast;
Precursor of a smiling day,
　It lulls his fears to peaceful rest.
No more in peril shall he roam,
　For night and danger now are far;
With steady helm he enters home,
　His guide the Bright and Morning Star!

Thus, when affliction's billows roll,
　And waves of sorrow and of sin
Beset the fearful, weeping soul,
　And all is dark and drear within—
'Tis Jesus, whispering strains of peace,
　Drives every doubt and fear afar;
He bids the raging tempests cease,[Star!
　And shines the Bright and Morning

Glory of God in his Works. L. M.
WATTS.

The heavens declare thy glory, Lord;
　In every star thy wisdom shines;
But when our eyes behold thy word,
　We read thy name in fairer lines.
The rolling sun, the changing light,
　And nights, and days, thy power confess;
But that blest volume thou hast writ
　Reveals thy justice and thy grace.

Sun, moon, and stars, convey thy praise
　Around the earth, and never stand,
So, when thy truth began its race,
　It touched and glanced on every land,
Nor shall thy spreading gospel rest,
　Till through the world thy truth has run,
Till Christ has all the nations blest
　That see the light or feel the sun.

Great Sun of Righteousness, arise·
　O bless the world with heavenly lig..,
Thy gospel makes the simple wise;
　Thy laws are pure, thy judgments right.
Thy noblest wonders here we view,
　In souls renewed and sins forgiven,
Lord, cleanse my sins, my soul renew,
　And make thy word my guide to heaven.

The Star of Bethlehem. L. M.
BY WM. B. TAPPAN.

Star of the East! the tempest-tost,
　On life's uncertain billows borne,
Is by rude gales of trouble crossed,
　By hidden rocks of sorrow torn—
When breaks the cheering Star of Morn,
　When night and thrall forever flee,
O, where the doubts and fears forlorn
　Of him, the wanderer of the sea?

Break out, blest Star! with peaceful ray;
　And if our steps to Truth incline,
Oh, help and guard our weeping way!
　Along these doubtful waters shine!
The heavenly beacon-light of thine
　That trembled once on Bethlehem's plain,
Shall guide us to the Source Divine,
　Shall lead us to the Child again.

10 DEATH AND RESURRECTION OF CHRIST. L. M.

Poetry by Watts. (*Ward.*)

1. He dies! the Friend of sinners dies; Lo! Salem's daughters weep a-round;
A solemn darkness veils the skies; A sudden trembling shakes the ground
2. Ye saints, approach! the anguish view Of him who groans beneath your load;
He gives his precious life for you; For you he sheds his precious blood.

Here's love and grief beyond degree;
The Lord of glory dies for men;
But, lo! what sudden joys we see!
Jesus, the dead, revives again.

The rising God forsakes the tomb;
Up to his Father's court he flies;
Cherubic legions guard him home,
And shout him welcome to the skies.

Break off your tears, ye saints, and tell
How high our great Deliverer reigns;
Sing how he spoiled the hosts of hell,
And led the tyrant Death in chains.

Say, "Live forever, glorious King,
Born to redeem, and strong to save!"
Then ask, "O Death, where is thy sting?
And where thy victory, boasting Grave?"

Christ in Gethsemane. L. M.
BY WM. B. TAPPAN.

'Tis midnight; and on Olive's brow
The star is dimmed that lately shone;
'Tis midnight; in the garden, now,
The suffering Saviour prays alone.

'Tis midnight; and, from all removed,
The Saviour wrestles lone, with fears
E'en that disciple whom he loved
Heeds not his master's grief and tears.

'Tis midnight; and for other's guilt
The man of sorrows weeps in blood;
Yet he that hath in anguish knelt
Is not forsaken by his God.

'Tis midnight; and from ether plains
Is borne the song that angels know;
Unheard by mortals are the strains
That sweetly soothe the Saviour's woe.

Trust in God. L. M.
BY REV. J. H. CLINCH.

Lord, when the mists of doubt arise,
And error's night around me lies,
May faith's sure *compass* point the way,
And guide me to the realms of day!

When strong temptation shakes my soul,
And waves of passion round me roll,
And storms of grief my heart o'erwhelm,
Stand Thou, my Saviour, at the *helm*.

When borne by sin's resistless tide,
Where dangers lurk on every side,
Lord, may Thy *anchor*, strong and sure,
My troubled soul securely moor!

And when my voyage shall cease at last,
And life's wide ocean has been passed,
O, may I reach that haven blest,
The *port* of peace and endless rest!

Sailor, Speed thee. L. M.
BY REV. D. C. EDDY.

Oh! sailor speed thee o'er the sea,
Thy home and friends are far away,
Those fervent prayers ascend for thee,
While o'er the earth thy footsteps stray.

Oh! sailor speed thee o'er the sea,
While breakers roar and billows dash;
Soon shall thy vessel anchored be,
Where not one wave the shore shall lash.

Oh! sailor speed thee o'er the sea,
The deep, dark sea of human life;
Where nought the voyager's eye can see
But gloom and terror, sin and strife.

Oh! sailor speed thee o'er the sea,
And let thy toilsome wand'ring cease;
Soon shall thy heavy spirit be
Safe anchored in the port of peace.

The Gospel Ship. L. M.

Float gently on, thou blessed bark,
Touch every land and ship-lined shore·
Shed light where teeming millions sigh,
Unfold the Gospel's sacred store.

Show from the topmast's tallest peak,
The great Redeemer's glorious name;
Display the blessed, bleeding Cross;
Its love, its agony, its shame.

Proclaim the life-restoring Word;
Pour all the energy of Prayer;
Disturb the blest baptismal Wave;
The Bread, the Wine, of Life, prepare

Arrest the thoughtless, check the rash,
Win home the wanderer from his ways;
The broken hearted bind with balm,
And fill the penitent with praise

Like clouds, that fly before the storm,
Like doves, that to their windows come,
Crowd, brothers, to the glorious Cross,
And find the Church, the Sailors' Home.

Pray, Sailor, Pray. L. M. J. H. H.

When launched upon the briny tide,
You o'er its ample bosom glide,
From home and kindred far away,
Then look above, pray, sailor, pray.

When tossed on ocean's broad domain,
The sport of danger, toil and pain,—
As borne along the watery way,
Then pause awhile, pray, sailor, pray.

When troubled depths disparted yawn,
And death's embrace is round thee drawn;
When thy pure soul would leave its clay,
O gladly soar, pray, sailor, **pray.**

12. WHAT IS LOVE? L. M.

Words by J. Rusling. (*Hebron.*)

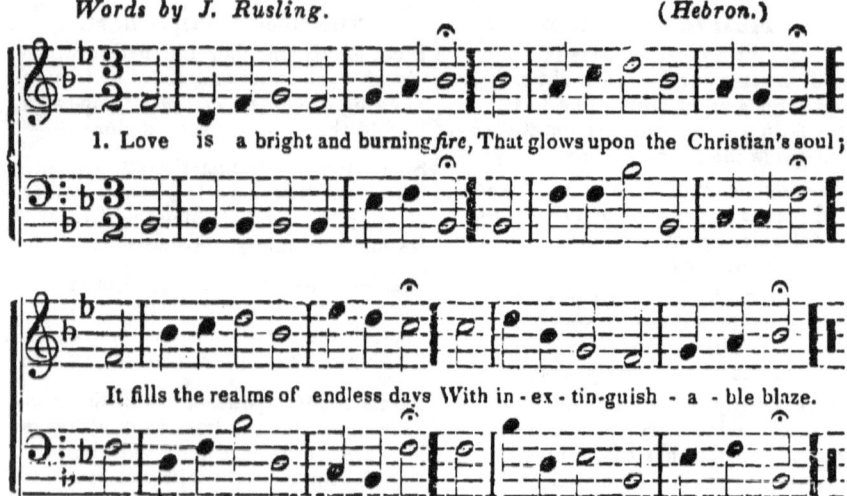

1. Love is a bright and burning *fire*, That glows upon the Christian's soul;
It fills the realms of endless days With in-ex-tin-guish-a-ble blaze.

Love is a deep expansive *sea*,
Where flow the swells of gospel grace—
Pleasures in wid'ning circles heave,
Respondent as the yielding wave.

Love is the radiant *rainbow*, seen
Suspended in the vault of heav'n;
Jesus and glory here combine,
To form a harmony divine.

Love is the grand *ecliptic* way,
Where faithful souls describe their course,
On beams of light they mount on high,
To shine meridian in the sky.

Love forms the splendors of the throne,
The glory of the courts above;
The Christian's *all* his portion this;
Heaven is his *home*, and *love* his *bliss*.

Devotion. L. M.

Morn wakes and waves her purple wing,
Bright glancing over earth and sea,
And happy forms and beauty spring
To life from rock, and stream, and tree.

The sunlit billow's glowing breast
Heaves like the bosom gushing o'er
With joy—and, shaking its proud crest,
Comes shouting onward to the shore.

Oh! at this hour, when, from above,
The light cloud o'er the mirrored deep
Comes floating from that sea of Love,
Where crystal waters ever sleep

When the glad sounds of Nature's mirth,
Are swelling o'er the deep blue sea,
My heart from all the bliss of earth,
Exulting turns great God to Thee

OCEAN MELODIES. 13

Sabbath Morning. L. M.

Earth glorious wakes, as o'er her breast
The morning flings her rosy ray,
And blushing from her dreamless rest,
Unveils her to the gaze of day.

The night-winds to their mountain caves
The morning mists to heaven's blue sleep,
And to their ocean-depths the waves,
Are gone, their holy rest to keep.

Each tree that lifts its gems in air,
Or hangs its pensive head from high,
Seems bending at its morning prayer,
Or whispering with the hours gone by.

This holy morning, Lord, is thine!
Let silence sanctify the praise;
Let heaven and earth in love combine,
And morning stars the music raise.

Sabbath Evening, L. M.

Earth sleeps, with all her glorious things
Beneath the Holy Spirit's wings,
And, rending back the hues above,
Seems resting in a *trance* of love.

Bright creatures of a better sphere
Came down at noon to worship here,
And from their sacrifice of love,
Returned to their home above.

And she for depths of earthly beam
So passing fair, we almost dream
That we can rise, and wander through
There open *path* of *trackless* blue.

May holy aspirations start,
Like blessed angels, from the heart,
And bid—when earth's dark ties are riven,
Our Spirits to the gates of heaven.

The Converted Sailor. L. M. ; H. H.

A cheering ray of hope has gleamed
Around the hardy sailor's way,
The gospel light at last has beamed,
And sheds afar the glorious ray.

On ocean's heaving billows borne,
The Christian seaman bows in prayer;
Submissive kneels before the throne,
And joys to meet his Saviour there.

Tho' winds may howl and tempests beat,
And lightnings glare, and surges roar,
He calmly bows at Jesus' feet,
Nor fears in danger's darkest hour.

O let loud songs of praise ascend
To our exalted, mighty King;
Let heaven and earth in union blend,
And every tongue in chorus sing.

The Bethel Flag. L. M.

Let our united voices rise,
The Bethel Flag streams on the air!
The herald bird has left the skies,
And bears her blessed mission here.

" Peace to the world, Jehovah's love,
Exulting souls, look up and bless,
The holy leaf, the heavenly dove,
Emblems of peace and tenderness."

Hushed nature brightens at the view;
Glad angels check their hymns to see;
Triumphant voices wake anew,
For " Sailor, there is hope for thee."

Then let loud anthems long ascend!
Shout hallelujahs to the Lord;
Landsmen, and sailors, angels, blend;
Rejoice and praise with one accord.

14 GOD'S DOMINION OVER THE SEA. L. M.
(Way-faring Man.)

1. God of the seas, thy mighty voice, Bids all the roaring waves rejoice;
At thy command they upward tend, Or quick to yawning depths descend
If but a Mo-ses wave his rod, The sea divides and owns its God;
The stormy floods their Maker knew, And let his chosen armies through.

OCEAN MELODIES. 15

The finny tribes, that sport and play,
To thee, their Lord, a tribute pay;
The humblest fish beneath the flood,
Proclaims the praise of Thee, O God,
O for a signal of thy hand!
Shake all the seas, Lord shake the land!
Great Judge, descend, lest man deny
That there's a God who rules on high.

Poor Way-faring Man. L. M.

A poor way-faring man of grief
Hath often cross'd me on my way,
Who sued so humbly for relief,
That I could never answer nay;
I had not power to ask his name,
Whither he went or whence he came;
Yet there was something in his eye,
That won my love, I knew not why.

Once when my scanty meal was spread,
He entered, not a word he spake,
Just perishing for want of bread,
I gave him all—He blest it, brake,
And ate but gave me part again,
Mine was an angel's portion then—
And while I fed with eager haste,
The crust was manna to my taste.

I spied him where a fountain burst
Clear from the rock—his strength was gone,
The heedless water mocked his thirst,
He heard it, saw it hurrying on;
I ran, and raised the sufferer up,
Thrice from the stream he drained my cup,
Dipped, and returned it running o'er,
I drank, and never thirsted more.

'Twas night. The floods were out; it blew
A wintry hurricane aloof;
I heard his voice abroad, and flew
To bid him welcome to my roof;
I warmed, I clothed, I cheered my guest,
Laid him on mine own couch to rest,
Then made the earth my bed, and seemed
In Eden's garden while I dreamed.

Stripped, wounded, beaten nigh to death
I found him by the high-way side;
I roused his pulse, brought back his breath,
Revived his spirit, and supplied
Wine, oil, refreshment, he was healed,
I had myself a wound concealed,
But from that hour forgot the smart,
And peace bound up my broken heart,

In prison I saw him next, condemned
To meet a traitor's doom at morn;
The tide of lying tongues I stemmed,
And honored him mid shame and scorn.
My friendship's utmost zeal to try,
He asked if I for him would die;
The flesh was weak, my blood ran chill,
But the free spirit cried "I will!"

Then, in a moment, to my view
The stranger started from disguise;
The tokens in his hands I knew,—
My SAVIOUR stood before my eyes!
He spake, and my poor name he named,—
"Of me thou hast not been ashamed;
These deeds shall thy memorial be,
Fear not, thou didst it unto me."

THE SOUND OF THE SEA. C. M.

Words by Mrs. Hemans. (*Nichols.*)

1. Thou'rt sounding on, thou mighty sea, For-ev-er and the same! The an-cient rocks, still ring to thee, Whose thunders nought can tame, Whose thunders nought can tame.

Oh! many a glorious voice is gone,
From the rich bow'rs of earth,
And hushed is many a lonely one,
Of mournfulness or mirth.

But thou art swelling on, thou deep,
Through many an olden clime.
Thy billowy anthem, ne'er to sleep
Until the close of time.

Thou liftest up thy solemn voice
To every wind and sky,
And all the earth's green shores rejoice
In that one harmony.

OCEAN MELODIES. 17

"Which Hope we have as an Anchor of the Soul." C. M. A. M. C.

Child of the Sea! hast thou this Hope,
  This Anchor of the soul;
Or dost thou yet desponding grope
  Where stormy billows roll?

Tossed to and fro by every blast,
  On every troubled wave;
This, this alone can hold thee fast,
  Thy bark from ruin save.

What tho' thick darkness shroud the sky,
  Robed in the tempest's wrath,
And not one burning star on high,
  Can light the watery path;

This Hope, thy Anchor, thou canst bide
  The storm's severest shock,
And slumber on the raging tide
  Firm as a mountain rock.

In wildest perils on the sea
  'Twill never, never fail,
When paleness on the cheek shall be,
  And bravest spirits quail.

Where icy rocks, and cliffs, and caves
  The Arctic billows form,
Or where the sunny tropic waves
  Roll by in currents warm.

Oh Sailor! make this Anchor thine,
  And cast it from thy deck,
Ere yet thy bark in ocean's brine
  Forever sinks a wreck;

And when thou hast a feeble breath,
  And life's strong cords are riven,
Then drop it in the port of death,
  And thou art moored in heaven!

[2]

The Christian Mariner. C. M.

I've launched upon the *sea of life*
  My little bark so frail,
Nor fear to meet the raging storm,
  The tempest and the gale.

For *Jesus* is my pilot now,
  My everlasting guide,
He'll bear me to the *port of peace,*
  O'er life's tempestuous tide.

Blow, *breezes* of the *spirit,* blow!
  And spread the *gospel sails;*
Waft down thy silent breath divine,
  In sweet, propitious gales!

For here I wait with Bible *chart*
  The *compass* God has given;
And soon I'll leave these shores of time
  To make the *port* of heaven.

No star shines on the brow of night,
  A cheering watch to me;
No moon hangs out her lamp to light
  My pathway o'er the sea.

And yet I have a Star to guide,
  More bright than sparkling gem;
It pierces through the darkest cloud
  "The Star of Bethlehem."

Land! land! the hopeful watcher cries
  In faith's extreme delight;
Land! land! each joyous soul replies,
  Fair Canaan heaves in sight.

Behold ten thousand on the shore!
  A shining host they stand;
To hail our glorious coming there,
  To that celestial land.

SEAMAN'S CONCERT.

Words by J. H. H. (*Coronation.*)

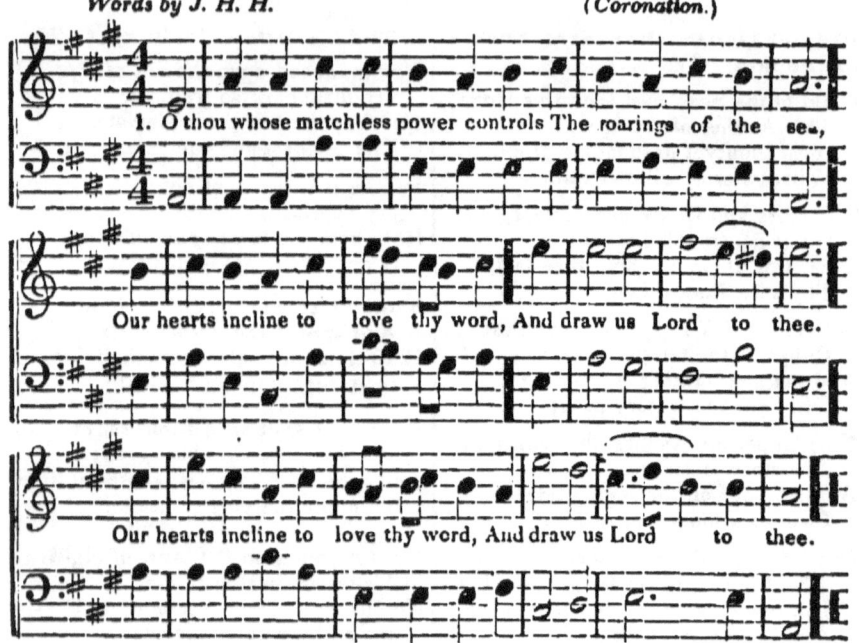

1. O thou whose matchless power controls The roarings of the sea, Our hearts incline to love thy word, And draw us Lord to thee. Our hearts incline to love thy word, And draw us Lord to thee.

Tempestuous billows often rise,
And stormy passions roar;—
O quell each hidden sinful thought,
And bid us upward soar.

Awake *anew* our souls to sing,
In strains of fervent love;
O wake again our fallen harps,
Attuned to those above.

May grateful tributes here ascend,
In sweet melodious lays,
Thy watch-care may we ever bless,
And joyous chant thy praise.

OCEAN MELODIES.

Sweet Home. C. M.

When on the ocean's towering foam
  My voyage I still pursue,
For the dear objects left at home,
  I'll nightly prayer renew.

If earthly home, with pleasure pure,
  So much delight the heart!
How happy they who heaven secure,
  As their rich better part?

To be at home, and there to stay,
  Where the blest Jesus reigns!
In that bright world of endless day,
  What higher joy remains?

For in that home the God of grace,
  His glory does display;
And saints and angels see his face
  Through an eternal day.

Seamen Singing. C. M.

How sweet the songs of Zion sound
  When seamen tune their voice
In praise to him who reigns on high,
  And bids the world rejoice.

They sing, to tell how God has sent
  Deliverance from the storm,
And brought them to their port in peace,
  By his almighty arm.

They sing, and tell of matchless love
  Of him who died to save;
Who now in glory reigns above,
  To rescue from the grave.

Sing on, dear seamen, sing and tell
  Of all Emanuel's love!
And may you rise and sit on high,
  And reign with him above.

My Father's House. C. M.
R. TURNBULL.

There is a place of sacred rest,
  Far, far beyond the skies,
Where beauty smiles eternally,
  And pleasure never dies.

My Father's house, my heavenly home,
  Where "many mansions" stand,
Prepared, by hands divine, for all
  Who seek the better land.

When tossed upon the waves of life,
  With fear on every side,—
When fiercely howls the gathering storm
  And foams the angry tide.

Beyond the storm, beyond the gloom,
  Breaks forth the light of morn,
Bright beaming from my Father's house,
  To cheer the soul forlorn.

Yes, even at that fearful hour,
  When death shall seize its prey,
And from the place that knows us now,
  Shall hurry us away.

The vision of that heavenly home
  Shall cheer the parting soul,
And o'er it, mounting to the skies,
  A tide of rapture roll.

In that pure home of tearless joy
  Earth's parted friends shall meet,
With smiles of love that never fade,
  And blessedness complete.

There, there adieus are sounds unknown,
  Death frowns not on that scene,
But life, and glorious beauty, shine,
  Untroubled and serene.

WONDERS OF THE DEEP. C. M.

Words by Mrs. Hemans. (*Peterborough.*)

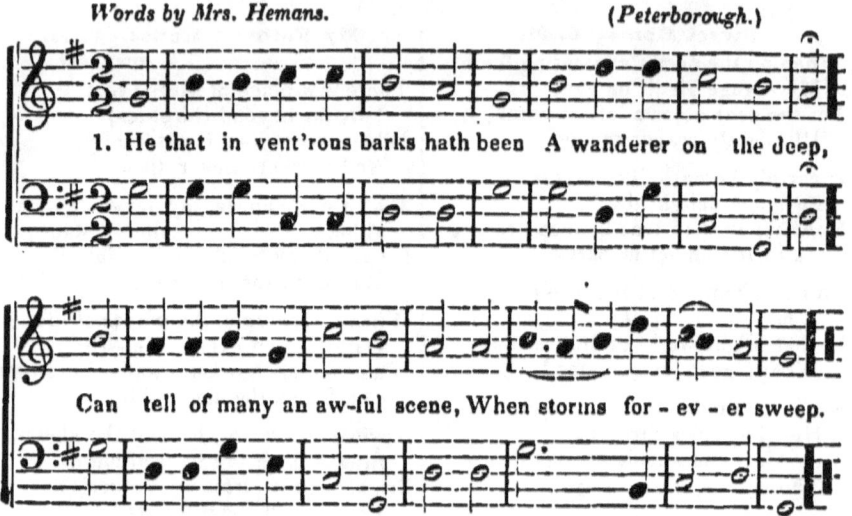

1. He that in vent'rous barks hath been
A wanderer on the deep,
Can tell of many an aw-ful scene,
When storms for-ev-er sweep.

Go ask him if the whirlpool's roar,
   Whose echoing thunder peals
Loud, as if rushed along the shore,
   An army's chariot wheels;—

Of sea-fires, which at dead of night,
   Shine o'er the tides afar,
And make th' response of ocean bright
   As heaven, with many a star.

If glorious be that awful deep,
   No human power can bind,
What then art Thou, who bid'st it **keep**
   Within its bounds confined!

OCEAN MELODIES.

Who is my Neighbor? C. M.

Thy neighbor? It is he whom thou
  Hast power to aid and bless—
Whose aching heart, or burning brow,
  Thy soothing hand may press.

Thy neighbor? 'tis the fainting poor,
  Whose eye with want is dim,
Whom hunger sends from door to door;
  Go thou and succor him.

Thy neighbor? 'tis that weary man,
  Whose years are at their brim,
But low with sickness, cares, and pain;
  Go thou and comfort him.

Oh, pass not, pass not heedless by—
  Perhaps thou canst redeem
The breaking heart from misery—
  Go, share thy lot with him!

God in the Sea. C. M.

The bard of Israel swept his lyre
  In praise, O Lord, to thee;
Sung, burning with the sacred fire,
  "Thy way is in the sea."

So bards may ever tune the string
  To ocean bounding free,
While "many waters" ever sing,
  "Thy way is in the sea."

Go, stand upon the wave-washed shore,
  Or on the sheltered lea,
And hear the bounding billows roar,
  "Thy way is on the sea."

Mark how the surges bound along
  And 'fore the surges flee!
Hear the wild tumult swell the song,
  "Thy way is in the sea."

Gaze on the shipwrecked mariner,
  And hear his fervent plea;
Exclaiming, as the ship goes down,
  "Thy way is in the sea."

Thy waters, Lord, from distant lands,
  Roll up their praise to thee;
Still singing o'er the golden sands,
  "Thy way is in the sea."

Courage from above. C. M.
BY DR. T. F. OAKES.

Say to the storms exhaust thy rage,
  What are thy gales to me?
The Saviour is my hope, my friend,
  No fear can rise from thee!

In fury lash the shore and sea—
  Cause guilty hearts to fear;
But why should I sink with dismay,
  While he I love is near.

Great God! thy love shall be my guide,
  While sailing o'er the sea;
Thy love in heaven shall be my song
  Through all eternity.

For Mariners. C. M.

When o'er the mighty deep we rode,
  By winds and storms assail'd;
We raised our cries to ocean's God,
  Whose mercy never fail'd.

The raging tempest heard thy voice,
  The winds obey'd thy will;
The elements withheld their noise,
  And all the floods were still.

With joy we hail'd the distant shore,
  And safe the vessel moor'd;
With grateful hearts, that happy hour,
  We praised the ocean's Lord.

THE THUNDER STORM. C. M

Words by Mrs. Hemans. (*Northfield.*)

1. Deep fiery clouds o'ercast the sky, Dead stillness reigns in air, There is not e'en a breeze on high The gos-sa-mer to bear.

The roar is hushed, the wave's at rest,
   The sea is dark and still,
Reflecting on thy shadowy breast
   Each form of rock and rill.
The thunder bursts! its rolling might
   Seems the ocean to shake;
And in terrific splendor bright,
   The gathered lightnings break

OCEAN MELODIES.

Christ stilling the tempest. C. M.

Behold, upon the raging sea,
  Tossed by the foaming wave,
A bark is struggling in the gale,
  Her valiant crew to save.

Behold the billows, raging high,
  Are breaking o'er her bow;
Those men who once disdained to fear,
  Are struck with frenzy now.

They look around with frightful gaze,
  As billows o'er them sweep,
While one, their Master and their Guide,
  Lies calmly down to sleep.

Now see the Saviour calmly rise,
  And ask them why they fear:
No harm to them can e'er befall,
  While Christ their Lord is near.

He bids the winds their fury cease;
  He bids the waves be still;
The raging wind, the swelling flood,
  Obey his sovereign will.

Though he in flesh no longer dwells,
  His power is still the same;
No winds nor waves need those dismay
  Who trust in Jesus' name.   J. F. R.

The Victor's Crown. C. M.

A bright unfading crown doth grace
  The victor's deathless head,
Who swift hath run the heavenly race,
  And to the goal hath sped.

Who for his brow that wreath would win
  Must lay aside each weight,
And cast away the robe of sin
  That would his feet beset.

Who runneth for the peerless prize,
  And would not run in vain,
Must keep before his eager eyes
  The garland he would gain.

He must forget who runs the race,
  The ground already passed,
And to the mark must forward press,
  With ever active haste.

Whose spirit would not faint, nor miss
  The joy of him that's crowned,
Must view the cloud of witnesses
  That compass him around.

But, most of all, be ever met
  The crowning Conqueror's eye,
Who, for the joy before him set,
  Won the great victory.

Christ the Ransom. C. M.
BY REV. S. HOWE

Sweet, on the mourning captive's ear
  The notes of ransom ring,
The broken, fainting heart to cheer,
  And hopes of freedom bring.

To sin-bound souls, O doubly blest!
  Is Jesus' precious name,
In whom to seek for joy and rest;
  Release from sin and shame.

And sweet to tell, to sinners lost,
  Of Him who freely gave
His blood, his life—how great the cost!
  Our rebel world to save.

Ye ransomed sinners, gladly swell
  The notes of joyful praise;
On Jesus' name still constant dwell,
  In ever rapturous lays.

OCEAN MELODIES.

Earthly and Heavenly Home. C. M.
BY D. RADFORD.

Where is thy home? I asked a child,
 Who in the morning air, [mild,
Was twining flowers most sweet and
 In garlands for her hair.

My home? the happy child replied,
 And smiled in childish glee,
Is on the sunny mountain's side,
 Where soft winds wander free.

Oh! blessings fall on artless youth,
 And all its rosy hours,
When every word is joy and truth,
 And treasures live in flowers.

Where is thy home thou lonely man?
 I asked a pilgrim gray;
Who came with furrowed brow and wan
 Slow musing on his way.

He paused;—and with a solemn mien
 Upturned his holy eyes,
The land I seek thou ne'er hast seen,
 My home is in the skies.

Oh! blest, thrice blest the heart must be,
 To whom such thoughts are given,
Who walks from worldly fetters free,
 Its only home is Heaven.

Grave of a Sea Captain. L. M.

Here in this lonely humble bed,
 Where myrtle and wild roses grow,
A son of ocean rests his head,
 For, reader, 'tis his watch below.

Long hath he done his duty well,
 And battled with the stormy blast;
But now when gentler breezes swell,
 He's safely moored in peace at last.

Tread lightly, sailors, o'er his grave,
 His virtues claim a kindred tear;
And yet why mourn a brother brave?
 He rests from all his labors here.

The Seaman's Song. L. M. WATTS

Would you behold the works of God,
 His wonders in the world abroad?
With hardy mariners survey
 The unknown regions of the sea.

They leave their native shores behind,
 And seize the favor of the wind;
Till God command, and tempests rise,
 That heaves the ocean to the skies.

When land is far, and death is nigh,
 Bereaved of hope to God they cry;
His mercy hears their loud address,
 And sends salvation in distress.

He bids the winds their wrath assuage,
 And stormy tempests cease to rage;
The grateful band their fears give o'er,
 And hail with joy their native shore.

O, may the sons of men record
 The wondrous goodness of the Lord;
Let them their purest offerings bring,
 And in the church his glory sing.

The Pious Fisherman's Hymn. C. M.

Great universal Lord of all
 Who formed the flowing deep,
And in its bosom, for our use
 A store of fish doth keep.

Thy providence has placed me here,
 To earn my daily bread;
By fishing I my wants supply,
 And so am richly fed.

O may I with returning day,
 To thee my tribute bring,
And with a heart replete with love
 Thy praise devoutly sing.

OCEAN MELODIES.

The Bereaved Parent's Consolation.
C. M.   BY L. F. BEECHER.

Yes! thou art gone from us away:
  Up to thy long abode,
Where thou shalt be forever near
  The palace of thy God.

Tis even so: this lovely flower
  Was nipped before it bloomed!
And an untimely blast has swept,
  This fair one to the tomb.

Thou wert too fair to bloom below,
  Midst groans and tears and sighs;—
So ministering Angels took thee hence,
  To plant thee in the skies!

Then we will gladly wipe away
  The tears for thee we shed;
And calmly lay thee down to sleep
  In silence with the dead.

Believing this, that He, in whom
  Is all our hope and trust,
Will send his guardian Angels down
  To watch thy sleeping dust.

And when the last great day shall come,
  He'll bid thee joyful rise,
Clothed in immortal vigor then;
  To bloom beyond the skies.

Happy Death.   L. M.

Which is the happiest death to die?
The Christian said if he might choose
Long at the gates of bliss would lie,
And feast his spirit ere it fly.

Fain would I catch a hymn of love,
From angel's harps that ring above;
That those around my bed might hear
The harp-notes of another sphere.

Voyage of Life.   C. M.   J. H. G.

As onward speeds the stately ship
  Across the watery main,
Frail man is hurried swift along,
  A distant shore to gain.

With varied course and struggled din,
  The devious way is traced;
Thick crowding dangers yawn around,
  Unseen, yet oft embraced.

Dark, threat'ning clouds may often frown,
  Portending sudden wrath;
Fierce lightnings dart and fervent glare
  Along the lurid path.

So sorrow's shades are o'er us thrown,
  And adverse billows flow;
The tempest's darts fall thick around,
  And scatter grief and wo.

Yet happy he, when toils are o'er,
  Who nears the port above,
Where sin and wo are never known,
  But all is bliss and love.

Hymn at Sea.   C. M.
BY MRS. L. H. SIGOURNEY.

God of the ever rolling deep,
  In thee is all our trust,
Who bidd'st the mighty surges sweep,
  Yet spare a child of dust.

God of the strong unfathomed tide,
  Whose billows, wild and dread,
May wreck the power of human pride,
  And whelm it with the dead.

Oh grant us, as the dove of old,
  Unto the ark did flee,
As seeks the lamb the shepherd's fold;
  To find repose in Thee.

Fair Wind. C. M.

O who can tell, that never sailed
  Among the glassy seas,   [morn
How fresh and welcome breaks the
  That ushers in a breeze!
Fair wind! Fair wind! alow, aloft,
  All hands delight to cry—
As leaping through the parted waves
  The good ship makes reply.

Then welcome to the rushing blast,
  That stirs the waters now—
Ye white plumed heralds of the deep
  Make music round her prow!
Good sea-room in the roaring gale—
  Let stormy trumpets blow—
But chain ten thousand fathoms down
  The sluggish calm below.

The Holy Spirit like the wind,
  Invisible to all,—
Comes from above and wafts the soul
  From danger's threatening pall.
May heavenly breezes waft me o'er
  This life's tempestuous sea,
To that bright land and peaceful shore,
  And rest eternally.

Free Protection for all Seamen.
C. M.   P. S.

The Father will protect and shield,
  By his all-powerful arm,
The children of his tender care,
  When gilded toys may charm.
The Son will intercede for them,
  And plead their cause above;
He freely them protects by grace,
  And plumes their soul with love.

The Holy Spirit cheers them on,
  And opens to their sight
Rich fields of beauty from above,
  And gives them pure delight.
His grace protects them on the sea,
  When angry billows roll;
His voice will dissipate their fear,
  And nerve their trembling soul.

The same protection all must have,
  And ratified by God;
He can alone protection grant,
  Who shed for us his blood.
All nations now may have this gift,
  Of every clime and tongue,
If they will bow before his throne,
  Free grace shall be their song.

The Sailor honored. C. M.

O honored saint, O glorious place,
  The bosom of our Lord!
What can so much display his grace
  To those he bought with blood?
But many a Sailor, poor and low,
  Weary of wandering here,
May I, though vile, be favored so,
  And dry up every tear?

O canst thou, wilt thou, dearest Lord,
  Give my poor soul this rest;
Shall I, when storms fulfil thy word,
  Repose upon thy breast?
Then farewell home, and foreign charms
  Your influence now shall cease,
Reclined in Christ my Saviour's arms,
  I rest in endless peace.

The Last Voyage. C. M.
BY WM. B. TAPPAN.

He tempts once more the smiling deep:
 Sad thoughts crowd on his joy—
That parting hour he saw her weep—
 The mother o'er her boy.

The gallant ship has spread her sail,
 With her did hope depart?
Day follows day, and wherefore fail
 Tidings to cheer the heart?

They know not of the ocean-caves,
 Where men and treasures lie,
Buried within their dreamless graves,
 Beyond e'en fancy's eye.

That noble ship—that cheerful crew—
 What in the storm befel,
Is it not hidden from our view?—
 The last great day shall tell.

That hour, of friends to sooth was none;
 Of shipmates, none to pray;
The gulf before them—each, alone,
 Must tread the trackless way.

O Saviour! hasten thou, and save;
 Of these let it be said:
"They lie in that unfathomed grave,
 With thy own faithful dead."

Christ revealeth the gospel. C. M.
BY N. COLVER.

God of the land and rolling flood,
 Throughout thy wide domain,
Thy works proclaim the mighty God,
 But *not* the Saviour's reign.

The raging storm, the heaving flood,
 The sun that shines above,
Proclaim the wise and powerful God,
 But not a Saviour's love.

The gospel only can impart
 The knowledge of thy grace;
No light can reach and cheer the heart,
 But from a Saviour's face.

O let the sons of ocean be
 Converted to the Lord;
Then shall they bear to realms of death,
 The knowledge of thy word.

The Sailor Invited. C. M.
C. A. WILSON.

Son of the ocean! stop and think,
 Before you further go;
Why linger on the fearful brink
 Of sin, despair, and woe?

Son of the ocean! you must die,
 How soon you cannot tell;
Be ready for Eternity;
 Tread not the path to Hell.

Son of the ocean! Jesus cries
 "My son give me thine heart;"
Hear, then, O sailor, and be wise,
 And choose the better part.

Son of the ocean! Christians pray,
 That you may hear his voice;
That you may come without delay,
 And in his love rejoice.

Son of the ocean! now's the time
 To seek your Father's face;
That you may with the ransomed shine
 In Heaven, that glorious place.

Son of the ocean! Angels wait
 To hear you say "I come;"
That they may shout in Heaven's gate,
 "This is the Sailor's Home!"

PARTING HYMN. S. M.

Words by J. H. H. (Laban.)

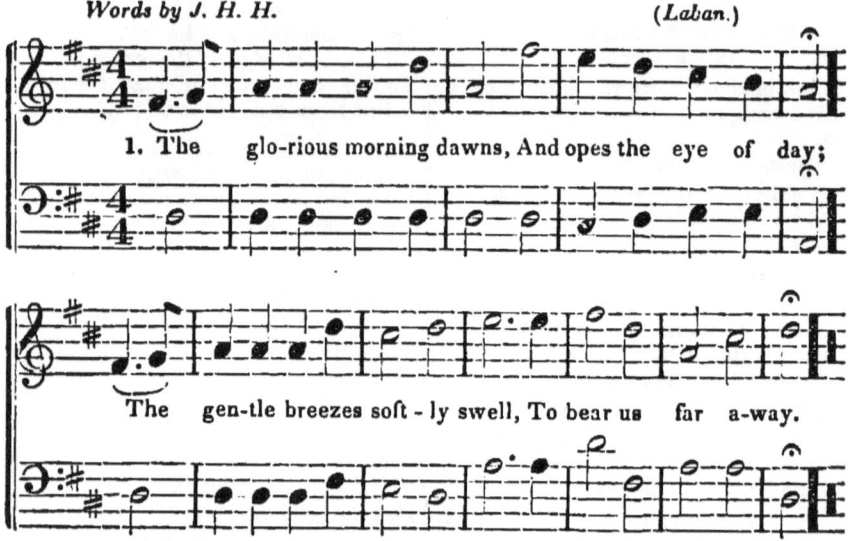

1. The glo-rious morning dawns, And opes the eye of day; The gen-tle breezes soft-ly swell, To bear us far a-way.

On ocean's treach'rous tide,
 Our bark must speed her way;—
Perchance contend with tempests wild,
 And lightning's vivid ray.

O, God in mercy hear,
 And thy rich blessings send;
Be thou around our devious way,
 Our guide and faithful friend.

And when life's voyage is o'er,—
 Its scenes forever past,
Around thy blissful throne above,
 May we appear at last.

OCEAN MELODIES. 29

Prayer at Sea. S. M. c. w. b.

Night cometh o'er the sea!—
 The stars are thick on high,
And every wave a casket is,
 Where their reflections lie.

Night o'er the treacherous sea!
 Who here shall see the light
Of the glad morn' when chased away
 Are all the mists of night?

Father! I bow to thee!
 I pray Thee guard my head,
While, sea-rocked, here I rest
 Upon a wandering bed.

Once, when the billows roll'd
 And rocked in midnight's hour,
Thy Son serenely trod the sea,
 And showed his wondrous power,

So guide us o'er the glassy deep—
 So watch our evening rest—
Or if we here must die,
 Grant we may join the blest.

Encouragement. S. M.

Your harps, ye trembling saints,
 Down from the willows take;
Loud, to the praise of love divine,
 Bid every string awake.

Though in a foreign land,
 We are not far from home;
And nearer to our house above,
 We every moment come.

His grace will to the end
 Stronger and brighter shine;
Nor present things, nor things to come,
 Shall quench the spark divine.

The Saviour on the Sea. S. M.
BY A. JORDAN.

I'm bound upon the sea
 Where Jesus reigns supreme;
I leave the shore at his command,
 Forsaking all for him.

The billows of the sea,
 The rocks, the waves, the wind,
Are small, whatever they may be,
 To those I leave behind.

The Lord himself will keep
 His people safe from harm;
Will hold the helm, and guide the ship
 With his almighty arm.

The Death of the Righteous. S. M.

O for the death of those
 Who slumber in the Lord!
O, be like theirs my last repose,
 Like theirs my last reward!

Their bodies in the ground,
 In silent hope, may lie,
Till the last trumpet's joyful sound
 Shall call them to the sky.

Their ransomed spirits soar,
 On wings of faith and love,
To meet the Saviour they adore,
 And reign with him above.

With us their names shall live
 Through long-succeeding years,
Embalmed with all our hearts can give,
 Our praises and our tears.

O for the death of those
 Who slumber in the Lord!
O, be like theirs my last repose,
 Like theirs my last reward!

30 THERE'S SORROW ON THE DEEP. S. M.

Music by J. M. Hewes. *Words by J. H. H.*

Slow, with expression.

1. A wail comes o'er the wave, And speaks of sighing there; It moans where billows never sleep, "There's sorrow on the deep," "There's sorrow on the deep."

Around the dying cot,
  Where raging fevers glow,
With bursting hearts fond shipmates weep,—
  "There's sorrow on the deep."

When threat'ning clouds appear,
  And winds and waves arise;
When o'er the main, wild tempests sweep,—
  "There's sorrow on the deep."

Great God of earth and skies
  In mercy deign to hear;
In danger's hour the sailor keep,—
  When "sorrow's on the deep."

Prayer for the Mariner. S. M.
BY MISS M. BALL.

Dear Saviour, teach our hearts
  To feel for those whose home
Is on the stormy ocean cast,
  Amid the tempest's foam.

When thunder peals around,
  And lightnings flash on high,
Oh cover them, and 'neath thy wing,
  Protected may they lie.

So shall they sing of Thee,
  And midst the calm rehearse
The great deliverance of thy hands,
  In humble grateful verse.

The Sailor's Prayer. S. M.

Father, the storm is loud,
  No light beams on our way,
Save when o'er yonder threat'ning cloud,
  The fearful lightnings play.

The frowning heavens above!
  The yawning deep below!
Far, far are those we fondly love
  Where can the Sailor go?

Father! to thee we turn,
  God of the earth and sea,
Our hearts are sad, our bosoms yearn,
  Our fears are known to thee.

O! let thine eye of love,
  Beam through the angry-storm,
And hope's bright image from above,
  Appear in dove-like form!

Father! to Thee we cry,
  God of the earth and sea,
Thy powerful arm is always nigh—
  Our hopes repose on Thee.

The Temperance Life Boat. S. M.

The storm is on the deep,
  The lightning hovers o'er
The seamen on the stricken mast,
  And raging breakers roar.

A cry of hope is heard,
  The Life-boat is at hand;
Again upon the steadfast shore
  The rescued sailors stand.

We see the raging tide
  Of double death—and send
Our Life boat in the simple Pledge,
  Which is the drunkard's friend.

To heaven we lift a prayer,
  And ply our watchful oar,
Convey him where his Saviour's praise,
  May greet him on the shore.

The Inebriate warned. S. M.

I heard a voice from heaven
  Address the thoughtless throng,
Who hasten downward to the tomb
  With revelry and song.

It warned them not to quench
  The deathless flame within,
And madly dare the fearful doom
  Of unrepented sin.

It warned them of the shame
  That haunts the drunkard's grave;
And of that leprosy of soul
  From which no skill can save.

I looked, and thousands fled
  The tempter's fatal snare;
But some were number'd with **the dead**
  Who shall their doom declare?

THE SAILOR'S RETURN. S. M.

Words by J. H. H.   (*Silver Street.*)

1. Great God! E-ter-nal King, Whose might con-trols the sea, In grate-ful strains we tune our hearts, And raise our thoughts to thee.

From all our toils and woes,
  And dangers on the main,
In kindness, O, Almighty God,
  We're safely moored again.

Around the sacred shrine,
  Of humble prayer and praise,
With kindred hearts we gladly join,
  And chant our grateful lays.

We sing thy mercies, Lord,
  And thy preserving care;
We near, our God, the mercy sea
  And fervent worship there

OCEAN MELODIES.

Attachment to the Church. S. M.
DWIGHT.

I love thy kingdom, Lord,
  The house of thine abode,
The church our blest Redeemer saved
  With his own precious blood.

I love thy church, O God;
  Her walls before thee stand,
Dear as the apple of thine eye,
  And graven on thy hand.

For her my tears shall fall;
  For her my prayers ascend;
To her my cares and toils be given,
  Till toils and cares shall end.

Beyond my highest joy
  I prize her heavenly ways,
Her sweet communion, solemn vows,
  Her hymns of love and praise.

Jesus, thou Friend divine,
  Our Saviour and our King,
Thy hand, from every snare and foe,
  Shall great deliverance bring.

Sure as thy truth shall last,
  To Zion shall be given
The brightest glories earth can yield,
  And brighter bliss of heaven.

Heavenly Joy on Earth. S. M.
WATTS.

Come, we that love the Lord,
  And let our joys be known:
Join in a song with sweet accord,
  And thus surround the throne.

The sorrows of the mind
  Be banished from the place;
Religion never was designed
  To make our pleasures less.

Let those refuse to sing
  Who never knew our God;
But children of the heavenly King
  May speak their joys abroad.

The hill of Zion yields
  A thousand sacred sweets,
Before we reach the heavenly fields,
  Or walk the golden streets.

Then let our songs abound,
  And every tear be dry;
We're marching thro' Immanuel's ground,
  To fairer worlds on high.

Active Piety. S. M.
SIGOURNEY.

Laborers of Christ, arise,
  And gird you for the toil;
The dew of promise from the skies
  Already cheers the soil.

Go where the sick recline,
  Where mourning hearts deplore;
And where the sons of sorrow pine,
  Dispense your hallowed lore.

Urge, with a tender zeal,
  The erring child along
Where peaceful congregations kneel,
  And pious teachers throng.

Be faith, which looks above,
  With prayer, your constant guest,
And wrap the Saviour's changeless love
  A mantle round your breast.

So shall you share the wealth
  That earth may ne'er despoil,
And the blest gospel's saving health
  Repay your arduous toil

OCEAN MELODIES.

And praise our great and might-y King.

our great and might-y King.

Thy bark he'll safely guide
  O'er the raging, trackless deep,
And lull the swelling tide—
  Thy soul in mercy keep:
He is thy Pilot on the wave,
He will from all thy dangers save.

Then trust in him alone,
  When storms around thee roar,—
To the celestial throne,
  On faith's bright pinions soar:
He'll moor thee safe on Canaan's shore
Where storms shall beat and rage no more.

The Seaman's Friend. H. M.
BY REV. D. C. EDDY.

God is the seamen's friend,
  When in the house of prayer;
The knee with soul he bends,
  And pours his homage there.
God is the firm and constant friend,
While quick to heaven his prayers ascend.

God is the seaman's friend,
  While home he seeks for rest;
He doth his mercy lend,
  To make his hearth-side blest;
God gives him wife and child to love,
And balmy blessings from above.

God is the seaman's friend,
  When billows dash on high;
He doth the life-boat send,
  When storms and death are nigh;
'Tis God's own hand that doth provide,
For him who roams upon the tide.

My own Ship's Company. H. M.
BY CAPT. T. ATWOOD.

O! God of sailors, hear,
  While we before thee bend,
And answer this our prayer;
  On us thy spirit send;
We have no plea before thy throne,
But trust in thee by faith alone.

O, hear the sailor now
  Confess his sins and grief,
Melting before thee bow,
  Grant, grant him quick relief;
Wash and control with Jesus' blood,
And fill the soul with love to God.

Thy promise, Lord, is sure,
  We claim it as our own;
And praying, still endure,
  To wrestle at thy throne,
Till thou shalt say, "Now sailor live;
My blood to-day new life shall give."

36. THE SAILOR A MISSIONARY. 8s, 7s & 4.
Words by J. H. H. (Siberia.)

Bear, O bear the blessed gospel, Th' ra-diant beams of heavenly light,
Haste thee on o'er raging billows, Spread the flowing canvas wide,
To the poor, enshrouded pagan, Groping in the dark-est night,
Haste to break the cru-el fetters, Stay the roll-ing, fear-ful tide,
Hardy sailor, Hardy sailor, Bear the glorious bread of life.
Christian sailor, Christian sailor, Gladly sound the gos-pel trump.

There, where blind, benighted pagans
Bow before their idol shrine,
Let the gospel's light be kindled,
And in all its beauty shine.
   Blessed gospel,
Let it spread from shore to shore.

Bear his name, the lowly Savior,
  To a dark and heathen shore,
Till the gloom of idol worship,
  Shrouds the souls of men no more.
    Pious sailor,
Bear the cross of Christ afar.

The Saviour Asleep. C. M.
BY MISS M. BALL.. (Balerma.)

But as they sailed He fell asleep,
 And on the sea there came
A storm of wind, whose furious sweep
 No vessel could sustain.
They haste in terror to his side,
 "Lord, save us from the storm,"
He rose, the furious, swelling tide
 Beheld its Maker's form.

And sank as childhood sinks to rest,
 Upon its mother's knee,
The winds to softest whispers lulled,
 Seemed lost in ecstacy.
That voice, its cadence was the same,
 As when of old it fell
On their chaotic waves, and gave
 Their form, their rise, their swell.

So Mariner in every hour,
 Call on his name who saves,
And thou shalt hear when dangers lower,
 His voice who calms the waves.

Midnight Prayer. 8s & 7s. M. B.

Hark! upon the midnight air,
 Comes the voice of grateful prayer,
'Tis the hour when sailors keep
 Lonely watches on the deep.

All alone he kneels to pray,
 To his God, whose trackless way,
Lieth where the boisterous sea,
 Uttereth its symphony.

Heaven attends the sailor's prayer,
 God our God is with him there,
And though midnight reigns around,
 He a Bethel there hath found

Deliverance from danger. 7s.
BY MRS. SIGOURNEY.

Ruler of the earth and sky,
 Who the mighty deep doth hold
In the hollow of Thy hand,
 By thy slightest word controlled;
Who the stormy winds dost curb,
 Rushing on their midnight path,
And the reeling vessel save
 From the tempest of their wrath;

Thou from shipwreck and despair
 Didst our souls in safety set,
When all human help was vain,
 May we ne'er thy love forget;
Ne'er the tender mercy grieve,
 That upheld us when we prayed,
Nor the sacred promise break,
 That in danger's hour we made.

Be not afraid. 7s. (Watchman tell us.)
BY MISS M. BALL.

Tossing on a stormy sea,
 Lay the men of Gallilee,
Loud and fiercely blew the wind,
 Fear oppressed each anxious mind.
But in peril's darkest hour,
 He was near of mighty power,
And in accents sweet He said,
 "It is I, be not afraid!"

Timid ones, oppressed with fear,
 Know ye not that He is near,
Who sublimely walked the wave,
 All omnipotent to save?
Cheer thee, Mariner,—Good cheer!
 As a spirit He is near;
Fear thee not, for He hath said.
 "It is I, be not afraid!"

MARINER'S PRAYER. 8s & 7s.

(*Bavaria.*)

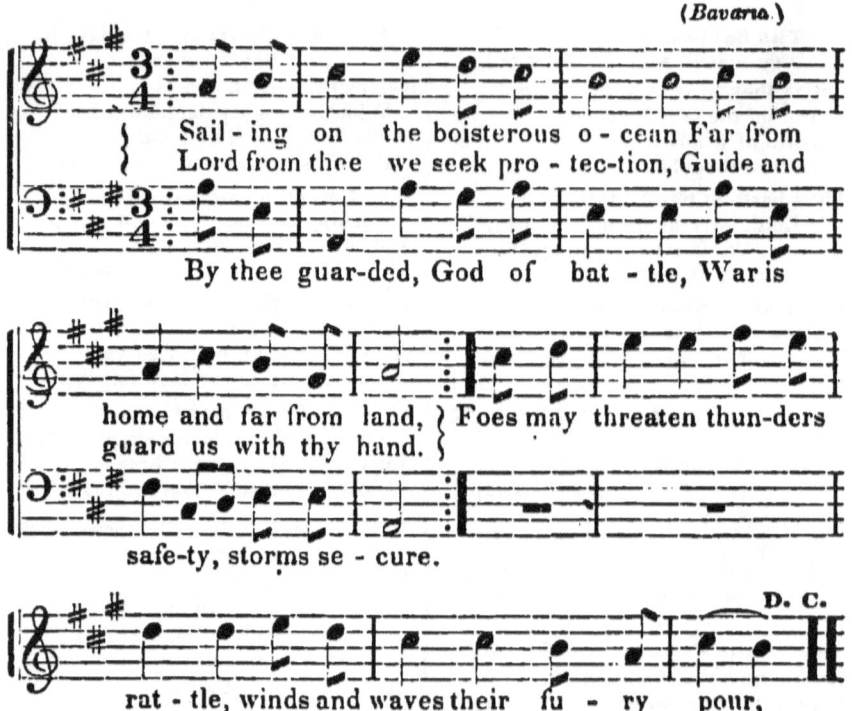

Sail-ing on the boisterous o-cean Far from home and far from land, Foes may threaten thun-ders rat-tle, winds and waves their fu-ry pour,

Lord from thee we seek pro-tec-tion, Guide and guard us with thy hand.

By thee guar-ded, God of bat-tle, War is safe-ty, storms se-cure.

When with fears and dangers compassed,
   May we find thee strong to save;
All our hope, our trust we centre,
   In his might who walked the wave;
May thy mercy safe return us,
   From the perils of the deep,
In the world's wide ocean keep us,
   Heav'n's the haven that we seek.

The Soul. C. M.

How beautiful the setting sun!
  The clouds how bright and gay!
The stars, appearing one by one,
  How beautiful are they!
And when the moon climbs up the sky,
  And sheds her gentle light,
And hangs her crystal lamp on high,
  How beautiful is night!

And can it be I am possessed
  Of something brighter far?
Glows there a light within this breast
  Outshining every star?
Yes: should the sun and stars turn pale,
  The mountains melt away,
This flame within shall never fail,
  But live in endless day.

The Jubilee. C. M.

What heavenly music do I hear,
  Salvation sounding free!
Ye souls in bondage lend an ear,
  This is the Jubilee.

*Good news, good news to Adam's race,
  Let Christians all agree;
To sing redeeming love and grace,
  This is the Jubilee.

The gospel sounds a sweet release,
  To all in misery,
And bids them welcome home to peace,
  This is the Jubilee.

Jesus is on the mercy seat,
  Before him bend the knee,
Let heaven and earth his praise repeat,
  This is the Jubilee.

Sinners be wise, return and come,
  Unto the Saviour flee;
The Saviour bids you welcome home,
  This is the Jubilee.

Come ye redeemed, your tribute bring,
  With songs of harmony,
While on the road to Canaan sing,
  This is the Jubilee.

A Psalm of Life. 8s & 7s

Tell me not in mournful numbers,
  Life is but an empty dream!
For the soul is dead that slumbers,
  And things are not what they seem.

Life is real! Life is earnest!
  And the grave is not its goal;
Dust thou art, to dust returnest,
  Was not spoken of the soul.

Not enjoyment, and not sorrow,
  Is our destined end or way;
But to act that each to-morrow
  Finds us further than to-day.

Art is long, and time is fleeting,
  And our hearts tho' stout and brave,
Still like muffled drums are beating
  Funeral marches to the grave.

Lives of great men all remind us
  We can make our lives sublime,
And, departing, leave behind us
  Footprints on the sand of time;

Footprints, that perhaps another,
  Sailing o'er life's solemn main,
A forlorn and shipwrecked brother,
  Seeing, shall take heart again.

Marriage Hymn. L. M. P. S.

With glowing hearts great God. our King,
Help us in joyous strains to sing,
And celebrate thy boundless love,
For sacred rights, from Heaven above,
When man, lone man, in Eden's bower,
Was musing on creative power,
And nature smiling with delight,
And all was lovely in His sight;
Before one *groan* had rent the air,
When God-like man was free from care,
A voice from the Celestial Throne
Says, "It is not good to be alone."
A "help meet" then for man He made,
To cheer his heart, and lend him aid;
While sailing o'er the sea of time,
By mutual love and strength combined.
Congenial spirits! may you glide,
In *union sweet* o'er life's rough tide,
And each arrayed in that bright land
In marriage robes at God's right hand.
There, those will meet who highly prize
The wedding garment of the wise,
Saints, like the angels, there will be,
In that sweet home—ETERNITY.

Flight of Time. S. M.

Another day is past,
  The hours forever fled,
And time is bearing us away
  To mingle with the dead.

Our minds in perfect peace
  Our Father's care shall keep;
We yield to gentle slumber now,
  For thou canst never sleep.

How blessed, Lord, are they
  On thee securely stayed!
Nor shall they be in life alarmed,
  Nor be in death dismayed.

Sabbath Evening Hymn. C. M.
BY MRS L. H. SIGOURNEY.

We thank thee, Father, for the day
  That, robed in twilight sweet,
Doth linger ere it pass away,
  And lead us to thy feet.

We thank thee for its healing rest
  To weary toil and care;
Its praise, within thy temple blest—
  Its holy balm of prayer.

Forgive us, if with spirit cold,
  We breathed the murmurer's moan,
Or failed to grasp the chain of gold,
  That links us to thy throne.

O grant, that when this span of life
  In evening shade shall close,
And all its vanity and strife
  Tend to their long repose,

We, for the sake of Him who died,
  Our Advocate and Friend,
May share that Sabbath at thy side
  Which never more shall end.

All one in Christ. S. M. BEDDOME.

Let party names no more
  The Christian world o'erspread:
Gentile and Jew, and bond and free,
  Are one in Christ, their Head.

Among the saints on earth
  Let mutual love be found—
Heirs of the same inheritance,
  With mutual blessings crowned.

Thus will the church below
  Resemble that above,
Where streams of endless pleasure flow,
  And every heart is love.

The gifts of God perverted. H. M.
God gave the gift to man;
But man with fatal skill,
Devised and formed the plan
To change the good for ill:
The poison, tortured from the cane,
Like Samson hath its thousands slain.

God gave the golden grain
To hungry man for food;
But querulous and vain,
He spurn'd the proffer'd good:
And Egypt's slothful sons, athirst,
Drew forth the maddening beverage first.

God gave the clustering vine:
Ingenious man perverse,
Exchang'd the boon for wine,
And wrought fair Canaan's cure;
The patriarch, who had safely past
The deluge, was o'erwhelmed at last.

To earth the cup be hurled,
That holds an adder's sting,
And let us pledge the world
With nectar from the spring;
That hence, like Rechab's ancient line,
Tho' prophets urge, we drink no wine.

The Temperance Ship. H. M.
Speed, speed the temperance ship!
Ye winds fill every sail,
Behold her on the deep,
Outriding every gale,
The tempest's fury she out-braves,
And hosts of deathless drunkards saves.

Speed, speed the Temperance ship!
Who joins us in the cry?
Mothers may cease to weep,
Our ship is passing by:

We wish to take you all on board—
A freight of mercy to the Lord.

Speed, speed the Temperance ship!
For her we'll ever pray,
'Tis God alone can keep
In safety, night and day;
On him we'll evermore depend,
Who is the contrite drunkard's friend.

Speed, speed the Temperance ship!
Ye young and aged shout,
Behold her o'er the deep,
With all her streamers out,
Bound for the true tee-total shore—
Where streams of death are drank no more

Temperance Hymn. 7s & 6s.
LYRE.

How long shall virtue languish,
How long shall folly reign,
While many a heart with anguish
Is weeping o'er the slain?

How long shall dissipation
Her deadly waters pour,
Throughout this favored nation,
Her millions to devour?

We hail with joy unceasing
The band whose pledge is given
Whose numbers are increasing
Amid the smiles of Heaven.

Their virtues, never failing,
Shall lead to brighter days,
Where holiness, prevailing,
Shall fill the earth with praise.

SAILOR'S HYMN. 8s & 7s.
(*Bounding Billows.*)

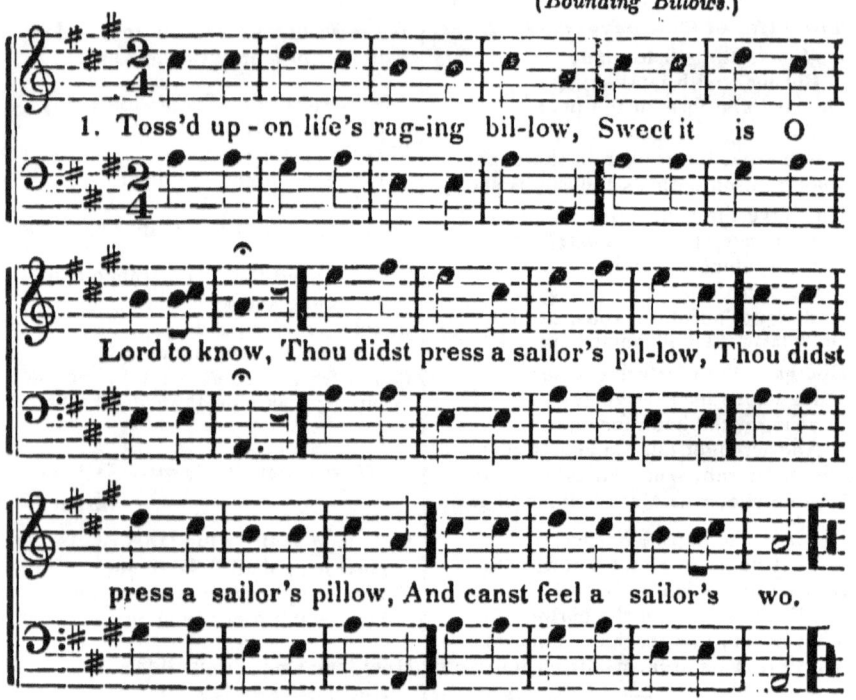

1. Toss'd up-on life's rag-ing bil-low, Sweet it is O Lord to know, Thou didst press a sailor's pil-low, Thou didst press a sailor's pillow, And canst feel a sailor's wo.

Thou canst calm the raging ocean,
  All its noise and tumult still;—
Hush the tempest's wild commotion,
Hush the tempest's wild commotion,
  At the bidding of thy will.

Thus my heart, the hope will cherish,
  While to thee I lift mine eye;
Thou wilt save me ere I perish,
Thou wilt save me ere I perish,
  Thou wilt, hear the sailor's cry.

OCEAN MELODIES. 43

Let Me Go. 8s & 7s. WM. BAXTER.

Let me go; my soul is weary
 Of the chain which binds it here;
Let my spirit bend its pinion
 To a brighter, holier sphere. [me
Earth, 'tis true, hath friends who bless
 With their fond and faithful love;
But the hand of angels beckon
 Me to brighter climes above,

Let me go; for earth hath sorrow,
 Sin, and pain, and bitter tears;
All its paths are dark and dreary—
 All its hopes are fraught with fears;
Short-lived are its brightest flowers,
 Soon its cherished joys decay;
Let me go; I fain would leave it
 For the realms of endless day.

Homeward Bound. 8s & 7s.

Whither goest thou sailor stranger,
 Roaming o'er the raging main?
Know'st thou not 'tis full of danger,
 And will not thy toils be vain?
"No, I'm bound for the kingdom, &c.

Storms may gather wild around thee,
 Winds and waves their wrath unite;
Then will not dread fear astound thee,
 Veil thy hopes in darkest night.
No, I'm bound, &c.

Storm at Sea. 8s & 7s. J. H. H.

Dark and fearful clouds appearing,
 Spread their mantling forms around,
Deep'ning, black'ning, and careering,
 Veiling earth in gloom profound;
Howling winds in fury driven,
 Fiercely rage and loudly roar,

Rending earth and shaking heaven,
 With their rude and frantic power.
Sadly heaves the mighty ocean,
 Far its moaning voice resounds,
As the tempest's wild commotion,
 O'er its restless bosom sweeps;
Billows mighty upward tending,
 Raise their crested heads on high,
Foaming, dashing and descending,
 Delving sea and spanning sky.
Hoarse the deep-toned thunders pealing,
 Roll afar in sullen wrath,
Flash on flash the lightnings stealing,
 Fitful trace their glowing path;
Then the hardy sailor gazes
 O'er the raging, troubled waves,
Fervently his cry he raises,
 While the tempest's power he braves

The Saviour's Invitation. 8s & 7s.

Toilworn Sailor, come and welcome,
 To my glorious feast of love,
I now stand with arms extended,
 Calling you to joys above;
I will light thee o'er life's ocean;
 By the Star of glory bright;
Fill thy heart with peace and rapture;
 Plume thy soul with wings of light.

When the voyage of life is over,
 Then you'll launch upon that sea,
Clear as crystal are its waters,
 Placid will its bosom be—
Can you still resist my spirit?
 Can you slight my love and grace?
Must you perish in your blindness?
 Come and run the heavenly race.

F. S

CHEERFUL HOPE. 7s & 6s.

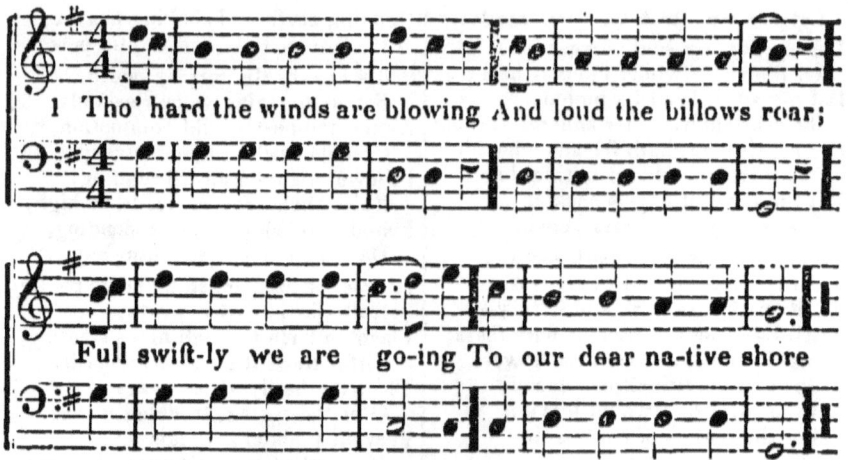

1 Tho' hard the winds are blowing And loud the billows roar; Full swiftly we are going To our dear native shore

The billows breaking o'er us,
  The storms that round us swell,
Are aiding to restore us
  To all we loved so well.

So sorrow often presses
  Life's mariner along,
Afflictions and distresses
  Are gales and billows strong

The sharper and severer
  The storm of life we meet,
The sooner and the nearer
  Is Heaven's eternal seat.

Come then, afflictions dreary,
  Sharp sickness pierce my breast;
You only bear the weary
  More quickly home to rest.

OCEAN MELODIES. 45

The Child on the Sea. 7s & 6s. P. S.

Just launched upon the ocean,
  Where billows madly rise,
And gloomy clouds are frowning,
  And veil youth's radiant skies.

Each child's frail bark is sailing
  Upon life's raging deep,
But winds and waves assail them,
  They sigh and groan and weep.

Behold! upon this ocean,
  A life-boat sweetly rides;
Its saving shipwrecked children,
  While o'er the sea it glides.

Kind teachers in this Life-boat,
  Sail round you with delight,
From wo and death to save you,
  They point where all is bright

The Saviour is this Life-boat,
  From heaven he came to save,
He walked upon the ocean,
  And calmed the mountain wave.

His arms embrace dear children,
  For them he shed his blood;
And died for your redemption;
  Behold! the Lamb of God!

Life rapidly passing away. 7s & 6s.
S. F. SMITH.

As flows the rapid river,
  With channel broad and free,
Its waters rippling ever,
  And hasting to the sea.

So life is onward flowing,
  And days of offered peace,
And man is swiftly going
  Where calls of mercy cease.

As moons are ever waning,
  As hastes the sun away;
As stormy winds, complaining,
  Bring on the wintry day.

So fast the night comes o'er us—
  The darkness of the grave;
And death is just before us:
  God takes the life he gave.

Say, hath thy heart its treasure
  Laid up in worlds above?
And is it all thy pleasure
  Thy God to praise and love?

Beware, lest death's dark river
  Its billows o'er thee roll,
And thou lament forever
  The ruin of thy soul.

Speak to the Sailor. 7s & 6s. P. S.

Go, speak to that brave seaman,
  He has a generous heart—
Your winning words may lead him
  To choose a " better part."

Speak to him of that Saviour,
  Who died and arose again,
And chose his first disciples,
  From sailors—fishermen.

A thrill of joy in heaven,
  Among that holy throng,
While angel-harps are ringing,
  And swell the pleasing song.

The lost has found the Saviour;
  The wanderer has come home;
" A *word* was *fitly* spoken,"
  Is echoed *round the throne*.

BETHEL. 7s & 6s.

This piece of music is respectfully dedicated to Rev. P. Stow, Pastor of the Boston Baptist Bethel Society, by Wm. Lock Brown, late Musical Director at N. Y. University.

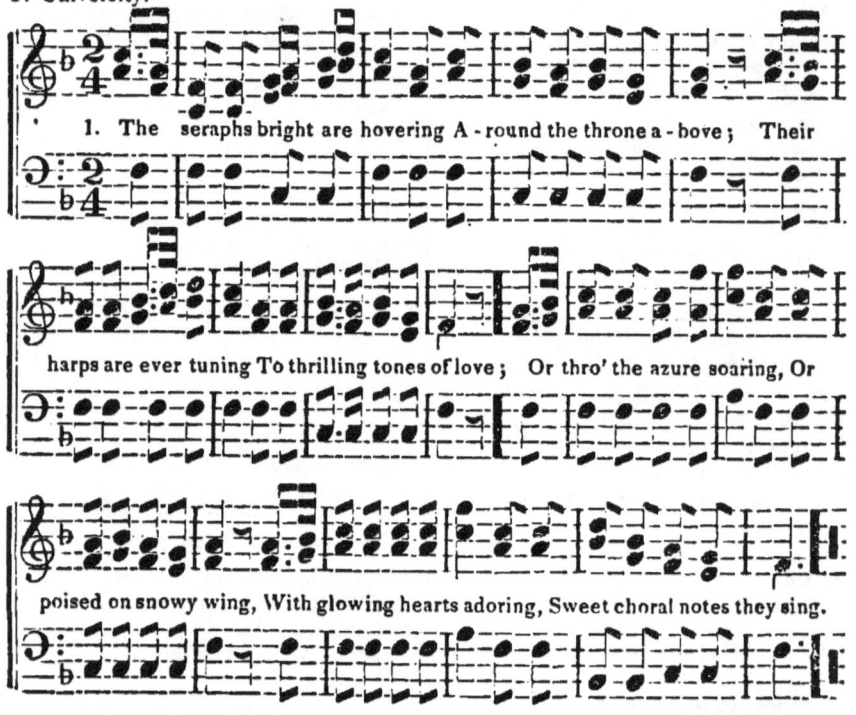

1. The seraphs bright are hovering A-round the throne a-bove; Their harps are ever tuning To thrilling tones of love; Or thro' the azure soaring, Or poised on snowy wing, With glowing hearts adoring, Sweet choral notes they sing.

From earth is daily rising
  A rich, harmonious song,
From sunny, perfumed flowers
  By breezes borne along.
From hills in sunlight glittering,
  From smooth, deep emerald seas,
A cloud of praise is rising,
  Like incense on the breeze.

And childhood's voice is chanting
  A full, harmonious song;
When morning light is breaking,
  Or evening sweeps along.
For should we fail proclaiming
  Our great Redeemer's praise,
The stones, our silence shaming
  Would their hosannas raise.

Prayer for Missionaries while on their Voyage. 7s & 6s WORCESTER'S SEL.

Roll on, thou mighty ocean
  And as thy billows flow,
Bear messengers of mercy
  To every vale of woe:
Arise, ye gales, and waft them
  Safe to their distant shore;
That men may sit in darkness
  And death's deep shade no more.

O thou Eternal Ruler,
  Who holdest in thine arm
The tempests of the ocean,
  Deliver them from harm!
Thy presence still be with them
  Wherever they may be:
Though far from those who love them,
  Let them be nigh to thee.

Confidence in God. 7s & 6s.
MONTGOMERY.

God is my strong salvation;
  What foe have I to fear?
In darkness and temptation,
  My light, my help, is near:
Though hosts encamp around me,
  Firm in the fight I stand;
What terror can confound me,
  With God at my right hand?

Place on the Lord reliance;
  My soul, with courage, wait;
His truth be thine affiance,
  When faint and desolate:
His might thy heart shall strengthen,
  His love thy joy increase;
Mercy thy days shall lengthen;
  The Lord will give thee peace.

We are scattered. 8, 7, 6.
BY W. H. BURLEIGH.

We are scattered—we are scattered—
  Though a joyful band were we!
Some sleep beneath the green-sod,
  And some are in the sea.
And time hath wrought his changes
  On the few who yet remain;
The joyous band that once we were
  We cannot be again!

We are scattered—we are scattered!
  Yet may we meet again,
In a brighter and a purer sphere,
  Beyond the reach of pain!
Where the shadow of this lower world
  Can never cloud the eye—
When the mortal hath put brightly on
  Its *immortality!*

Come to the Waters. 7s & 6s.
J. B. HAGUE.

Ho! every one that thirsteth,
  Come to the waters, come;
See life's pure stream—it bursteth
  From the eternal throne.
See! like a mighty river,
  Its crystal tide rolls by;
Thy soul haste to deliver!
  Come, drink, and never die

Come, then, thou poor and needy;
  Thy God will freely bless;
And haste with steps most speedy,
  While mercy gives access;
For as a mountain torrent,
  Life's stream is dashing by;
Then come, thou hast full warrant
  Come quickly, lest thou die

48 THE SICK CABIN BOY. 7s & 6s.
(*Watcher.*)

1. The night was dark and fearful, The blast swept wailing by, A watcher pale and tear-ful, Looked forth with anxious eye; How wist-ful-ly he gaz-eth, No gleam of morn is there, His eyes, to heaven he rais-eth, In ag-o-ny of prayer. How

OCEAN MELODIES.

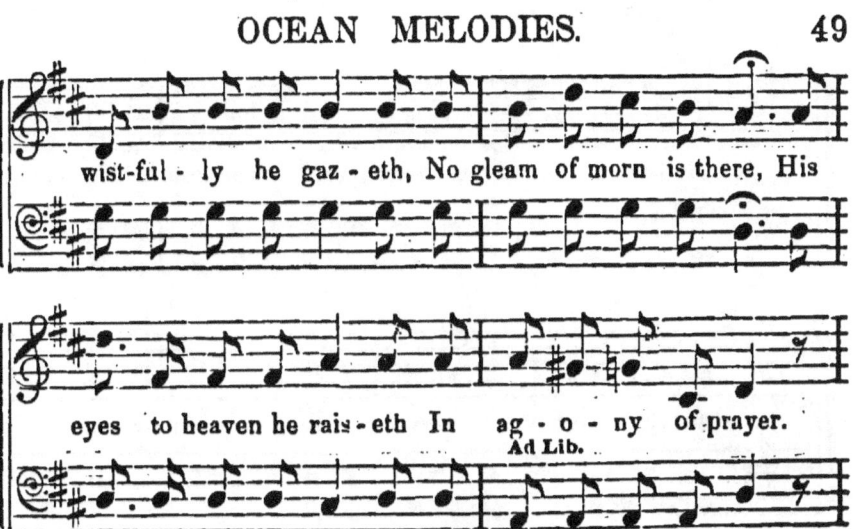

wist-ful-ly he gaz-eth, No gleam of morn is there, His eyes to heaven he rais-eth In ag-o-ny of prayer.

Within that cabin lonely,
   Where gloom and sickness reign,
The sailor boy, the only,
   Lay moaning in his pain,—
And death alone can free him —
   He feels that this must be,
But Oh! for one to see him,
   Before the spirit flee.

No mother kind wept o'er him
   The gushing tears of love;
No ray of hope before him,
   Save dawning joys above,
As beamed afar the morning
   Across the eastern sky,
The spirit saw its dawning
   In realms of bliss on high.

THE SAILOR BOY'S FAREWELL. 8s & 7s.

OCEAN MELODIES.

Storms may gather wild above me,
    Angry waves their fury pour,
Yet my mother, I will love thee,
    While the winds and surges roar ;—
Think of scenes in childhood's weakness,
    When I shared thy tender care,—
Bowed the knee in humble meekness,
    Gladly breathed my evening prayer.

Though in distant lands I'm bending,
    Low beneath a sultry sky ;—
When my mother's prayer's ascending,
    And her spirit's hovering nigh,—
Then thy smile shall ever cheer me,
    Be my solace and my joy ;—
Then I'll joy that thou'rt near me,
    Pleading for thy sailor boy.

DOXOLOGY.

May the grace of Christ our Savior,
    And the Father's boundless love,
With the holy Spirit's favor,
    Rest upon us from above ;
Thus may we abide in union,
    With each other and the Lord :
And possess in sweet communion,
    Joys which earth cannot afford.

52. SAILOR BOY'S EARLY GRAVE. P. M.

WORDS BY MRS. DANA.

1. Shed not a tear o'er your friend's early bier, When I am gone, When I am gone; Smile, if the slow tolling bell you should hear, When I am gone, I am gone. Weep not for me when you stand round my grave, Think who his died his be-

OCEAN MELODIES. 53

Plant ye a tree which may wave over me,
    When I am gone, when I am gone;
Sing me a song, if my grave you should see,
    When I am gone, I am gone.
Come at the close of a bright summer's day,
Come when the sun sheds his last lingering ray,
Come and rejoice that I thus pass'd away,
    When I am gone, I am gone.

THE LIGHT SHIP. 11s.

Words by A. M. Edmond. (Christ in the Garden.)

1. The Light Ship! how welcome the beacon to me When wild was the tem-pest, And dark was the sea; It soothed my sad spir-it's tu-mul-tu-ous fear, And told me the ha-ven I longed for was near.

I saw it again in the calm silent hour,
When twilight descends with mysterious power,
And the moonlight fell soft on the eddying wave,
That rolled o'er the mariner's sea-girt grave.

Then shone in the distance the Light Ship afar,
And paled, with its lustre, the glow of the star,—
The small, silver star, that with tremulous eye,
Looked down on the sea from its home, in the sky.

OCEAN MELODIES.

How blest was the beacon! how lovely it seemed,
As its watch-fires of crimson unceasingly gleamed,
Sweet assurance of safety in moments of calm,
And in seasons of peril a safeguard from harm.
O, would that while sailing on life's stormy sea,
The Star of Religion my beacon might be,
To warn me of danger, to soothe me in fear,
And tell me the haven I long for is near.

"O pray for the Sailor."
BY MRS. P. H. BROWN.

O pray for the sailor, now far on the billow,
 O think of his hardships, temptation and pain;
His home is the ocean, the hammock his pilllow,
 He toils for our pleasure, his loss is our gain.

While we are securely and peacefully sleeping,
 He stands at the helm, and his duty performs,
Now, walking the deck, and his painful watch keeping,
 Or sits at the mast head 'mid perils and storms.

O pray for the sailor, to banishment driven,
 Enduring privation, oppression and care,
Shut out from the gospel, a stranger to heaven,
 The victim of vice, and a prey to despair.

And while we thus pray for the sons of the ocean,
 A kind peaceful Home to him must be given,
The Mariner's Bethel allure to devotion,
 The Bible and Preacher direct him to heaven.

Look Above.

In the tempest of life, when th' wave and the gale
Is round and above, if thy footing should fail,
If thine eye should grow dim and caution depart,
Look above! and be firm, be fearless of heart.

If th' friend who embraced in prosperity's glow,
With a smile for each joy, a tear for each wo,
Should betray, when sorrow like clouds are arrayed,
Look above! to friendship that never shall fade.

THE APPEAL. 14s & 12s.

Words by Mrs. C. T. Putnam. (*The morning light is breaking.*)

1. From many a no-ble ves-sel that ploughs the mountain wave,
From many a thronged fore-cas-tle where crowd the reckless brave,
From many a gal-lant whaler, that lies a hope-less wreck,
Where clings the dy-ing sai-lor to mast, or spar, or deck;

From darker scenes of evil that meet him on the shore,
Where vice and ruin revel at many an open door
The seaman's cry is sounding in ev'ry listening ear,
The Christian landsmen rousing to bring salvation near.

Shall we who dwell securely at ease upon the land,
And taste those blessings freely that rise on every hand—
Shall we forget the sailor, that ploughs for us the deep,
And for the landsman's favor their painful vigils keep?

Shall we who feast so richly on Zion's choicest stores,
For whom so full and freely she opens all her doors,
Withhold in cruel hardness the help we might extend,
And to the siprit's sadness the news of peace not send?

O for the Spirit's fire to warm each Christian's heart,
A gracious zeal inspire, a love and strength impart!
Then shall the songs of gladness from Bethel temples rise,
And they that mourn in sadness, send praises to the skies.

Driving to Port.

Though hard the winds are blowing, and loud the billows roar,
Full swiftly we are going to our dear native shore :
The billows breaking o'us, the storms that round us swell,
Are bidding to restore us to all we loved so well.

So sorrow often presses life's mariner along;
Afflictions and distresses are gales and billows strong :
The sharper and severer the storms of life we meet,
The sooner and the nearer is Heaven's eternal seat.

OCEAN MELODIES.

Do not ask me why I hasten
  To each vessel that appears,
Why so anxious and so wildly
  I wait the cherished hope of years,
    No, no, no,
Though my search prove unavailing,
  What have I to do with tears.

Do not blame me when I seek him,
  With these worn and weary eyes,
Can you tell me where he perished,
  Can you show me where he lies?
    No, no, no,
Yet there surely is some record,
  When a youthful sailor dies.

VOICE FROM THE OCEAN.

The following beautiful poem was written by D. Radford, to his mother, while at sea. In a few months after it was written, he fell from the yard-arm, and found a watery grave. He was a native of Boston, and the fond mother still survives to mourn the loss of an affectionate son.

(*Sweet Home.*)

1. I think of thee, moth-er, When th' low rippling sea, As it sweeps 'cross our prow seems to whis-per to me. There's *one* whose sad thoughts thou on-ly canst smother; Then think of that one. O, for-get not thy

VOICE FROM THE OCEAN, Continued.

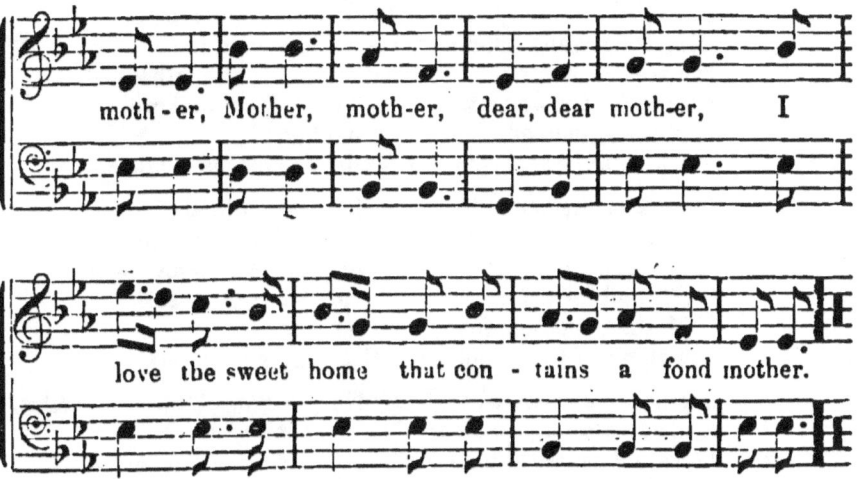

moth-er, Mother, moth-er, dear, dear moth-er, I love the sweet home that con-tains a fond mother.

I think of thee, too, when there's nought to be seen
Of the land I love best, and its bright sunny green;
When th' mirror-like surface of th' pure crystal water,
Reflects to my fancy *thine image*, my mother.
    Mother, mother, dear, dear mother.
    I love the sweet home that contains a fond mother.

When th' deep voice of thunder, and th' hoarse wind I hear,
'Mid the bright lightning's flash, that illumines the sphere,
My thoughts often tell me the heart of another
Ne'er possesses the feelings expressed by a mother,
    Mother, mother, dear, dear mother,
    I love the sweet home that contains a fond mother.

In th' bright sunny land of th' Italian's fair clime,
'Mid beauty and splendor, I'd hasten the time
My voyage will be ended, and th' home of another,—
I leave for the *home* which contains a fond mother.
    Mother, mother, dear, dear mother,
    I love the sweet home that contains a fond mother.

I think of thee, mother, when hardship attends,
When far o'er th' ocean, from dearly-loved friends,
Each voice of the sea-breeze still murmurs to me,—
" O, think of thy mother ! her prayer is for thee."
    Mother, mother, fond, fond mother,
    I think of thee, mother,—thy prayer is for me.

Should th' dreams wrought by fancy's conjectures prove false,
And some foreign malady then deaden my pulse,—
Were my sentence held forth in death's cruel grasp,—
I would think of thee, mother, while life's moments last.
    Mother, mother, fond, fond mother,
    I would think of thee, mother, while life's moments last.

When our barque is enshrouded by th' dark shade of night,
As she seeks her rough path by th' phosphoric light,—
On th' wild-dancing waves, that seem chasing each other,
My thoughts are all wandering to th' home of my mother
    Mother, mother, kind, kind mother,
    My thoughts are all wandering to the home of my mother.

I think of thee always, though time, in its flight,
Has taken thy home and thy form from my sight ;
Though long, weary days of toiling are mine,
My heart's meditations and thoughts are all thine.
    Mother, mother, kind, kind mother,
    My heart's meditations and thoughts are all thine.

OCEAN MELODIES.

Zion Nursed by Ships of the Sea.
Hymn sung at the Dedication of the First Baptist Mariner's Chapel, New York.
BY MRS. C. H. PUTNAM.—Tune, "*Sound the Loud Timbrel.*"

Praise to the grace which has triumph'd so freely
  Where sin had abounded and darkness had reign'd;
Praise to the word, which has spoken so fully
  Of blessings in store, which are yet to be gain'd.
    Sound the loud anthem o'er ocean and sea,
    The hand of Jehovah is stretched out to thee.

*For Zebulon's sons yet "shall call to the mountain,"
  The people from far to the house of the Lord,
To partake of that altar, and wash in that fountain
  Whose virtues their "going" shall herald abroad.
    Sound the loud anthem, &c.

The light of the promise already is dawning,
  For Zion is nursed by the ships of the sea;
Her temples the sailor now gladly is thronging,
  Rejoiced from the bondage of sin to be free.
    Sound the loud anthem, &c.

On the shore, where his footsteps too often were taken
  In snares which the wicked had set for his feet,
The Bethel now spreads for his welcome her beacon,
  And temples are rising his coming to greet.
    Sound the loud anthem, &c.

* Deut 33: 18, 19.

The Arbor of Prayer.—Tune, "*Home.*"

There is joy for our sorrows, and hope for our fears,
There is balm for our wounds, and a smile for our tears;
Though surrounded by grief, or low sunk in despair,
There is refuge from all in the arbor of prayer.
    Prayer, prayer, oh, sweet prayer,
    Let us fly to this arbor, the arbor of prayer.

Should the billows that never know quiet or rest,
Bear a part of our number afar on their breast,;
Tho' severed in body, our hearts may meet there,
To seek solace and peace in the arbor of prayer.
    Prayer, prayer, oh, sweet prayer, &c.

He who walks 'mid the waves and the storms at his will,
Can lash them to fury, or say, "Peace, be still!"
But we'll rest on His bosom, and seek the place where
He bestows his rich blessings—the arbor of prayer.
    Prayer, prayer, oh, sweet prayer, &c.

64 THE OMNIPOTENCE OF FAITH. L. M.

Music by Thorley. (*Portugal.*)

1. There is a faith, "the gift of God," The fruit of Je-sus' precious blood, That on the gos-pel's wondrous plan, Bestows omnip-o-tence to man.

This faith can every grace improve,
Command each mountain to remove,
And make each foe or barrier flee,
To sink beneath a boundless sea.

Victorious faith! each mountain flee,
Be swallowed up beneath the sea;
E'en more then conqueror I'll press on;
Begone, my fears, my doubts, begone.

Seamen, O seamen, Christ shall save,
And 'Bethel,' round the world shall wave;
Till winds and seas his praises "roar,"
On ocean waves from shore to shore.

The Voyage of Life. L. M.

The billows foam, the ocean rolls,
 And night in dismal darkness reigns;
I glide o'er seas in search of souls,
 The fruit of all my toil and pains.

We onward press, awake or sleep,
 In pain, or ease, in joy or woe,
Thus time, that mighty rolling deep,
 Pursues its fatal, ceaseless flow.

Propell'd along to Canaan's shore,
 All hail the tide that bears me on;
My toils and woes will soon be o'er,
 And angels shout " *his work is done.*"

O grateful pause in busy life,
 Free from its pain, and noise and din,
Its cares and woes, its cruel strife;
 Ah, let me now commune within.

Yes, onward still I guide my course,
 Through earth and hell's united flood·
Faith conquers heaven, *prayer* takes
  by force;
Thus, thus I urge my way to God.

OCEAN MELODIES.

The Wanderer Invited. L. M.
BICKERSTETH'S COLLECTION.

Wanderer from God, return, return,
And seek an injured Father's face;
Those warm desires, that in thee burn,
Were kindled by reclaiming grace.

Wanderer from God, return, return;
Thy Father hears that deep-felt sigh;
He sees thy softened spirit mourn,
And mercy's voice invites thee nigh.

Wanderer from God, return, return;
Renounce thy fears; thy Saviour lives;
Go to his bleeding cross, and learn
How freely, fully, he forgives.

Prayer at Sea. L. M. SIGOURNEY.

Prayer may be sweet in cottage homes,
Where sire and child devoutly kneel,
While through the open casement nigh
The vernal blossoms fragrant steal.

Prayer may be sweet in stately halls,
Where heart with kindred heart is blent,
And upward to th' eternal throne
The hymn of praise melodious sent.

But he who fain would know how warm
The soul's appeal to God may be,
From friends and native land should turn,
A wanderer on the faithless sea;—

Should hear its deep, imploring tone
Rise heavenward o'er the foaming surge
When billows toss the fragile bark,
And fearful blasts the conflict urge.

Nought, nought appears but sea and sky,
No refuge where the foot may flee:
How will he cast, O Rock divine,
The anchor of his soul on thee!

The Middle Watch. L. M.

Yes, Lord, my grateful voice I'll raise,
At midnight, in my watch at sea,
The floods shall hear me sing thy praise
And tell what grace has done for me

The moon, the stars, the deep shall hear,
Millions shall catch the grateful sound,
And winds shall o'er the ocean bear
The praise, till earth and heav'n rebound.

I'll praise for grace already given,
I'll praise for grace I'm yet to have,
I'll praise for grace '*reserved in heaven*,'
With glory crown'd beyond the grave.

Mariners' Hymn. L. M.

Great God! we will thy name adore;
And seek thy love, and grace implore;
May all who plough the sparkling sea,
Enjoy thy love and worship *Thee*.

While o'er the raging deep they ride,
Be thou their helper and their guide;
When thoughts impure annoy the soul,
Let matchless grace their minds control.

Prayers fervant often will ascend
To him who is the Sailor's Friend,
For their return to native clime,
Where love's sweet bow will brightly shine

Hopes brighter than the evening star,
Will cling around them when afar;
Affection's brilliant star will shed
Its beauty o'er the sailor's head.

When life's short voyage with them is
  o'er, [shore,
May they arrive on heaven's bright
There toilsome days and sleepless nights
Are known not in celestial heights.

66 SABBATH MORNING. C. M.

Music by Wm. Mather. (*Medfield.*)

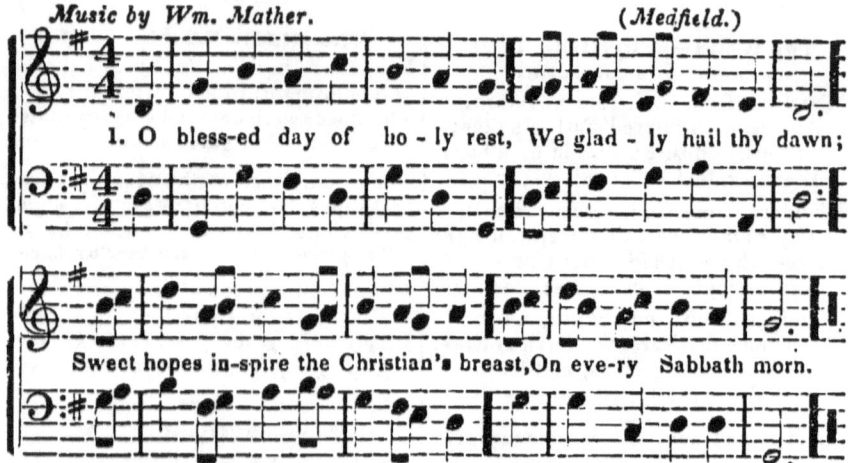

1. O bless-ed day of ho-ly rest, We glad-ly hail thy dawn; Sweet hopes in-spire the Christian's breast, On eve-ry Sabbath morn.

The little bark of Christian love,
O Father guide to-day;
Faith at the helm, and hope above,
And Christ the dear main-stay.

O God, on Ocean's treach'rous waves,
Thy glory oft we saw,
And now we sing the power that saves
'Mid dang'rous scenes afar.

Our Father bless the widows here,
The orphan too, O God,
Most graciously to them be near,
In sorrow's lone abode.

We would remember those afar
Upon the boundless deep;—
O keep them Saviour, ever near,
Nor let thy watch-care sleep.

And when our sabbaths all are past,
Then in the port above,
O anchor all our souls at last,
Where all is peace and love.

Pray for the Sailor. C. M. J. H. H.

O, pray for hardy sailors, pray,
While bounding o'er the wave;
Should storms and tempests round them play,
Then plead with God to save.

When black'ning clouds the sky o'erspread,
And vivid lightnings glare,
Then raise the soul to Zion's Head,
And ask his tender care.

O pray for wand'rers on the deep,
When dangers round them press,
That He the raging waves may keep,
Who bids their roarings cease.

Where'er he goes, 'neath foreign skies,
Or ploughs the briny main,
Let spirits yearn, and prayer arise,
And plead his safe return.

When life's short course of toil is o'er,
And dangers all are past,—
Then bid the soul in peace to soar,
And dwell in bliss at last

"Peace, be still." C. M.
BY MRS. A. M. C. EDMOND.

Fierce was the storm that rent the air,
 And shook the troubled sea;—
And redly gleamed the lightning's glare
 O'er gloomy Gallilee.

Within a fragile bark that rode,
 The sport of wind and wave,
Serenely slept the Son of God,
 Whose arm alone could save.

"Help, Lord!" the pale disciples cry,
 And cherish hope's last ray;
Death and destruction linger nigh,
 O guide us in thy way.

He speaks, "peace, peace," amazing word!
 Quenched are the lightning fires;
The tempest's voice no more is heard,
 The wrathful sea retires.

O thou who didst that fearful strife,
 With but thy voice assuage,
Calm thou the wilder storms of life,
 When sin and folly rage.

Speak, and the stormy breast shall be
 Calm as the lake at even,
And beams celestial caught from thee
 Shall mirror back to heaven.

The Sailor's Bible. C. M. J. H. H.

I love my bible,—precious boon,
 To sinful wand'rers given;—
A beacon light, to earth sent down
 To guide us safe to heaven.

I love, when darkness round us spreads,
 And ocean's lulled to rest,
To scan the page that ever sheds
 A halo round the blest.

I love, when adverse billows rise,
 And storms around me roar,—
Here to receive divine supplies,
 And upward gladly soar.

I love each promise so divine,
 On puny man bestowed,—
Whose mercies round our hearts entwine,
 And lead us to our God.

I love the bible—perfect chart
 Of life's meandering way,
A guiding star, our souls to lead
 To realms of endless day.

The Christian Mariner safe. C. M.
ADDISON.

How are thy servants blest, O Lord!
 How sure is their defence;
Eternal Wisdom is their guide,
 Their help, Omnipotence.

In foreign realms, and lands remote,
 Supported by thy care,
Thro' burning climes they pass unhurt,
 And breathe in tainted air.

When by the dreadful tempest borne
 High on the broken wave,
They know thou art not slow to hear,
 Nor impotent to save.

The storm is laid; the winds retire,
 Obedient to thy will;
The sea, that roars at thy command,
 At thy command is still.

In midst of dangers, fears, and deaths,
 Thy goodness we'll adore;
We'll praise thee for thy mercies past,
 And humbly hope for more.

68. CONFIDING TRUST. S. M.

Words by J. H. H. Music by Stanley. (*Shirland.*)

1. Great God at thy command, We launch up-on the deep;
O guide us in our devious way, Our souls in safety keep.

When dangers round us crowd,
 And toils our course attend,
Be thou our help, our sure defence,
 Our everlasting friend.

Should stormy winds arise,
 And tempests madly beat,
O grant us grace to trust in thee,
 And near the mercy-seat.

And though in distant climes,
 O'er raging seas we ride,
We trust in thee, thou gracious God,
 Our Saviour and our Guide.

And should our fragile bark,
 To ocean's depths be hurled:—
O may we reach a sheltering port,—
 A fairer, brighter world.

The power of God. S. M.

The boundless power of God
 Pour'd forth the noisy deep;
Whose billows lash the affrighted strand,
 Or hush'd by him, they sleep.

He guaged the mounds of sand,
 That smoothly line the shore;
And curb'd th' impetuous, lawless waves,
 While all enraged they roar.

His fingers spann'd the sky—
 Assign'd each star its place;
He smooth'd for each a spacious road
 Through vast, unbounded space

O praise him all ye orbs,
 And sound his fame abroad;
Proclaim his power, thou mighty deep,
 And own the hand of God.

OCEAN MELODIES. 69

Salvation by Grace. S. M.
Grace! 'tis a charming sound—
Harmonious to the ear;
Heaven with the echo shall resound,
And all the earth shall hear.

Grace first contrived the way
To save rebellious man;
And all the steps that grace display
Which drew the wondrous plan.

Grace led my roving feet
To tread the heavenly road;
And new supplies, each hour I meet,
While pressing on to God.

Grace all the work shall crown,
Through everlasting days;
It lays in heaven the topmost stone,
And well deserves the praise.

Deliverance. S. M. J. H. H.
When o'er the restless deep,
My bark has bounded high,
Thou mighty God, the Sailor's friend
Hast ever hovered nigh.

Though winds have round me howled,
And all was dark and drear,
My God, in love hast been my friend,
And ever lingered near.

When tempests dark assailed,
And thunders shook the sphere;
My gracious God hast heard my prayer,
And calmed each rising fear.

'Mid chilly arctic blasts,
And tropic's sultry glow,
Thou e'er hast been my sure defence,
My portion here below.

When far in distant climes,
I've groped in pagan night,
My Saviour's been my guiding star,
A gracious peering light,

And O, when life declines,
And earthly ties are riven;
My rescue then O deign to be,
And guide me safe to heaven.

Little Faith. S. M.
O thou of little faith,
On seas of trouble toss'd,
Depend on what the Saviour saith,
And you can ne'er be lost.

He bids you to him come,
Why should you yield to fear?
The winds may blow, and billows foam,
But Jesus Christ is there.

Though storms of sorrow rise,
And winds may adverse prove,
Yet, "Wherefore dost thou doubt?"
he cries,
"Mine is unchanging love."

Ark of Safety. S. M.
O, cease, my wandering soul,
On restless wing to roam;
All this wide world, to either pole,
Has not for thee a home

Behold the ark of God;
Behold the open door;
O, haste to gain that dear abode,
And rove, my soul no more.

There safe thou shalt abide,
There sweet shall be thy rest,
And every longing satisfied,
With full salvation blest

70. JOY AT IMMANUEL'S BIRTH. H. M.

Reed's Coll. (*Music from the Psaltery.*) (*Newman.*)

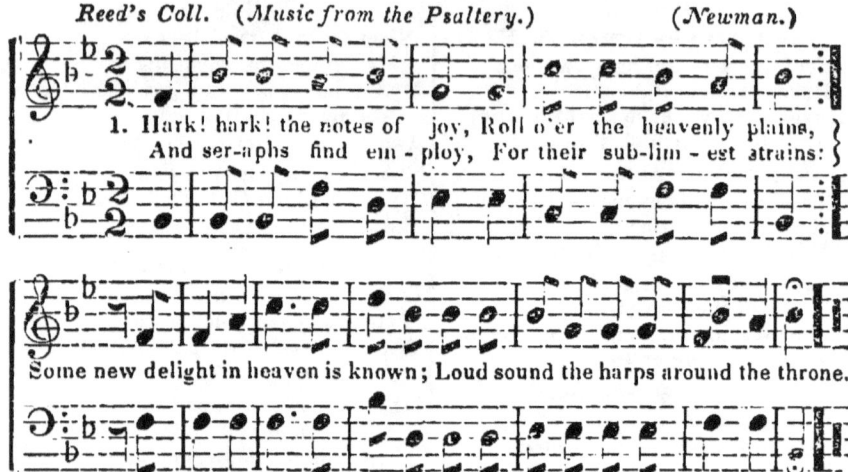

1. Hark! hark! the notes of joy, Roll o'er the heavenly plains,
And ser-aphs find em-ploy, For their sub-lim-est strains:
Some new delight in heaven is known; Loud sound the harps around the throne.

Hark! hark! the sounds draw nigh;
 The joyful hosts descend
The Lord forsakes the sky;
 To earth his footsteps bend:
He comes to bless our fallen race;
He comes with messages of grace.

Bear, bear the tidings round;
 Let every mortal know
What love in God is found,
 What pity he can show:
Ye winds that blow, ye waves that roll,
Convey the news from pole to pole.

Strike, Strike the harps again,
 To great Immanuel's name;
Arise, ye sons of men,
 And all his grace proclaim:
Angels and men, wake every string;
'Tis God the Saviour's praise we sing.

Repairing to Christ. H. M.

Hail, everlasting Spring!
 Celestial Fountain, hail!
Thy streams salvation bring;
 The waters never fail;
Still they endure, | For all our woe
And still they flow, | A sov'reign cure.

Blest be his wounded side,
 And blest his bleeding heart,
Who all in anguish died,
 Such favors to impart;
His sacred blood | From every sin,
Shall make us clean | And fit for God.

To that dear source of love,
 Our souls this day would come:
And thither, from above,
 Lord, call the nations home;
That Jew and Greek, |On all their tongues,
With rapturous songs,|Thy praise may
 [speak.

OCEAN MELODIES. 71

God's wonders of creation. H. M.

Give thanks to God most high,
The universal Lord;
The sovereign King of kings;
And be his grace adored.
His power and grace | And let his name
Are still the same; | Have endless praise.

How mighty is his hand!
What wonders hath he done!
He form'd the earth and seas,
And spread the heavens alone!
Thy mercy, Lord, | And ever sure
Shall still endure; | Abides thy word.

His wisdom framed the sun,
To crown the day with light;
The moon and twinkling stars
To cheer the darksome night.
His power and grace | And let his name
Are still the same; | Have endless praise.

God's Goodness and Truth. H. M.

Sing to the Lord most high;
Let every land adore;
With grateful voice make known
His goodness and his power;
With cheerful songs | And let his praise
Declare his ways, | Inspire your tongues.

Enter his courts with joy;
With fear address the Lord;
He formed us with his hand,
And quickened by his word;
With wide command, | O'er every sea
He spreads his sway | And every land.

His hands provide our food,
And every blessing give;
We feed upon his care,
And in his pastures live:
With cheerful songs | And let his praise
Declare his ways, | Inspire your tongues.

The Mariner's Prayer. H. M. H. W

O Lord, to thee we bow,
Hear thou our humble prayer,
We come before thee now,
To seek thy guardian care,
Ere leaving far behind, our home,
O'er ocean's swelling waves to roam

O, be our Guide and stay,
When foaming surges rise;—
When lurid lightnings play
Across the frowning skies;
And when soft winds our sails shall fill,
Be thou our Father, with us still.

'Tis thus we would implore,
Thy guidance on life's sea,
Until we reach that shore
Where we shall dwell with thee,
Unless thou should'st direct, we stray
Where shoals and quicksands fill the way.

But with thy presence near,
To light us o'er the sea,
No danger will we fear,
While looking unto thee,
For nought, our bark can overwhelm,
While thou, O Lord art at the helm.

Sabbath Morning. H. M. HAYWARD

Welcome, delightful morn,
Sweet day of sacred rest,
I hail thy kind return;
Lord, make these moments blest:
From low desires | I soar to reach
And fleeting toys | Immortal joys.

Now may the King descend,
And fill his throne of grace;
Thy sceptre, Lord, extend,
While saints address thy face:
Let sinners feel | And learn to know
Thy quickening word. | And fear the Lord.

72. MERCIES ACKNOWLEDGED. 8s & 7s.
(*Sicily.*)

1. Come, thou Fount of eve-ry blessing, Tune my heart to sing thy grace.
Streams of mer-cy, nev-er ceasing, Call for songs of loudest praise.

Teach me some melodious measure,
  Sung by raptured saints above;
Fill my soul with sacred pleasure,
  While I sing redeeming love.

By thy hand sustained, defended,
  Safe through life, thus far, I've come;
Safely, Lord, when life is ended,
  Bring me to my heavenly home.

Jesus sought me when a stranger,
  Wandering from the fold of God;
He, to save my soul from danger,
  Interposed his precious blood.

O, to grace how great a debtor
  Daily I'm constrained to be!
Let thy grace, Lord, like a fetter,
  Bind my wandering heart to thee.

God is Love. 8s & 7s.   BOWRING.

God is love; his mercy brightens
  All the path in which we rove,—
Bliss he wakes, and woe he lightens;
  God is wisdom, God is love.

Chance and change are busy ever;
  Man decays, and ages move;
But his mercy waneth never;
  God is wisdom, God is love.

E'en the hour that darkest seemeth,
  Will his changeless goodness prove;
From the gloom his brightness streameth;
  God is wisdom, God is love.

He with earthly cares entwineth
  Hope and comfort from above;
Every where his glory shineth;
  God is wisdom, God is love.

OCEAN MELODIES.

Sacred Song. 8s & 7s.   C. M. A.

Wand'rers o'er a stormy ocean,
  Star of Bethlehem be our guide;
Following thee with pure devotion,
  Fear we not the swelling tide.

Rudely though our bark be heaving,
  Dangers round, beneath, above!
Fiercer dangers gladly leaving,
  Onward to our port we move.

Every billow breaking o'er us,
  Nearer brings the land of rest;
Fair the haven lies before us,
  Bright the mansions of the blest.

There the stormy wind is sleeping,—
  Calm and peaceful is that shore;
There shall be no pain or weeping,
  There the weary toil no more.

Mariner's Hymn. 8s & 7s.   T. D.

See the sailor just embarking,
  For some distant foreign shore,
Blessed Jesus! Oh protect him,
  When the waves and billows roar.

When afar from christian teachers,
  Sailing through the trackless deep;
Gracious Savior! then instruct him,
  And his soul in safety keep.

If his grave be in the ocean,
  Far remote from home's lov'd shore;
Oh! receive his deathless spirit,
  Where the tempests rage no more.

Friend of seamen! deign to hear us,
  Listen to our fervent prayer:
Bear him to the port of glory,—
  May we meet the sailor there.

Source of Blessings. 8s & 7s.
NOEL'S COLLECTION.

Holy Source of consolation,
  Light and life thy grace imparts;
Visit us in thy compassion,
  Guide our minds, and fill our hearts.

Heavenly blessings, without measure,
  Thou canst bring us from above;
Lord, we ask that heavenly treasure,
  Wisdom, holiness, and love.

Dwell within us, blessed Spirit;
  Where thou art no ill can come;
Bless us now, through Jesus' merit;
  Reign in every heart and home.

Saviour, lead us to adore thee,
  While thou dost prolong our days;
Then, with angel hosts before thee,
  May we worship, love, and praise.

At Sea. 8s & 7s.   W. COLTON.

Lonely wand'rer on the ocean,
  Fainting for a place of rest;
Canst no longer keep in motion,
  Durst not trust the billow's breast.

Feeling fast thy strength diminish,
  Yet canst spy no friendly shore,
And must sink ere thou canst finish
  One returning circle more.

Rest thee then, I'll softly pillow,
  Thy too faint and feeble form,
Bear thee safely o'er the billow,
  Through this night of cloud and storm.

I was once like thee a ranger,
  Searching for a place of rest,
But to peace and hope a stranger,
  Till I found the Saviour's breast.

74 GRATEFUL ACKNOWLEDGMENTS. 8s, 7s & 4s.

Poetry by Mrs. T. P. Smith. (Zion.)

1. God of heaven, earth and ocean, We to-day thy praises sing;
Saved 'mid wind and wave's commotion, Grateful anthems we would bring.
Lord we praise thee, For thy goodness and thy grace, Lord we praise thee, For thy, &c.

Mercy guards us, mercy saves us,
 God's rich mercy is our song;
Buffeting temptation's breakers,
 Gracious mercy bears us on—
 God in heaven,
 Thy great mercy is our song.

When life's voyage shall be ended—
 Anchored in the port of rest,
With the Captain, Christ ascended,
 And the millions of the blest,
 There we'll praise thee,
 God of mercy and of grace.

Cheering Prospects. '8s, 7s & 4s. s.

Blessed Saviour! we adore thee,
 For the tokens of thy love,
It inspires the soul with rupture,
 While we muse on joys above.
 Shine upon us,
 Father, Son, and Heavenly Dove.

Great Redeemer! may the seamen,
 On the bosom of the deep,
Feel the flow of thy blest Spirit,
 And a golden harvest reap.
 Light is breaking
 For the children of the deep.

Yes, the long neglected sailor,
 Far from home and kindred dear,
Toiling when the raging ocean
 Fills his mind with gloom and fear,
 He is worthy
 Of the Christian's constant praye

When the sea shall yield her treasure,
 At the voice of God the Son!
Then, a noble band of seamen
 From their coral grave will come,
 Robed in splendor,
 By the Lamb, whose will is done

When the voyage of life is over,
  And we reach that heavenly land;
Where no raging billows harm us,
  Safe in port, a happy band;
    We will praise Thee,
  Holy, blessed Three in One.

Encouraging Prospects. 8s, 7s & 4.
Yes, we trust the day is breaking;
  Joyful times are near at hand;
God, the mighty God, is speaking,
  By his word, in every land:
    When he chooses,
  Darkness flies at his command.

While the foe becomes more daring,
  While he enters like a flood,
God, the Saviour, is preparing
  Means to spread his truth abroad:
    Every language
  Soon shall tell the love of God

O, 'tis pleasant, 'tis reviving
  To our hearts, to hear, each day
Joyful news, from far arriving,
  How the gospel wins its way,
    Those enlightening
  Who in death and darkness lay.

God of Jacob, high and glorious,
  Let thy people see thy hand;
Let the gospel be victorious,
  Through the world, in every land:
    Then shall idols
  Perish, Lord, at thy command.

Prayer for a Blessing. 8s, 7s & 4. JAY.
Come, thou soul-transforming Spirit,
  Bless the sower and the seed;
Let each heart thy grace inherit;

Raise the weak, the hungry feed;
  From the gospel
  Now supply thy people's need.

O, may all enjoy the blessing
  Which thy word's designed to give;
Let us all, thy love possessing,
  Joyfully the truth receive,
    And forever
  To thy praise and glory live.

Christ coming to Judgment.
        8s, 7s & 4.   OLIVER.
Lo! he comes, with clouds descending,
  Once for favored sinners slain;
Thousand thousand saints attending,
  Swell the triumph of his train:
    Hallelujah!
  Jesus shall forever reign.

Every eye shall now behold him,
  Robed in dreadful majesty:
Those who set at nought and sold him,
  Pierced, and nailed him to the tree,
    Deeply wailing,
  Shall the true Messiah see.

When the solemn trump has sounded,
  Heaven and earth shall flee away;
All who hate him must, confounded,
  Hear the summons of that day—
    "Come to judgment!—
  Come to judgment!—come away!"

Now the Saviour, long expected,
  See, in solemn pomp, appear,
All his saints, by man rejected,
  Now shall meet him in the air:
    Hallelujah!
  See the day of God appear.

76 TRIUMPH IN DEATH. 7s.

Poetry by Rev. A. T. (*Nuremburg.*)

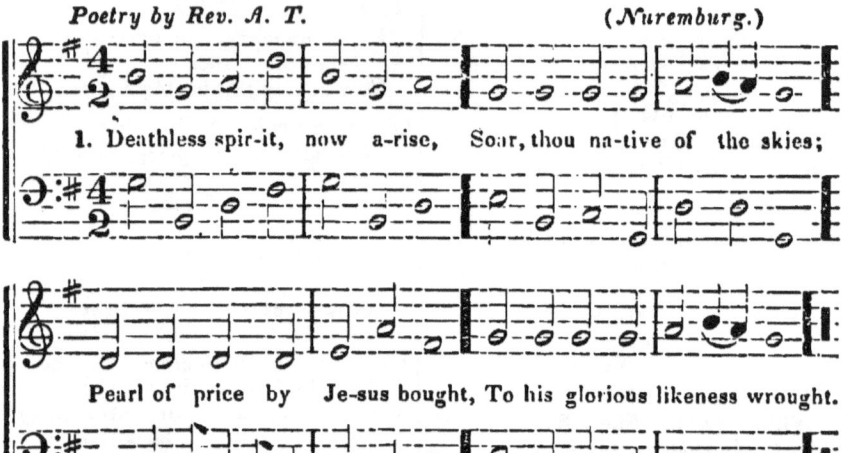

1. Deathless spir-it, now a-rise, Soar, thou na-tive of the skies;
Pearl of price by Je-sus bought, To his glorious likeness wrought.

Burst thy shackles, drop thy clay,
Sweetly breathe thyself away;
Singing, to thy crown remove,
Swift of wing and fired with love.

Shudder not to pass the stream;
Venture all thy care on him;
Him, whose dying love and power,
Stilled its tossing, hushed its roar.

Safe as the expanded wave,
Gentle as the summer's eve;
Not one object of his care,
Ever suffered shipwreck there.

See the haven full in view!
Love divine shall bear thee through;
Trust in that propitious gale,
Weigh thy anchor, spread thy sail.

Deliverance from Danger. 7s. L. M. s.

Ruler of the earth and sky,
Who the mighty deep doth hold,
In the hollow of thy hand,
By thy slightest word controlled.

Who the stormy winds dost curb,
Rushing on their midnight path,
And the reeling vessel save
From the tempest of their wrath.

Thou from shipwreck and despair,
Didst our souls in safety set,
When all human help was vain,
May we ne'er thy love forget.

Ne'er the tender mercy grieve,
That upheld us when we prayed,
Nor the sacred promise break
That in danger's hour we made.

The church going Bell. * 7s.
BY A SAILOR.

Praise to Heaven! peace to men!
Holy Sabbath comes again:
Day of thankfulness and prayer,
Sweet relief from lurking care.
Telling of that distant bourne
Whence to earth there's no return,
Bless'd of Him, by men adored,
Holy Sabbath of the Lord!

Innocence is in the swell
Of the holy Sabbath bell,
For it speaks of early time,
E'er we know of sin or crime.
And it brings around us here,
Forms and faces that were dear;
There's a sweet and sacred spell
In the holy Sabbath bell.

Simple, humble be the rhyme,
Singing of the Sabbath chime,
Though more stately numbers roll,
Sounding praise from pole to pole;
Still the bosom may be stirred,
By the humblest measure heard:
Peace to all of peaceful will,
Hope and joy are living still.

The Storm. 7s.

Fearful lightnings break the gloom,
And the deafening thunders roar,
Yawns the deep, unfathomed tomb,
Frowns the clifted craggy shore!
Death, in its terrific forms,
Rides the maddening waves of fire;
The wild genius of the storms,
Spends the fury of his ire.

Struggling hope now sinks and dies,
In the gloom of black despair,
Now the sailor lifts his eyes,
And his heart, to heaven in prayer.
Such the feelings of the soul,
When the power divine appeared;
He that could the storm control,
Spake, the driving tempest veered.

Swift along the craggy shore,
Fearfully the wreck was driven;
'Mid the bursting, breaker's roar,
To a safe, commodious haven.
So when time bears *us* along,
To Jordan's darkening flood;
May we join the glorious throng,
And chant the praises of our God.

Christ's Invitation. 7s. PRATT'S COL.

Come, saith Jesus' sacred voice,
Come, and make my paths your choice;
I will guide you to your home;
Weary pilgrims, hither come.
Hither come; for here is found
Balm for every bleeding wound,
Peace which ever shall endure,
Rest, eternal, sacred, sure.

Communion with God. 7s. EPIS.COL.

Softly now the light of day
Fades upon our sight away;
Free from care, from labor free;
Lord, we would commune with thee.
Soon for us the light of day
Shall forever pass away;
Then, from sin and sorrow free,
Take us, Lord, to dwell with thee.

* Lines composed by a Sailor on hearing the sound of the church going bell, whilst lying at anchor near the shore at *Salt Key, Turk's Island.*

78 PRAY WITHOUT CEASING. 7s & 6s.

Music by L. Mason. (*Missionary Hymn.*)

1. Go when the morning shineth, Go when the noon is bright, Go when the eve declineth, Go in the hush of night; Go with pure mind and feeling, Fling earthly thought away, And, in thy closet kneeling, Do thou in secret pray.

Remember all who love thee,
  All who are loved by thee;
Pray, too, for those who hate thee,
  If any such there be;
Then for thyself, in meekness,
  A blessing humbly claim,
And blend with each petition
  Thy great Redeemer's name.

Or, if 'tis e'er denied thee
  In solitude to pray,
Should holy thoughts come o'er thee
  When friends are round thy way,
E'en then the silent breathing,
  Thy spirit raised above,
Will reach his throne of glory,
  Where dwells eternal love

O, not a joy or blessing
  With this can we compare—
The grace our Father gave us
  To pour our souls in prayer:
Whene'er thou pin'st in sadness,
  Before his footstool fall;
Remember, in thy gladness,
  His love who gave thee all.

Confidence in God. 7s & 6s.
MONTGOMERY.

God is my strong salvation;
  What foe have I to fear?
In darkness and temptation,
  My light, my help, is near:
Though hosts encamp around me,
  Firm in the fight I stand,
What terror can confound me,
  With God at my right hand?

Place on the Lord reliance;
  My soul, with courage wait;
His truth be thine affiance,
  When faint and desolate;
His might thy heart shall strengthen,
  His love thy joy increase;
Mercy thy days shall lengthen;
  The Lord will give thee peace.

Praise to the Saviour. 7s & 6s.

To thee, O blessed Saviour,
  Our grateful songs we raise;
O, tune our hearts and voices
  Thy holy name to praise;
'Tis by thy sovereign mercy
  We're here allowed to meet,
To join with friends and teachers
  Thy blessing to entreat.

O, may thy precious gospel
  Be published all abroad,
Till the benighted heathen
  Shall know and serve the Lord,
Till o'er the wide creation
  The rays of truth shall shine,
And nations now in darkness
  Arise to light divine.

To my Sailor Boy. 7s & 6s. (Peculiar.)

When sailing on the ocean,
  In foreign climes you roam,
Oh! think with fond devotion,
  Upon your distant home;
And never strive to smother,
  But treasure up with joy,
Remembrance of a Mother,
  Who loves her Sailor boy.

When thunders loud are roaring
  And vivid lightning fly.
The rain in torrents pouring,
  Sleep will not greet my eye;
Tears will bedew my pillow,
  You all my thoughts employ,
'Toss'd on the angry billow,
  A little Sailor boy.

Kind Providence protect you,
  And bring you back again,
Your Mother will expect you,
  Safe from the troubled main;
No heaven will not distress me,
  The widow's hope destroy;
Return once more to bless me,
  My little Sailor boy.

PRAYER AT SEA. 6s & 4s.

Words by Mrs. A. M. C. Edmond. (*America.*)

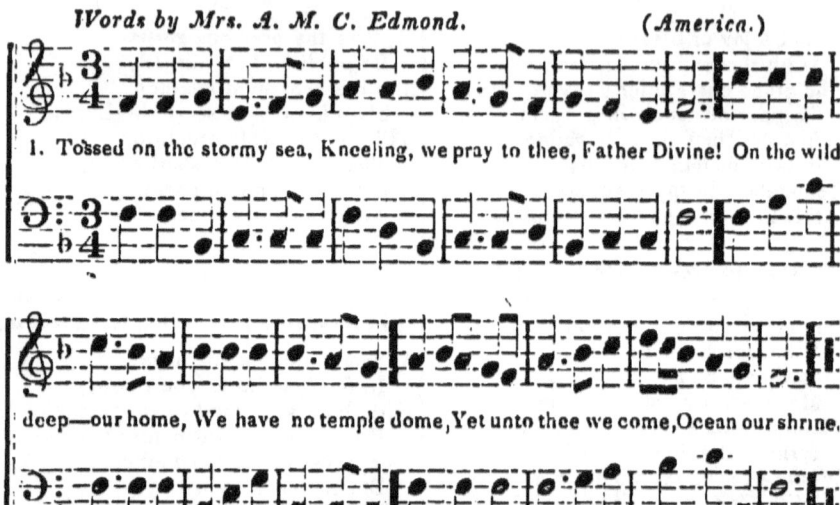

1. Tossed on the stormy sea, Kneeling, we pray to thee, Father Divine! On the wild deep—our home, We have no temple dome, Yet unto thee we come, Ocean our shrine.

Be thou our guard and guide
On the dark heaving tide,
  Pathless and free;—
When angry waves arise,
Hope in the bosom dies,
Where shall we turn our eyes,
  Lord! but to thee!

Hear thou our earnest prayer,
Through Him who once did bear
  Our weight of woe,—
Him, on the cross who died
When free salvation's tide,
Forth from his wounded side,
  For us did flow.

Grant his dear cross may be
On life's uncertain sea,
  Anchor secure;
So shall we breast the waves,
Where the fierce tempter craves
Souls for eternal graves,
  Death evermore.

Joyful our bark shall ride,
Safe from the raging tide,
  On to her haven,—
O when with weary breath,
But with exulting faith,
Near we the port of death,
  Moor us in heaven.

Christ our confidence. 6s & 4s.
R. PALMER.

My faith looks up to thee,
Thou Lamb of Calvary:
 Saviour divine,
Now hear me while I pray;
Take all my guilt away;
O, let me, from this day,
 Be wholly thine.

May thy rich grace impart,
Strength to my fainting heart;
 My zeal inspire;
As thou hast died for me,
O, may my love to thee
Pure, warm, and changeless be—
 A living fire.

While life's dark maze I tread,
And griefs around me spread,
 Be thou my Guide;
Bid darkness turn to day,
Wipe sorrow's tears away,
Nor let me ever stray
 From thee aside.

When ends life's transient dream,
When death's cold, sullen stream,
 Shall o'er me roll,
Blest Saviour, then, in love,
Fear and distress remove;
O, bear me safe above,—
 A ransomed soul.

Praise in the Courts of the Lord.
6s & 4s.   SACRED LYRICS.

Praise ye Jehovah's name;
Praise through his courts proclaim;
 Rise and adore;
High o'er the heavens above,
Sound his great acts of love,
While his rich grace we prove,
 Vast as his power.

[6]

Now let the trumpet raise
Triumphant sounds of praise,
 Wide as his fame;
There let the harp be found;
Organs, with solemn sound,
Roll your deep notes around,
 Filled with his name.

Christ's final Triumph. 6s & 4s.

Let us awake our joys;
Strike up with cheerful voice;
 Each creature, sing;
Angels, begin the song;
Mortals, the strain prolong,
In accents sweet and strong,
 "Jesus is King."

Proclaim abroad his name;
Tell of his matchless fame;
 What wonders done;
Above, beneath, around,
Let all the earth resound,
Till heaven's high arch rebound,
 "Victory is won."

He vanquished sin and hell,
And our last foe will quell;
 Mourners, rejoice;
His dying love adore;
Praise him, now raised in power;
Praise him forevermore,
 With joyful voice.

All hail the glorious day,
When through the heavenly way,
 Lo, he shall come,
While they who pierced him wail
His promise shall not fail;
Saints, see your King prevail:
 Great Saviour, come.

82. GOD'S WAY IN THE SEA. L. M.

Poetry by Rev. E. Mudge. Music by J. Hatton. (Duke Street.)

1. God of cre-a-tion! Lord of might, Thou hold'st thy universal sway.
O'er the broad fields of boundless light, And in the sea thou hast thy way.

Thy trump the awful thunders sound,
 Thine arrows forked lightnings are,
Thy march in earthquakes shake the ground
 And clouds ethereal are thy car.

Thy grace is an unbounded sea,
 Where tides of mercy ever roll,
In endless plenty rich and free,
 For every needy, thirsty soul.

"Thy way is in the sea," to guide
 Thy servants, who count all things loss,
To bear the gospel o'er the tide,
 In heathen lands to raise the cross

Thy way is in the raging sea,
 Where nations rise, and empires fall,
Tho' kings and emperors own not thee,
 Thou art the sovereign Lord of all

Christian Voyager. L. M.

The Christian voyager strikes the rock
 That lies conceal'd beneath the wave;
Yet safely he survives the shock,
 For Jesus ready stands to save.

His destined land he sometimes sees,
 And thinks his toils will soon be o'er,
Expects a gentle balmy breeze
 Will waft him quickly to the shore

But hark!—the midnight tempest roars
 He seems forsaken, and alone:
But Jesus, whom he then implores,
 Unseen preserves and leads him on.

Though fear his heart should overwhelm,
 He'll reach the port to which he's bound,
For Jesus holds and guides the helm,
 And soon the haven will be found.

OCEAN MELODIES.

Seamen Sing Praises. L. M.

Sing, seamen, sing to God on high!
 And let his praise on every breeze,
Sound to all lands, both far and nigh,
 O'er swelling floods and raging seas

So He ordains that you should sing,
 And tell the world his power to save;
To heathen lands his gospel bring,
 To cheer their passage to the grave.

Then sing, ye seamen, sing and tell
 Of all the goodness of the Lord,
In saving men from sin and hell,
 By his good spirit and his word.

By land or sea, at home, abroad,
 In christian or in heathen lands:
Lift up your voice and praise your God,
 In all the labour of your hands.

Sailor Boy to his Mother. L. M.

My mother! many a year has fled,
 Since first I left my native shore;
Now the dark ocean is my bed,
 And my night hymn the billows' roar.

No longer, as in days gone by,
 I feel thy hand upon me laid;
And see the tear-drop fill thine eye,
 As thou call'd blessings on my head.

No longer does thy prayer at even,
 In thy lov'd voice so sweet, and low,
Like a kind angel, sent from heaven,
 The way to truth and virtue show.

But as the lonely deck I pace,
 And gaze into the calm blue sky,
I seem to see thy well known face,
 And meet thy gentle, loving eye.

And then the voice of evening prayer
 In thrilling tones I know full well,
Comes like sweet music to my ear,
 And chains me with its holy spell.

And as I list that prayer at even,
 Its pleading, supplicating tone,
Bids me to hope my sins forgiven
 By the All Faithful holy One.

My mother's voice so full of love;
 My mother's heart so full of prayer
Whene'er they reach a throne above
 Will find thro' Christ acceptance there

FLORA.

Broken Vows. L. M.   s.

Men vow to Him who rules on high,
 And to him for protection cry:
When tempest howls, and thunder roll
 Then fear alarms their deathless soul

But when he calms the raging sea,
 They do not bow to him the knee;
They break the solemn vows they mad
 When lightnings flashed, and tempes
  raged.

Those vows men make in trouble, w
 One day their hearts with sorrow fill;
It will be then too late to say,
 I now my broken vows will pay.

God does remember every vow,—
 And though we scoff and trifle now
With judgment and eternal hell,
 There, those who break their vows mus
  dwell.

Now is the time to pay your vows,
 His bow of mercy round you throws
Its golden rays, O, heed this bow,
 And God will grace on you bestow

84 FAITH, THE SOUL'S SPY GLASS. L. M.

Music by Ch. Zeuner.   Poetry by P. Stow.   (Missionary Chant.)

1. Faith is a spy-glass for the soul; It shows where foaming billows roll;

Where rocks and whirlpools line the way, To drown the ship that sails astray.

Thro' this clear glass the soul may see
The bleeding Lamb of Calvary;
That sight will dissipate the gloom,
Which sin has gathered o'er the tomb.

While sailing o'er the sea of time,
Faith eyes a pure and blissful clime;
Far, far beyond life's stormy deep;
Where howling winds wake not from sleep.

Faith casts an anchor in that Bay,
Where gentle, balmy breezes play;
And moors the soul to *his* white throne,
Who will the faithful victors crown.

Sons of the deep! behold the cross,
Believe in Christ, our Righteousness,
He'll give strong faith, and light the way,
That leads to heaven's eternal day.

The Sailor's Chapel. L. M.

We kindle here a beacon light
For those whose home is on the wave,
To guide the seaman's course at night,
On treach'rous coasts, where tempests rave.

Dangers and death in forms untold,
The daring sons of ocean seize;
Their life-blood chilled by polar cold,
By ice fields crushed in northern seas.

When storms terrific rouse the swell
Of angry billows mountain high,
Far up the crested waves they go,
Then sink to coral depths below.

They need the cheering hope of heaven,
The peace of God within their breast,
An anchor, when by rough winds driven,
A pole star, pointing unto rest.

OCEAN MELODIES. 85

The Sailor. L. M.

Sailor! we need thee, to extend
Thy hand to lost and ruined men;
Thy noblest efforts to expend,
To bring our race to God again.

The eyes of Christians turn to thee,
  While they would fill the world with light,
And Jesus, also, looks to see
  Thee labor with a sailor's might.

Sailor! a gospel herald be!
  Enter the service of the Lord,
Rich freight bear to eternity,
  Which, there, shall be 'thy great reward.'

Good tidings of salvation take
  To those who are the slaves of sin,
Their iron fetters haste to break,
  Let now this blessed work begin.

God a Rock. L. M.

When thickly beat the storms of life,
  And heavy is the chastening rod,
The soul, beyond the waves of strife,
  Views the eternal rock—her God.

What hope dispels the spirit's gloom,
  When sinking 'neath affliction's shock?
Faith, through the vista of the tomb,
  Points to the everlasting rock.

Is there a man who cannot see
  That joy and grief are from above?
O, let him humbly bend the knee,
  And own his Father's chastening love.

Hope, Grace, and Truth, with gentle hand,
  Shall lead a bleeding Saviour's flock,
And show them, in the promised land,
  The shelter of th' eternal Rock.

Blessedness of the Righteous. L. M.
BARBAULD.

How blest the righteous when he dies!
When sinks a weary soul to rest!
How mildly beam the closing eyes!
How gently heaves th' expiring breast!

So fades a summer cloud away;
So sinks the gale when storms are o'er;
So gently shuts the eye of day;
So dies a wave along the shore.

Farewell, conflicting hopes and fears,
Where lights and shades alternate dwell,
How bright th' unchanging morn appears
Farewell, inconstant world, farewell!

Life's labor done, as sinks the clay,
Light from its load the spirit flies,
While heaven and earth combine to say,
'How blest the righteous when he dies!'

Parting with carnal Joys. L. M.
WATTS.

I send the joys of earth away;
Away, ye tempters of the mind,
False as the smooth, deceitful sea
And empty as the whistling wind.

Your streams were floating me along
Down to the gulf of dark despair;
And while I listened to your song,
Your streams had e'en conveyed me there.

Lord, I adore thy matchless grace,
That warned me of that dark abyss,
That drew me from those treach'rous seas,
And bade me seek superior bliss.

Now to the shining realms above
I stretch my hands and glance my eyes;
O for the pinions of a dove,
To bear me to the upper skies!

86 POWER AND MAJESTY OF GOD. C. M.
Poetry by H. K. White. Music by Gardiner. (*Dedham.*)

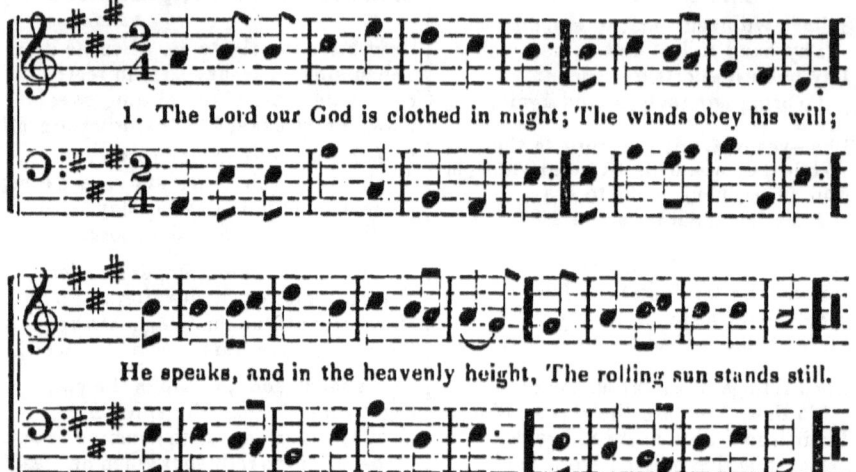

1. The Lord our God is clothed in might; The winds obey his will;
He speaks, and in the heavenly height, The rolling sun stands still.

Rebel, ye waves, and o'er the land
  With threatening aspect roar;
The Lord uplifts his awful hand,
  And chains you to the shore.

Ye winds of night, your force combine;
  Without his high behest,
Ye shall not, in the mountain pine,
  Disturb the sparrow's rest.

His voice sublime is heard afar;
  In distant peals it dies;
He binds the whirlwinds to his car,
  And sweeps the howling skies.

Ye nations, bend; in reverence bend;
  Ye monarchs, wait his nod,
And bid the choral song ascend
  To celebrate our God.

Paul's Voyage. C. M.

If Paul in Cesar's court must stand,
  He need not fear the sea;
Secured from harm on every hand
  By the divine decree.

Although the ship in which he sail'd,
  By dreadful storms was toss'd;
The promise over all prevail'd,
  And not a life was lost.

Jesus! the God whom Paul adored,
  Who saves in time of need;
Was then confess'd by all on board,
  A present help indeed!

Believers thus are toss'd about,
  On life's tempestuous main;
But grace assures beyond a doubt;
  They shall their port attain.

OCEAN MELODIES.

The Sailor at home again. C. M.
BY N. COLVER.

Hail to the precious Sabbath morn!
 Hail to this *bethel* home!
Saviour, to meet thy kind return,
 We wand'rers gladly come.

Toss'd on the billowy road of life,
 With suns, and stars, unblest;
From clouds, and storms, and tempests rife,
 We come, to seek thy rest.

Here let our weary spirits find,
 The God of Jacob still;
With promised grace to cheer the mind,
 Our hearts with comfort fill.

Spirit divine, on us descend,
 Make this a time of love,—
The pledges of thy grace renew,
 Seal'd from thy courts above.

Save the Sailor. C. M.

The Sailor's home is on the wave,
 And there his grave may be;
O christian stretch thy hand and save
 This pilgrim of the sea.

O haste ye, for his life is brief,
 Those "wild waves" roaring free—
May sink to everlasting death,
 The pilgrim of the sea

His heart is gen'rous, kind and brave—
 Landsmen! he toils for thee;
For thee he finds an early grave,
 Lone pilgrim of the sea.

Our God has pledged a bright reward
 To those who'll set him free;
And blest are they, who turn to God,
 One pilgrim of the sea.

The Sailor's Grave. C. M. REL. ALM

O place me not in sordid dust,
 When life shall cease to be;
For where could I this body trust,
 But in the deep blue sea?

In thy broad bosom, mighty deep,
 So quietly I'll lie;
And, resting with my fathers, sleep,
 While wild winds o'er me sigh.

The weeds shall be my winding-sheet,
 My coffin be of shell;
And when I sleep in caverns deep,
 No chiseled words shall tell.

Roll on, roll on! ye mountain waves,
 My dirge is in your roar,—
Roll on, till all within their graves
 Shall wake to sleep no more!

The sea shall then restore her dead,
 And from its depths I'll rise;
Then may I mount with Christ my head,
 And dwell above the skies.

Seaman's Concert. C. M. P. H. B.

We come, O Lord, before thy throne,
 And, with united pleas,
We weep, we pray for those who roam,
 Far off upon the seas.

Oh may the Holy Spirit bow
 The Sailor's heart to thee,
Till tears of deep contrition flow,
 Like rain-drops on the sea.

Then may a Saviour's dying love,
 Pour peace into his breast,
And waft him to the port above;—
 The port of glorious rest.

88. PRAISE TO GOD. C. M.

Poetry by Mrs. Hemans.   Music by Tansur, 1735.   (St. Martin's.)

It was his word which gave you birth,
   And majesty and might;
Praise ye the Highest from the earth,
   And let the deeps unite!

The fire and vapor, hail and snow,
   Are servants of his will;—
And stormy winds, that fiercely blow,
   His mandate they fulfil.

Mountains and rocks, to heaven that rise,
   And restless mighty flood;
Creatures of life, that wing the skies,
   Or track the plain for food.

Praise ye his name, to whom alone
   All homage should be given;
When glory from th' eternal throne,
   Spreads wide o'er earth and heaven.

God's Power on the Ocean. C. M.

To thee O God! whose just command
   Earth, sea, and air obey;
We gladly meet a joyful band,
   And here our homage pay.

We've seen thy works upon the sea,
   Thy wonders in the deep;
When thou didst loose the stormy winds,
   O'er raging waves to sweep.

We've sunk in Ocean's fearful depths,
   Then rose on mountain waves;
We've clung to rocks o'er the bright seas,
   That yawn'd like watery graves.

Then from the deep we called on God,
   The raging winds to stay;
The angry winds were hushed to sleep,
   At his almighty sway.

OCEAN MELODIES.

The Bethel Flag. C. M. F. S. KEY.

To thee O God, whose awful voice,
  The sea and air obey;
This humble house of prayer we raise,
  And here our homage pay.

Here, in this house high hymns of joy,
  Thy rescued sons shall raise;
And glowing hearts, and ready tongues,
  Their great Protector praise.

They called on Thee, and th' raging sea
  Sunk down at Thy command!
Their troubled souls Thou didst set free,
  By thine Almighty Hand.

Here let them come, and th' holy flag
  Shall float in sainted air;
As high they raise the hymn of praise,
  And breathe the solemn prayer.

Wonders of the Deep. C. M.

Oh God! thy name they well may praise,
  Who to the deep go down;
And trace the wonders of thy ways,
  Where mountain billows frown.

For them the fair majestic sight,
  Hath met their wand'ring eyes,
Beneath the streaming northern light,
  Or blaze of Indian skies.

If glorious be that awful deep,
  No human power can bind,
What then art Thou, who bid'st it keep
  Within its bounds confined?

Let heaven and earth in praise unite,
  Eternal praise to Thee,
Whose word can rouse the tempest's
    might,
Or still the raging sea!

The Sea of Gallilee. C. M.
BY MISS M. ROBINSON.

Bow down my spirit, and adore,
  While thus I gaze on thee,
Thou favored spot of all the earth,
  Thrice hallowed Gallilee.

Bow down my spirit and adore,
  As in the courts above;
Behold the place the Saviour trod,
  In sorrow and in love.

There is no sound along thy shore;
  No murmur of thy wave;
But tells of Him who left the skies,
  And life eternal gave.

Methinks among those stirring leaves
  His accents linger yet,
And fancy sees each glittering shrub
  With tears of pity wet.

How great that love, thy silver waves,
  The tale can well attest,
As from a simple seaman's boat,
  That floated on thy breast.

The God who reared those lofty hills,
  And gave the seas their birth;
There deigned to teach the outcast poor;
  The ignorant of earth.

Thy conscious waters knew their God,
  And yielded to his will,
As moved along the troubled deep,
  The gentle words, "Be still,"

Or when beneath the starless sky,
  Upon the stormy wave,
He went in mercy's fairest guise,
  To succor and to save.

90. DIVINE CONDESCENSION. S. M.

Poetry by Dr. Watts.   Music by L. Mason.   (*Boylston.*)

1. O Lord, our heavenly King, Thy name is all di-vine;
Thy glo-ries round the earth are spread, And o'er the heavens they shine.

When to thy works on high
  I raise my wondering eyes,
And see the moon, complete in light,
  Adorn the evening skies,—

When I survey the stars,
  And all their shining forms,—
Lord, what is man, that worthless thing,
  Akin to dust and worms?

Lord, what is worthless man,
  That thou shouldst love him so?
Next to thine angels is he placed,
  And lord of all below.

How rich thy bounties are,
  How wondrous are thy ways,
That, from the dust, thy power should frame
  A monument of praise!

Living by Faith. S. M.

If on a quiet sea
  Toward heaven we calmly sail,
With grateful hearts, O God, to thee,
  We'll own the favoring gale.

But should the surges rise,
  And rest delay to come,
Blest be the sorrow, kind the storm,
  Which drives us nearer home.

Soon shall our doubts and fears
  All yield at thy control;
Thy tender mercies shall illume
  The midnight of the soul.

Teach us, in every state,
  To make thy will our own,
And, when the joys of sense depart,
  To live by faith alone.

OCEAN MELODIES. 91

The Mission Ship. S. M. J. H. H.

Behold that stately ship,
  With pennon streaming wide;
Her canvas spread, with giant strides,
  She plows the briny tide.

The fanning breeze speeds on,
  A sacred, precious trust;
The gospel heralds bear his name,—
  The Holy and the Just.

In drear benighted climes,
  When rayless billows roll,—
The lamp of life reflects its beams,
  To light the darkened soul.

The gospel's joyful sound,
  Falls sweetly on the ear;
A Saviour's love proclaimed abroad,
  Bids idols disappear.

Kindness to our Frailty. S. M.

The pity of the Lord,
  To those that fear his name,
Is such as tender parents feel;
  He knows our feeble frame.

He knows we are but dust,
  Scattered with every breath;
His anger, like a rising wind,
  Can send us swift to death.

Our days are as the grass,
  Or like the morning flower;
When blasting winds sweep o'er the field,
  It withers in an hour.

But thy compassions, Lord,
  To endless years endure;
And children's children ever find
  Thy words of promise sure.

The Grace of Christ. S. M.

We sing the Saviour's love,
  Who pitied wretched man,
Delighting in the thought of peace,
  Ere time and worlds began.

We see its smiling beams,
  Forthshining at his birth,
And trace its lustre day by day,
  While he sojourned on earth.

But, in his closing hour,
  How infinite his grace,
When, bowed beneath the curse, he died
  To save the chosen race!

Ten thousand thousand songs,
  With high, seraphic flame,
Fall far below the boundless praise
  Of our Immanuel's name.

Preparation for the Judgment. S. M.

And will the Judge descend?
  And must the dead arise?
And not a single soul escape
  His all-discerning eyes?

How will my heart endure
  The terrors of that day,
When earth and heaven, before his face,
  Astonished, shrink away?

But, ere the trumpet shakes
  The mansions of the dead,
Hark! from the gospel's cheering sound
  What joyful tidings spread!

Come, sinners, seek his grace,
  Whose wrath ye cannot bear;
Fly to the shelter of his cross,
  And find salvation there.

92. APPEAL OF THE SAILOR. C. M.

Poetry by Mrs. Sigourney. (*Rochester.*)

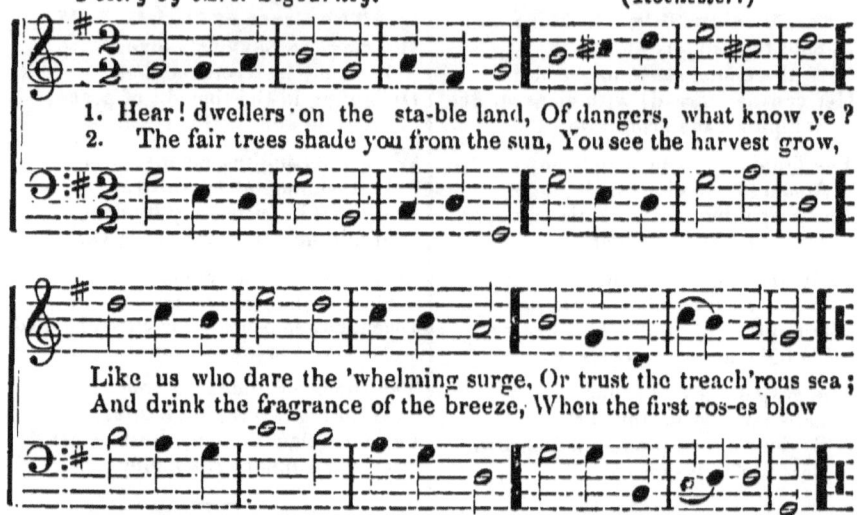

1. Hear! dwellers on the sta-ble land, Of dangers, what know ye?
2. The fair trees shade you from the sun, You see the harvest grow,

Like us who dare the 'whelming surge, Or trust the treach'rous sea;
And drink the fragrance of the breeze, When the first ros-es blow

But still, what know ye of the joy
  That lights our ocean strife—
When on its way the gallant ship
  Sweeps like a thing of life

And gaily, to the wished-for port,
  With fav'ring breeze we stand,
Or first your misty line descry,
  Hills of my native land!

Yet oh! there's peril in our path,
  Beyond the wrecking blast;
A peril that may reach the soul,
  When life's short voyage is past.

Send us your Bibles when we go
  Forth on the foaming wave,
Your men of prayer, to teach us how
  To meet a wat'ry grave.

A Mariner's Hymn. C. M.

While on the swelling sea of life,
  Proud mortals heedless sail;
Their guilty passions drive them far,
  Till cheering prospects fail.

Then gloomy storms, and fearful roar
  Of tempests, threaten death,
And yet all hands love not the name
  Of God who gives them breath.

May seamen for this haven steer,
  And see their Jesus there,
Behold his bloody sweat, and hear
  His agonizing prayer.

Be then this port my chief delight,
  'Till moor'd in heaven above;
Weeping I'll gaze upon the sight,
  And be dissolved in love.

God seen in his Works. C. M.
WALLACE.

There's not a star whose twinkling light
  Illumes the distant earth,
And cheers the solemn gloom of night,
  But goodness gave it birth.

There's not a cloud whose dews distil
  Upon the parching clod,
And clothe with verdure vale and hill,
  That is not sent by God.

There's not a place in earth's vast round,
  In ocean deep, or air,
Where skill and wisdom are not found;
  For God is every where.

Around, beneath, below, above,
  Wherever space extends,
There Heaven displays its boundless love,
  And power with goodness blends.

Swiftness of Time. C. M.
J. Q. ADAMS.

How swift, alas! the moments fly!
  How rush the years along!
Scarce here, yet gone already by—
  The burden of a song,

See childhood, youth, and manhood, pass,
  And age, with furrowed brow;
Time was—time shall be—but, alas!
  Where, where in time is now?

Time is the measure but of change;
  No present hour is found;
The past, the future, fill the range
  Of time's unceasing round.

Where, then, is now? In realms above,
  With God's atoning Lamb,
In regions of eternal love,
  Where sits enthroned I AM.

The Mariner's Psalm. C. M.

Thy works of glory, mighty Lord,
  Thy wonders in the deeps,
The sons of courage shall record,
  Who trade in floating ships.

At thy command, the winds arise,
  And swell the towering waves;
The men, astonished, mount the skies,
  And sink in gaping graves.

Sailors rejoice to lose their fears,
  And see the storm allay'd;
Now to their eyes the port appears,
  There let their vows be paid.

O that the sons of men would praise
  The goodness of the Lord!
And those that see thy wondrous ways,
  Thy wondrous love record.

The Sailor Sorrowing for Sin. C. M
BY REV. E. MUDGE.

Come, sailor, come with all the grief,
  With which thy soul is riven,
And though earth yields thee no relief,
  There's hope for thee from heaven.

Though you have run a wild career,
  By passion's whirlwind driven;
Come, change your course, and you
    may wear,
  A sparkling crown in heaven.

O, let your future life declare
  That you to God have given
Your heart, to live a life of prayer,
  And seek a rest in heaven.

O come, before life's day declines,
  In clouds of darkest even;
Secure a place where glory shines,
  In endless day in heaven.

94 THE MORAL LIGHT HOUSE. L. M.
Words by P. Slow. (*Uxbridge.*)

1. God's moral lights, his children are, From them a radiance streams a-far;

O'er sea and land in eve-ry clime, The Star of Hope o'er them will shine.

Now they receive their light and bliss
From Christ, the Sun of righteousness;
His mellow light illumes the soul,
When rayless billows madly roll.

They were in sin and darkness too,
But Jesus did their souls renew;
He gave them light, from heav'n above,
And o'er them spread his bow of love.

God will impart this light to all,
If we obey his winning call;
He will array in bright attire,
And give us pure, celestial fire.

But if we heed not moral light,
And choose to grope in nature's night,
Our bark will dash upon *that* shore,
Where light will greet the soul no more.

Birth day Hymn. L. M.

My years roll on: the tide of time
Bears me thro' many a changing clime:
I've summers, winters, heat and cold,
Winds, calms, and tempests ten times to d.

My years roll on: and with them flows
That mercy which no limit knows;
'Tis mercy's current makes me glide,
In hope of safety, down the tide.

My years roll on: then let me know
The great design for which they flow;
And as the ship floats o'er the wave,
The vessel, Lord, in mercy save.

My years roll on: my soul be still,
Guided by love thy course fulfil:
And when life's anxious voyage is past,
My rest shall be with Christ at last.

OCEAN MELODIES.

The Bethel. L. M.   P. S.

The Bethel is the place for thee,
Thou wand'rer o'er the pathless sea;
Here you may have your spirit blest,
And find in Jesus perfect rest.

The Bethel is the place for thee,
For God is here, and he will see
Thy tearful eye and throbbing heart,
And bid thy load of guilt depart.

The Bethel is the place for thee,
To pay the vows you made at sea;
When crested billows o'er you roll'd,
You mercy crav'd with sighs untold.

The Bethel is the place for thee,
Dear seamen, now to Jesus flee;
Then when the storms of life are past,
You'll go where all the weary rest.

God's Presence. L. M. N. COLVER.

God's voice is heard when thunders roar,
I see him in the lightning's blaze;
The earth stands trembling at his pow'r,
And owns his hand, and speaks his praise.

He rides upon the stormy blast,
That howls along its billowy road;
The staggering hulk, the shiv'ring mast,
Proclaim the great, and dreadful God.

Nor less, his goodness, shines abroad,
In smiling suns, and falling showers;
He writes his name upon the cloud,
And seals the promised blessing ours.

In all his works, my God I see;
But still I feel his glory more,
When e'er I gaze on Calvary,
And my redeeming God adore.

Security in God. L. M. WATTS.

How oft have sin and Satan strove
To rend my soul from thee, my God
But everlasting is thy love,
And Jesus seals it with his blood.

The oath and promise of the Lord,
Join to confirm the wondrous grace;
Eternal power performs the word,
And fills all heaven with endless praise.

Amidst temptations, sharp and long,
My soul to this dear refuge flies;
Hope is my anchor, firm and strong,
While tempests blow and billows rise.

The gospel bears my spirit up;
A faithful and unchanging God
Lays the foundation for my hope,
In oaths, and promises, and blood.

True Friend. L. M. P. S.

There is a Friend who's always nigh,
To those who on his word rely;
When storms arise, and billows roll,
He will protect the humble soul.

When dangers in their pathway lie,
And howling tempests rage and sigh;
He then will keep with watchful care,
All those who seek his face by prayer.

When sickness rends their mortal frame,
And human aid appears in vain;
He'll prove a friend in time of need
To all who will his promise plead.

Come, then, bold seamen, seek this Friend!
He'll constant prove till time shall end;
And when the voyage of life is o'er,
He'll land you safe on Canaan's shore.

HOLY FORTITUDE. C. M.

Poetry by Dr. Watts. (*Balerma.*)

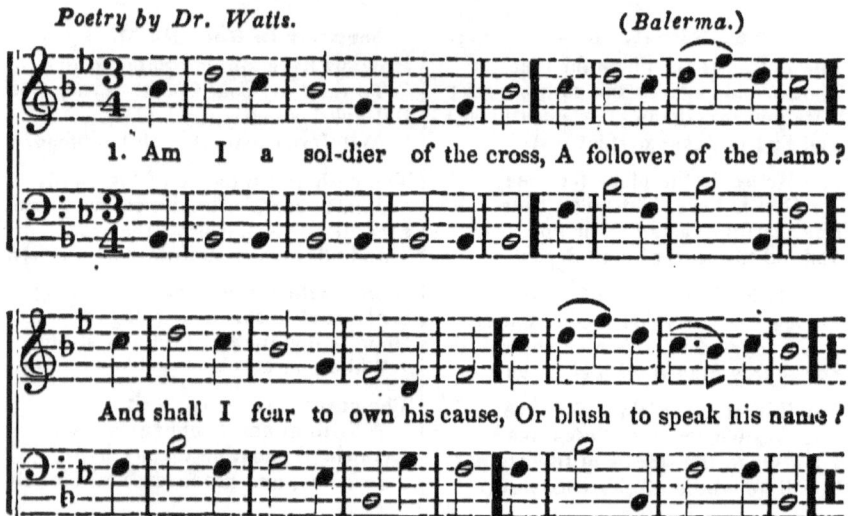

1. Am I a sol-dier of the cross, A follower of the Lamb? And shall I fear to own his cause, Or blush to speak his name?

Must I be carried to the skies
  On flowery beds of ease?
While others fought to win the prize,
  And sail'd through bloody seas?

Are there no foes for me to face,
  Must I not stem the flood?
Is this vile world a friend to grace,
  To help me on to God?

Thy saints in all this glorious war
  Shall conquer, though they die;
They see the triumph from afar,
  And seize it with their eye.

When that illustrious day shall rise,
  And all thy armies shine
In robes of victory through the skies,
  The glory shall be thine.

Light is breaking. C. M.

How changed the vision of the sea,
  The dim cloud floating o'er,
Spreads on the azure canopy,
  And breaks in mercy's shower.

Thus when the ocean wanderer feels
  The Law's fierce lightning-flame,
And hears its bursting thunder-peals
  The doom of death proclaim;—

The light of heavenly mercy plays
  On his Redeemer's brow,
There's life immortal in its rays,
  And he's forgiven now.

We bless the goodness of our Lord,
  Who sends his light to thee,
O, love his name, believe his **word,**
  Our brother of the sea!

OCEAN MELODIES. 97

The Sailor's Friend. C. M.

Of old did Jesus condescend
  To calm the raging sea,
O, he was then the Sailor's Friend,
  And such he still would be.

He does but wait to hear us crave,
  As they besought him then—
'Master, we perish! come and save,
  For we are dying men!'

Not to sustain our mortal breath,
  We raise the earnest cry;
Lord save our precious souls from death,
  And make us fit to die.

Then blow, ye winds, ye surges roar!
  'Twill not our souls appal;
Tho' waves and billows pass us o'er,
  And deep to deep should call.

Miracles of Christ. C. M.

And didst thou, Jesus, condescend,
  When veiled in human clay,
To heal the sick, the lame, the blind,
  And drive disease away?

Didst thou regard the beggar's cry,
  And cause the blind to see?
Thou Son of David, hear—O, hear—
  Have mercy, too, on me.

And didst thou pity mortal woe,
  And sight and health restore?
O, pity, Lord, and save my soul,
  Which needs thy mercy more.

Didst thou thy trembling servant raise,
  When sinking in the wave?
I perish, Lord; O, save my soul;
  For thou alone canst save.

Power of God. C. M.

With reverence let the saints appear,
  And bow before the Lord,
His high commands with reverence hear,
  And tremble at his word.

The northern pole and southern rest
  On thy supporting hand;
Darkness and day from east to west
  Move round at thy command.

Thy words the raging winds control,
  And rule the boisterous deep;
Thou mak'st the sleeping billows roll,
  The rolling billows sleep.

Justice and judgment are thy throne,
  Yet wondrous is thy grace;
While truth and mercy, joined in one,
  Invite us near thy face.

The Tree with Golden Fruit. C. M.
BY C. S. BARTH

Upon a hill there stands a tree
  Where golden fruit is found,—
'Tis meant for ev'ry land to see,
  It shines for all around.

Here many come by day and night,
  Its gold their fond pursuit,
They shake its branches with delight,
  And bear away the fruit.

And yet its riches always stay,
  The tree is never bare;
Whatever fruit is borne away,
  As much still glitters there.

What is its name? and where its place?
  How can this wonder be?
Who now will tell us? who can guess?
  The *Bible is that tree.*

7

98. HOPE OF REUNION IN HEAVEN. C. M.

Poetry from the Psalmist. (*Marlow.*)

1. When floating o'er life's troubled sea, By storms and tempests driven,
Hope, with her radiant finger points To brighter scenes in heaven.

She bids the storms of life to cease,
  The troubled breast be calm;
And in the wounded heart she pours
  Religion's healing balm.

Her hallowed influence cheers life's hours
  Of sadness and of gloom;
She guides us through this vale of tears,
  To joys beyond the tomb.

And when our fleeting days are o'er,
  And life's last hour draws near,
With still unwearied wing she hastes
  To wipe the falling tear.

She bids the anguished heart rejoice:
  Though earthly ties are riven,
We still may hope to meet again
  In yonder peaceful heaven.

The Sailor Missionary. C. M.

Upon the waters, glorious Lord,
  Thy path of light has been,
The *mariner* thy voice has heard,
  Thy works of mercy seen.

Thou hast disciples from the sea,
  A bold and ardent band,
Who *love* to tell the *world* of thee,
  Who wait on *thy* command.

O, send them to the lands afar,
  As heralds of thy grace;
Give them thy truth to scatter there,
  That yields a large increase.

The seed on many waters cast,
  Shall spring to life and bloom,
The harvest day will come at last,
  And sheaves be gathered home.

OCEAN MELODIES.

Divine aid Implored. C. M.
DR. T. F. OAKES.

God of the earth and boundless sea,
  Thou Maker of my soul,
Whose kingdom fills immensity,
  Wilt thou my thoughts control.

Inspire my voice to sing thy praise
  My heart to love thy word,
That I may high thy banner raise,
  And triumph in the Lord.

Teach me to feel thy truth divine,
  Engraven on my heart;
Teach me to know that I am thine,
  Say to my doubts, depart.

Then, will I love thy cause, my King;
  Praise thee from shore to shore—
And then in heaven thy glory sing,
  When time shall be no more.

Purposes of God. C. M.

God moves in a mysterious way,
  His wonders to perform;
He plants his footsteps in the sea,
  And rides upon the storm.

Judge not the Lord by feeble sense,
  But trust him for his grace;
Behind a frowning providence
  He hides a smiling face.

His purposes will ripen fast,
  Unfolding every hour;
The bud may have a bitter taste,
  But sweet will be the flower.

Blind unbelief is sure to err,
  And scan his work in vain;
God is his own interpreter,
  And he will make it plain.

The Hope, the Star, the Voice. C. M.
H. H. HAWLEY.

There is a hope, a blessed hope,
  More precious and more bright
Than all the joyless mockery
  The world esteems delight.

There is a star, a lovely star,
  That lights the darkest gloom,
And sheds a peaceful radiance o'er
  The prospects of the tomb.

There is a voice, a cheering voice,
  That lifts the soul above,
Dispels the painful, anxious doubt,
  And whispers, "God is love."

That voice, aloud from Calvary's height,
  Proclaims the soul forgiven;
That star is revelation's light;
  That hope, the hope of heaven.

Call to pious seamen. C. M. T. B. B.

Seamen who love the Saviour's name,
  Go forth and make it known;
Where'er you go his love proclaim,
  Point upward to his throne.

Bear, bear to India's sunny clime,
  The knowledge of his name;
Bid China in the chorus chime,
  And catch the heavenly flame.

On Afric's dark benighted shore,
  Kindle the gospel light;
The Islands of the sea implore,
  To break from satan's might.

Exalt his name o'er land and sea,
  Make known his matchless grace;
And soon the captives shall be free;
  Freedom that brings true peace.

100. DEATH AT SEA. S. M.

Poetry by J. H. H.   Music by A. Williams.   (St. Thomas.)

1. Far, far from childhood's home, And cherished kindred dear; In lone-liness the sai-lor lies, And wipes the falling tear.

His languid form is pale,
  And crumbles slow away,
For wan disease with fearful grasp,
  Has seized his trembling prey.

The feeble ebbing tide,
  Now nears a distant shore;
Life's sun is sinking 'neath the wave,
  On earth to beam no more.

A dread and icy spell,
  Has chilled life's current now;
And death has fixed his final seal
  Upon that pallid brow.

Thus speeds our earthly course,
  As borne by rushing wind,
Thus soon the destined haven's made,
  Where all an entrance find.

Burial at Sea. S. M.   J. H. H.

A hardy mariner
  Has bid to earth adieu;
Loved shipmates fondly gather round,
  To take a final view.

That cold and lifeless form,
  From which the soul has fled,
In death's habiliments is clad,
  To sleep in ocean's bed.

The bubbling waters yawn
  To receive the sacred trust,
Beneath the closing wave it sinks
  In silence there to rest.

Amid the sparkling gems
  Of ocean's choicest store,
Where coral monuments arise
  O'er millions gone before.

The Spirit Inviting. S. M.

The Spirit, in our hearts,
  Is whispering, "Sinner, come;"
The bride, the church of Christ, proclaims
  To all his children, "Come!"

Let him that heareth say
  To all about him, "Come;"
Let him that thirsts for righteousness
  To Christ, the fountain, come.

Yes, whosoever will,
  O, let him freely come,
And freely drink the stream of life;
  'Tis Jesus bids him come.

Lo! Jesus, who invites,
  Declares, "I quickly come:"
Lord, even so; we wait thy hour;
  O blest Redeemer, come.

Active Effort to do Good. S. M.

Sow in the morn thy seed;
  At eve hold not thy hand;
To doubt and fear give thou no heed;
  Broadcast it o'er the land;—

And duly shall appear,
  In verdure, beauty, strength,
The tender blade, the stalk, the ear,
  And the full corn at length.

Thou canst not toil in vain;
  Cold, heat, and moist, and dry,
Shall foster and mature the grain
  For garners in the sky.

Thence, when the glorious end,
  The day of God, shall come,
The angel-reapers shall descend,
  And heaven cry, "Harvest home!"

Now the accepted Time. S M.

Now is th' accepted time;
  Now is the day of grace;
Now, sinners, come, without delay,
  And seek the Saviour's face.

Now is th' accepted time;
  The Saviour calls to day;
To-morrow it may be too late;
  Then why should you delay?

Now is th' accepted time
  The gospel bids you come,
And every promise in his word
  Declares there yet is room.

Lord, draw reluctant souls,
  And feast them with thy love;
Then will the angels swiftly fly
  To bear the news above.

Office of Faith. S. M

Faith is a precious grace,
  Where'er it is bestowed;
It boasts a high, celestial birth,
  And is the gift of God.

Jesus it owns as King,
  And all-atoning Priest;
It claims no merit of its own,
  But looks for all in Christ.

To him it leads the soul,
  When filled with deep distress,
Flies to the fountain of his blood,
  And trusts his righteousness.

Since 'tis thy work alone,
  And that divinely free,
Lord, send the Spirit of thy Son,
  To work this faith in me

CHRIST THE PILOT. L. M.

Poetry by Cowper. (*Effingham.*)

1. The billows swell; the winds are high; Clouds overcast my wintry sky;
Out of the depths to thee I call, My fears are great, my strength is small.

O Lord, the pilot's part perform,
And guide and guard me thro' the storm;
Defend me from each threatening ill;
Control the waves; say, "Peace! be still."

Amidst the roaring of the sea,
My soul still hangs her hope on thee;
Thy constant love, thy faithful care,
Is all that saves me from despair.

Dangers of every shape and name
Attend the followers of the Lamb,
Who leave the world's deceitful shore,
And leave it to return no more.

Tho' tempest-tossed, and half a wreck,
My Saviour through the floods I seek;
To him alone will we complain,
Amid the winds, and stormy main.

The Precious Bible. L. M. P. S.

The Bible! is a *Polar Star*—
It sheds its brightness from afar,
And cheers the soul with rays divine!
O'er life's rough sea, in every clime.

It is a *Chart*, by which we may
Shun hidden rocks, and find that bay
Where angry billows never rise,
And gloomy clouds veil not the skies.

It is a *Compass* for the soul,
When tempests howl and surges roll,
Its *magnet* power attracts the heart;
While *quiv'ring* with affliction's dart.

Most precious Book! in thee we find
Knowledge and wisdom for the mind;
May all who plough the boist'rous deep,
A *Mother's Bible* search and keep.

OCEAN MELODIES.

God's Protection. L. M.

Launch'd on blue ocean's restless waves,
My bark expands its feeble wing;
And flies o'er countless watery graves,
A trembling, frail, precarious thing.

Enclosed within its tender shell,
I hear the waters yawn below;
I feel it quiver to the swell,
I feel it to the breezes bow.

Yet on this couching, helpless thing,
Th' Atlantic's stormy wrath I brave;
Beneath the shadow of his wing,
Stretch'd out in mercy o'er the wave.

Though cloudy day and darksome night,
Succeed upon a shoreless sea;
Tho' "Hope deferred" denies my sight
The distant land where I would be:

There is a hope, which guilds for me
The awful surges of the deep;
And in the gloomiest cloud I see
The pledge, that God will safely keep.

The Cross. L. M.

Inscribed upon the cross we see,
In glowing letters, "God is love;"
He bears our sins upon the tree;
He brings us mercy from above.

The cross! it takes our guilt away,
It holds the fainting spirit up;
It cheers with hope the gloomy day,
And sweetens every bitter cup;—

The balm of life, the cure of woe,
The measure and the pledge of love,
The sinner's refuge here below,
The angel's theme in heaven above.

The Sailor Boy. L. M.

The sailor boy, how hard his lot!
The angry winds have nursed his form!
Rocked on the ocean's heaving breast,
His playmate is the giant storm!

Roams he a silent wave alone?
Earth's noblest scenes are all his own,
But ah! the heart can ne'er forget
She is a weary wanderer yet.

Oh! while he gazes, fondly rise,
The happy home now left behind,
Those lips, with smiles of love enwreathed,
Those hearts with sweet affections
[twined;

His bosom throbs, he bends to hear
Glad voices steal upon his ear,
Lured by the whisper of the breeze,
And far off murmur of the seas.

The shipwrecked Sailor. L. M.

What fearful cry, so wild and shrill,
In loneliness bursts up to heaven?
'Tis heard no more, the winds are hush'd,
The tempest-clouds asunder riven!

The moon looks down with placid eye,
On surge and fragment hurrying by:
A faithful watch should ever keep
Above the shipwrecked sailor's sleep.

While round his corpse the foam shroud
[cling,
For him warm tears are gushing fast,
For him a mother's longing eye
In silent grief to heaven is cast,

Though o'er his form no tomb is piled,
Think you unwept is ocean's child,
While beating hearts with love can burn
His memory shall find an urn.

104 SAILOR, IS IT WELL WITH THEE? 7s.

Music by Pleyel.   (*Pleyel's Hymn.*)

1. Sail-or, is it well with thee? In thine own im-mor-tal soul? If the Saviour makes you free, Grace will all your powers control.

Seamen, is it well with thee?
  Blind by nature, poor and lame,
Jesus Christ can make you see
  All the beauties in his name

Sailor, is it well with thee?
  Is thy soul now moored above?
Have you sought true liberty?
  Do you know a Saviour's love?

Seamen, is it well with thee?
  Were thy sins on Jesus laid,
When he bled on Calvary,
  Died and bow'd his sacred head?

Sailor, is it well with thee?
  Christ in glory waits to save.
Pardons rich, and full, and free,
  Wilt thou now from Jesus have?

God's Protection to Mariners. 7s.

They that toil upon the deep,
  And in vessels light and frail,
O'er the mighty waters sweep,
  With the billow and the gale.

Mark what wonders God performs,
  When he speaks, and, unconfin'd,
Rush to battle all his storms,
  In the chariots of the wind.

Then unto the Lord they cry·
  He inclines a gracious ear;
Sends deliv'rance from on high,
  Rescues them from all their fear.

Oh that men would praise the Lord
  For his goodness to their race;
For the wonders of his word,
  And the riches of his grace!

OCEAN MELODIES.

A Refuge. 7s. C. WESLEY.

Jesus, refuge of my soul,
　Let me to thy bosom fly,
While the raging billows roll,
　While the tempest still is high:

Hide me, O my Saviour, hide,
　Till the storm of life is past;
Safe into the haven guide;
　O, receive my soul at last.

Other refuge have I none;
　Hangs my helpless soul on thee;
Leave, ah, leave me not alone;
　Still support and comfort me:

All my trust on thee is stayed,
　All my help from thee I bring;
Cover my defenceless head
　With the shadow of thy wing.

Expostulation. 7s.

Sinner, what has earth to show
Like the joys believers know?
Is thy path, of fading flowers,
Half so bright, so sweet, as ours?

Doth a skilful, healing friend
On thy daily path attend,
And, where thorns and stings abound,
Shed a balm on every wound?

When the tempest rolls on high,
Hast thou still a refuge nigh?
Can, O, can thy dying breath
Summon one more strong than death?

Canst thou, in that awful day,
Fearless tread the gloomy way,
Plead a glorious ransom given,
Burst from earth, and soar to heaven?

Danger of Delay. 7s.

Haste, O sinner; now be wise;
　Stay not for the morrow's sun;
Wisdom if you still despise,
　Harder is it to be won.

Haste, and mercy now implore;
　Stay not for the morrow's sun,
Lest thy season should be o'er,
　Ere this evening's stage be run.

Haste, O sinner; now return;
　Stay not for the morrow's sun,
Lest thy lamp should cease to burn
　Ere salvation's work is done.

Haste, O sinner; now be blest;
　Stay not for the morrow's sun,
Lest perdition thee arrest,
　Ere the morrow is begun.

Pleading for Acceptance. 7s

On that great, that awful day,
This vain world shall pass away,
And before the Maker stand,
All the creatures of his hand.

Then shall all the nations meet
At th' eternal judgment-seat,
And, unveiled before his eye,
All the works of man shall lie.

O, in that destroying hour,
Source of goodness, Source of power,
Show thou, of thine own free grace,
Help unto a helpless race.

Hear, and pity; hear, and aid;
Spare the creatures thou hast made;
Fold us with the sheep that stand
Pure and safe at thy right hand.

106. THE WINGS OF FAITH. C. M

Poetry by Dr. Watts. Music by Tucker.   (*Devizes.*)

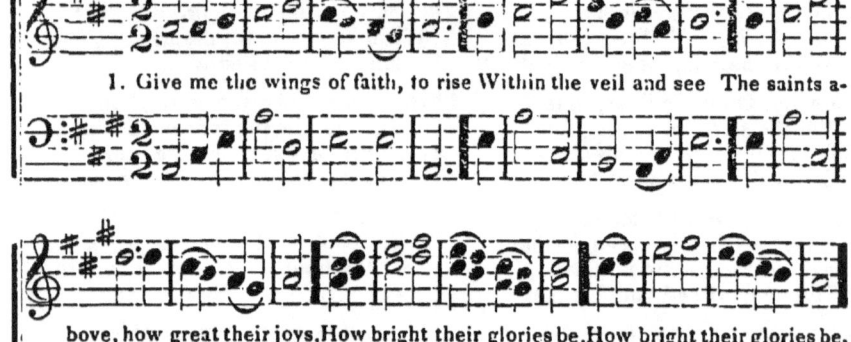

1. Give me the wings of faith, to rise Within the veil and see The saints above, how great their joys, How bright their glories be, How bright their glories be.

Once they were mourning here below,
And bathed their couch with tears;
They wrestled hard, as we do now,
With sins, and doubts, and fears.

I ask them whence their victory came;
They, with united breath,
Ascribe their conquest to the Lamb,
Their triumph to his death.

They marked the footsteps that he trod;
His zeal inspired their breast;
And, following their incarnate God,
Possessed the promised rest.

Our glorious Leader claims our praise,
For his own pattern given,
While the long cloud of witnesses
Shows the same path to heaven.

Christ the Resting Place. C. M.

Jesus! delightful, charming name!
It spreads a fragrance round;
Justice and mercy, truth and peace,
In union here are found.

He is our life, our joy, our strength;
In him all glories meet;
He is a shade above our heads,
A light to guide our feet.

When storms arise and tempests blow,
He speaks the stilling word,
The threatening billows cease to flow,
The winds obey their Lord.

The thickest clouds are soon dispersed,
If Jesus shows his face;
To weary, heavy-laden souls
He is the resting-place.

OCEAN MELODIES.

Christ our Guide. C. M.

Bright was the guiding star that led,
 With mild benignant ray,
The Gentiles to the lowly shed
 Where the Redeemer lay.

But lo! a brighter, clearer light
 Now points to his abode;
It shines through sin and sorrow's night,
 To guide us to our Lord.

O haste to follow where it leads;
 The gracious call obey,
Be rugged wilds, or flowery meads,
 The Christian's destined way.

O gladly tread the narrow path
 While light and grace are given;
We'll meekly follow Christ on earth,
 And reign with him in heaven.

Prayer for Strong Faith. C. M.

O for a faith that will not shrink
 Though pressed by every foe,
That will not tremble on the brink
 Of any earthly woe!—

That will not murmur nor complain
 Beneath the chastening rod,
But, in the hour of grief or pain,
 Will lean upon its God;—

A faith that shines more bright and clear,
 When tempests rage without;
That when in danger knows no fear,
 In darkness feels no doubt;—

Lord, give us such a faith as this,
 And then, whate'er may come,
We'll taste, e'en here, that hallowed bliss,
 Of an eternal home.

Hope. C. M.

Borne o'er the ocean's stormy wave,
 The beacon's light appears,
When yawns the seaman's watery grave,
 And his lone bosom cheers.

Then, should the raging ocean foam,
 His heart shall dauntless prove,
To reach, secure, his cheerful home,
 The haven of his love.

So when the soul is wrapt in gloom,
 To worldly grief a prey,
Thy beams blest hope, beyond the tomb,
 Illume the pilgrim's way.

They point to that serene abode
 Where holy faith shall rest,
Protected by the sufferer's God,
 And be forever blest.

The Crown of Glory. C. M.

Awake, my soul, stretch every nerve,
 And press with vigor on,
A heavenly race demands thy zeal,
 And an immortal crown.

A cloud of witnesses around,
 Hold thee in full survey;
Forget the steps already trod,
 And onward urge thy way.

'Tis God's all-animating voice,
 That calls thee from on high;
'Tis his own hand presents the prize
 To thine aspiring eye.

My soul, with all thy wakened powers,
 Survey the heavenly prize;
Nor let the glitt'ring toys of earth
 Allure thy wandering eyes.

108 THE CONVERTED SAILOR. L. M.

Poetry by P. Stow. (*Hamburg.*)

1. Behold the spir-it from a-bove, Renews the sailor's heart with love, The li-on has the lamb become, No more with hatred will he roam.

He serves his Captain with delight,
At home, abroad, for him he'll fight;
With weapons tempered by the Lord,
He wields a glorious heavenly sword.

If seamen round him reckless are,
The mellow ray from Bethlehem's star,
Illumes his soul and cheers his heart,
And hope's sure anchor joys impart.

The Bible, the *celestial Chart,*
Directs him to a blessed port,
Where raging billows never rise,
And gloomy clouds vail not the skies.

His mind is tranquil in that hour,
When death's dark waves around him roar,
A sweet majestic voice says come,
And rest from toil in thy bright home.

The Sabbath Bell. L. M. s. a. b.

Though to the wanderer o'er the sea,
No Sabbath bell may peal its chime,
Nor sweetly on his spirit steal
Those sounds that mark this holy time.

Though from the bosom of the deep,
No Bethel spires shall point above,
Nor whisper to his listening ear,
The story of redeeming love.

Yet if the heart be tuned to hear,
At each return of holy time,
That Sabbath bell anew shall sound,
And Memory bring the sacred chime.

And though no temple "made with hands,"
Shall then upon their vision break,
The Spirit may a dwelling find,
And in his *heart* a *Bethel* make.

OCEAN MELODIES.

A Peaceful Conscience. L. M.

While some in folly's pleasures roll,
And court the joys that hurt the soul,
Be mine that silent, calm repast,
A conscience peaceful to the last.

With this companion in the shade,
My soul no more shall be dismayed;
But fearless meet life's dreariest gloom,
And the pale monarch of the tomb.

Amidst the various scenes of ills,
Each blow some kind design fulfils;
And can I murmur at my God,
While love supreme directs the rod?

His hand will smooth my rugged way,
And lead me, to the realms of day;
To milder skies, and brighter plains,
Where everlasting pleasure reigns.

Breathings of Grace. L. M.

Like morning, when her early breeze
Breaks up the surface of the seas,
That, in their furrows, dark with night,
Her hand may sow the seeds of light.

Thy grace can send its breathings o'er
The spirit, dark and lost before;
And freshening all its depths, prepare
For truth divine to enter there.

Till David touched his sacred lyre,
In silence lay th' unbreathing wire;
But when he swept its chords along,
E'en angels stooped to hear the song.

So sleeps the soul, till thou, O Lord,
Shall deign to touch its lifeless chord;
Till, waked by thee, its breath shall rise
In music worthy of the skies.

Asleep in Jesus. L. M.

Asleep in Jesus! O, how sweet
To be for such a slumber meet!
With holy confidence to sing
That Death has lost his venomed sting

Asleep in Jesus! peaceful rest,
Whose waking is supremely blest:
No fear, no woe, shall dim that hour
That manifests the Saviour's power.

Asleep in Jesus! time nor space
Affects this precious hiding-place:
On Indian plains or Lapland snows,
Believers find the same repose.

Asleep in Jesus! O, for me
May such a blissful refuge be:
Securely shall my ashes lie,
And wait the summons from on high.

The River of Life. L. M.

There is a pure and peaceful wave,
That issues from the throne of love,
Whose waters gladden as they lave
The bright and heavenly courts above.

In living streams behold that tide
Thro' Christ the rock profusely burst;
And in his word, behold supplied
The fount for which our spirits thirst.

The pilgrim faint, who seems to sink
Beneath the sultry sky of time,
May here repose, and freely drink
The waters of that better clime.

And every soul may here partake
The blessings of the fount above;
And none who drink will e'er forsake
The crystal stream of boundless love.

110 VICTORY OF THE SAINTS. 7s. DOUBLE.
Poetry by Montgomery. (*Eltham.*)

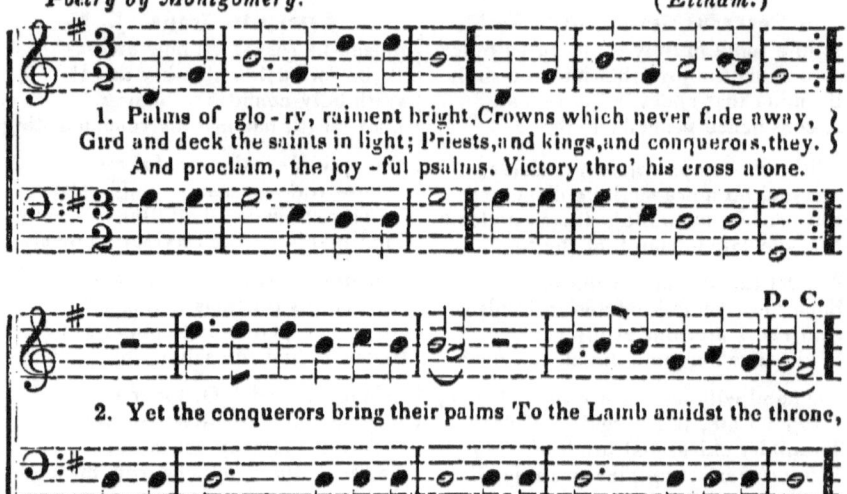

1. Palms of glo-ry, raiment bright, Crowns which never fade away,
Gird and deck the saints in light; Priests, and kings, and conquerors, they
And proclaim, the joy-ful psalms, Victory thro' his cross alone.

2. Yet the conquerors bring their palms To the Lamb amidst the throne,

Kings for harps their crowns resign,
 Crying, as they strike the chords,
"Take the kingdom; it is thine,
 King of kings and Lord of lords."

Round the altar priests confess,
 With their robes made white as snow
'Twas their Saviour's righteousness,
 And his blood, which made them so.

Who were these? on earth they dwelt,
 Sinners once of Adam's race;
Guilt, and fear, and suffering, felt,
 But were saved by sovereign grace.

They were mortal, too, like us;
 And when we, like them, shall die,
May our souls, translated thus,
 Triumph, reign, and shine, on high.

The hour of Prayer. 7s.

Hark! the bell! the hour of prayer,
Morning signal, sweet and clear;
Welcome, welcome not to me,
Th' Sailor's call to prayer at sea.
Ready in the cabin hall,
At the mercy seat now fall;
Ready, he's your Captain there,
Raise the soul in fervent prayer
Tremble while Jehovah speaks,
Bend as Sinai's thunder breaks;
Pardoned, tearful sinner, hear;
Meekly bow in holy fear.
Sailor bless the hour of prayer,
Bless the bell that calls thee there;
So shall Jesus prosper thee
In the hour of prayer at sea.

Watchman's Chorus. 7s.

Watchman! tell us of the sea,
  Have ye signs of promise now?
Does the wand'ring sailor flee
  To God's altar with his vow?

Does your flag yet float the breeze,
  High in air its story tell?
"Sons of ocean, rivers, seas,
  Come and enter, come and dwell."

Christian! yes, on every wind,
  Signs of promise are at hand;
Weary sons of ocean find
  Peace and joy, within our band.

To the breeze our banner's thrown,
  In the storm our light is high,
Guiding sailors to their "Home,"
  And the home of God on high.

Watchman! tell us of the sea,
  Of the ships of Tarshish there;
Will they join the conflict free,
  And with God the battle share?

Christian! yes; the mighty sea,
  Speaks the praises of our God,
And her flag waves proudly free,
  Where the sailor's foot hath trod.

Watchman! Christian! join in one,
  High to God your voices raise,
To the Father and the Son,
  Tune alike your harps of praise.

Guide, O God, the ocean's son;
  Saviour, let him dwell with thee,
Where thou art no storm can come,
  In thy rest, there's no more sea.

The Messengers of God. 7s.

Go, ye messengers of God;
  Like the beams of morning, fly;
Take the wonder-working rod;
  Wave the banner-cross on high.

Go to many a tropic isle,
  In the bosom of the deep,
Where the skies forever smile,
  And th' oppressed forever weep.

O'er the pagan's night of care
  Pour the living light of heaven;
Chase away his wild despair;
  Bid him hope to be forgiven.

Where the golden gates of day
  Open on the palmy east,
High the bleeding cross display,
  Spread the gospel's richest feast.

Christ coming to save his People. 7s.

Hark! that shout of rapturous joy,
  Bursting forth from yonder cloud;
Jesus comes, and, through the sky,
  Angels tell their joy aloud.

Hark! the trumpet's awful voice
  Sounds abroad o'er sea and land;
Let his people now rejoice;
  Their redemption is at hand.

See, the Lord appears in view;
  Heaven and earth before him fly,
Rise, ye saints; he comes for you;
  Rise to meet him in the sky.

Go and dwell with him above,
  Where no foe can e'er molest,
Happy in the Saviour's love,
  Ever blessing, ever blest.

112. ENCOURAGED TO HOPE. C. M.

Poetry by P. Stow. Music by N. D. Gould. (Woodland.)

When earthly visions fade in gloom,
  And sun and stars are gone,
The soul a wreck, a splendid wreck,
  Lies hopeless and forlorn—

When sin revives, and billows roll,
  And hope's last ray has fled,
While sinking in a sea of wo,
  Lost, hopeless, blind, and dead—

A sweet, majestic voice is heard
  Above the roaring sea:
Listen! he calls who freely bled,
  " Come, hopeless, come to me."

His voice gives life, hope, joy, and peace,
  Then peerless glories shine,
His love benign illumes the soul,
  And gives a hope divine.

All hope of safety but in Him
  Who rules o'er sea and land,
Is taken from the sinner's mind,
  Whose ' house is on the sand.'

Sunless and starless is our sky,
  Until the Holy Dove
New plumes the soul with pinions strong,
  To soar and dwell above.

Seeking a rest. C. M.

We seek a rest beyond the skies,
  In everlasting day;
Thro' floods and flames the passage lies,
  But Jesus guards the way.

The swelling flood, and raging flame,
  Hear and obey his word;
Then let us triumph in his name,
  Our Saviour is the Lord.

OCEAN MELODIES.

Heaven Anticipated. C. M.

Come, Lord, and warm each languid
Inspire each lifeless tongue; [heart;
And let the joys of heaven impart
Their influence to our song.

Then to the shining realms of bliss
The wings of faith shall soar,
And all the charms of Paradise
Our raptured thoughts explore.

There shall the followers of the Lamb,
Join in immortal songs,
And endless honors to his name
Employ their tuneful tongues.

Lord, tune our hearts to praise and love;
Our feeble notes inspire,
Till, in thy blissful courts above,
We join the heavenly choir.

The final Adieu. C. M. BEDDOME.

There is a world of perfect bliss
  Above the starry skies;
Oppressed with sorrows and with sins,
  I thither lift my eyes.

'Tis there the weary are at rest,
  And all is peace within;
The mind, with guilt no more oppressed,
  Is tranquil and serene.

Discord and strife are banished thence,
  Distrust and slavish fear;
No more we hear the pensive sigh,
  Or see the falling tear.

Farewell to earth and earthly things:
  In vain they tempt my stay:
Come, angels, spread your joyful wings,
  And bear my soul away.

[8]

Heaven in Prospect. C. M.
STENNETT.

On Jordan's stormy banks I stand,
  And cast a wishful eye
To Canaan's fair and happy land,
  Where my possessions lie.

O'er all those wide-extended plains
  Shines one eternal day;
There, God the Son, forever reigns,
  And scatters night away.

When shall I reach that happy place,
  And be forever blest?
When shall I see my father's face,
  And in his bosom rest?

Filled with delight, my raptured soul,
  Would here no longer stay;
Tho' Jordan's waves should round me
  I'd fearless launch away. [roll,

There's Hope for Thee. C. M.

Blest be that voice now heard afar,
  O'er the dark, rolling sea,
That whispers in the sailor's ear,
  'Sailor, there's hope for thee!

Blest be that pure, that Christian love,
  That boundless charity,
Which bears the olive like the dove,
  Brave, generous man for thee.

Blest be those lips, in accents mild,
  From sordid motives free,
That first proclaimed to Ocean's child,
  'Sailor, there's hope for thee.'

Long hadst thou rode the foamy wave,
  From sin nor danger free,
Till mercy stretched her arm to save—
  To save, brave sailor, thee.

114 THE PIOUS SAILOR'S REQUEST. L. M.

Words by T. B. B.   (Wells.)

1. O how I love thy name my Lord, How precious is thy ho-ly word; Come friends and own his gracious reign,"Take not my Saviour's name in vain."

At the beginning he was there,
He formed the sea, he made the air;
He lights the sun, he sends the rain,
"Take not my Saviour's name in vain."

He loved our fallen race so well,
He died to save our souls from hell;
He died for us, but rose again,
"Take not his blessed name in vain."

In heaven he lives, for us he pleads,
Our souls by grace divine he feeds;
Our sins are by his sorrow slain,
"Take not my Saviour's name in vain."

Once more to judge the world he'll come,
And take his ransomed people home,
Would you with him in glory reign,
"Take not his hallowed name in vain."

God's Voice upon the deep. L. M.

Upon the waters glorious God,
Thy voice sublime is often heard
Proclaiming in the Sailor's ear,
Of power and love and constant care.

Thy voice is echoed o'er the sea,
By minds attuned to worship thee,
They speak of pardon bought with blood
While sailing o'er the raging flood.

When seamen shall obey thy voice,
And in thy boundless love rejoice,
Thy truth shall triumph o'er the earth,
From east to west, from north to south.

We hail with joy that glorious day,
When all who plow the foaming way,
Shall sound thy voice o'er sea and land;
And on the Rock of Ages stand.   P. S.

OCEAN MELODIES.

The Bethel Flag. L. M.

Flag of the pure and azure heaven!
  How lovely is thy bearing here;—
Free as the breezes round thee driven,
  Is thy sweet errand on the ear.

For unto thee are gathered men,
  Whose only panoply is prayer;
And where thou wavest, lofty hymns
  Discourse along the listening air.

It tells unto the ocean-tossed,
  That He who span its floods can save,
And that for him, the well nigh lost,
  The ark yet lingers on the wave.

It heralds joy to the oppress'd,
  And ransom to the sons of thrall,
And shadow forth to labor rest,
  In music of Salvation's call.

With voice of psalms, then to the skies
  Unfurl the flag—a type of love;
The answering anthem's shout shall rise
  When they reveal the Holy Dove.

Eye the Heavenly Compass. L. M.

While o'er the angry sea of time,
We need to eye in ev'ry clime,
The glorious Compass from above,
This Magnet from the God of love.

O may this Compass be my guide,
While I am sailing o'er life's tide;
Let me not go upon the sea,
Without the Bible, guide for me.

If we this Compass eye with care,
Whirlpools and rocks we oft shall clear;
And onward glide to that bright land,
Where joyful spirits sweetly blend.
  P. S.

Pouring Oil on the Waters. L. M.

The glorious gospel now allays
  The angry waves of bitter strife,
And ushers in those golden days,
  When wo and tumult are not rife.

Like oil upon the foaming deep,
  On which the furious winds do play,
In vain the wrathful waves now leap,
  The oil holds them in perfect sway.

So oil divine new power imparts,
  And calms the tumult of the soul,
Gives peace and joy to troubled hearts,
  Subdues by love and gains control.

May seamen with a cheerful will,
  Pour oil divine on sin's dark sea,
Kind words the hardest heart can thrill,
  And bid all angry passions flee.

This holy oil o'er sea and land, [roll,
  Shall calm woe's crested waves that
All nations shall in union blend,
  And love abound from pole to pole.
  P. S.

No Peace for the Wicked. L. M.

No peace! no peace! Jehovah cries,
To those who do my love despise;
Their mind is like the restless deep,
Whose turbid waters never sleep.

In the deep fountain of the soul,
The waves of sorrow madly roll,
They beat upon the smitten heart,
And peace and joy will *then depart.*

But Jesus can the tumult calm,
And thro' the soul transfuse his balm;
Bid peace and love possess the breast,
And give the troubled mourner rest. P. S.

116. THE SAILOR'S TOMB. C. M.

Music by D. Dutton, jr. (*Woodstock.*)

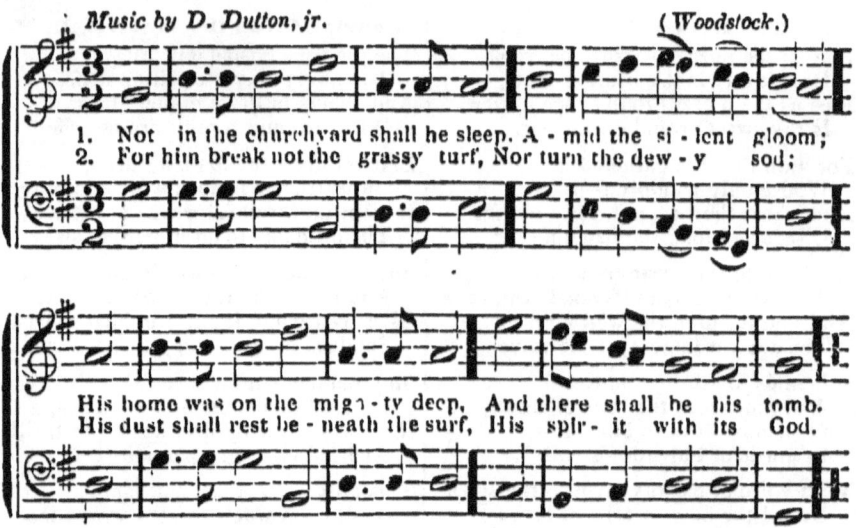

1. Not in the churchyard shall he sleep, A-mid the si-lent gloom;
2. For him break not the grassy turf, Nor turn the dew-y sod;

His home was on the migh-ty deep, And there shall be his tomb.
His dust shall rest be-neath the surf, His spir-it with its God.

He loved his own bright, deep blue sea,
O'er it he loved to roam;
And now his winding-sheet shall be
That same bright ocean's foam.

Tho' sea and sky fierce war would wage,
And howling thunder roll,
He heeded not the tempest's rage,—
'Twas music to his soul.

He acted well the sailor's part,
So generous and brave,
And boundless as his noble heart,
So wide shall be his grave.

No village bell shall toll for him
Its mournful, solemn dirge;
The winds shall chant a requiem
To him beneath the surge.

Remember Me. C. M. L. M.

"Remember me," my Saviour God,
Whilst here on earth I stay;
Give strength to bear affliction's rod,
A faith to watch and pray.

"Remember me," when fortune smiles,
And scenes are bright and fair;
Lest I should fall, through Satan's wiles,
Beneath his baneful snare.

"Remember me," thy voice I'll greet
In all thy dealings here;
O let thy Spirit guide my feet,
And I shall never fear.

"Remember me," stand by my side,
Where'er my lot may be;
And when by Jordan's swelling tide,
Dear Lord, "Remember me."

Influence. C. M.
BY WM. CUTTER.

What if the little rain should say—
 "So small a drop as I
Can ne'er refresh those thirsty fields—
 I'll tarry in the sky."
What if a shining beam of noon
 Should in its fountain stay,
Because its feeble light alone
 Cannot create a day?

Doth not each rain-drop help to form
 The cool, refreshing shower;
And every ray of light to warm
 And beautify the flower?
Go thou— and strive to do thy share;
 One talent—less than thine—
Improved with steady zeal and care,
 Would gain rewards divine.

Reaping in Joy. C. M.
BY W. B. TAPPAN.

There is an hour of hallowed peace
 For those with care oppressed; [cease
When sighs and sorrowing tears shall
 And all be hushed to rest.
'Tis then the soul is freed from fears
 And doubts that here annoy;
Then they that oft had sown in tears,
 Shall reap again in joy.

There is an hour of sweet repose,
 When storms assail no more;
The stream of endless pleasure flows
 On that celestial shore.
There purity with love appears,
 And bliss without alloy;
There they that oft had sown in tears,
 Shall reap eternal joy.

The Doomed Man. C. M.
BY REV. J. G. COCHRAN.

There is a time, we know not when;
 A point we know not where;
That marks the destiny of men,
 To glory or despair.

There is a time, by us unseen;
 That crosses every path:
The hidden boundary between
 God's patience and his wrath.

To pass that limit is to die;
 To die as if by stealth;
It does not quench the beaming eye,
 Nor pale the glow of health.

The conscience may be still at ease:
 The spirit light and gay;
That which is pleasing, still may please,
 And care be thrust away.

And yet the doomed man's course below
 Like Eden may have bloomed;
He did not, does not, will not know
 Or feel that he is doomed.

He knows, he feels that all is well,
 And every fear is calmed;
He lives, he dies, he wakes in hell,
 Not only doomed but damned.

How far may we go on in sin;
 How long will God forbear;
Where does hope end, and when begin,
 The confines of despair?

An answer from the skies is sent,
 Ye who from God depart,
While it is called to-day, repent,
 And harden not your hearts.

118 CHRIST THE GUIDE. 8s & 7s. (DOUBLE.)

Poetry by Miss S. Augusta Brown. (*Greenville.*)

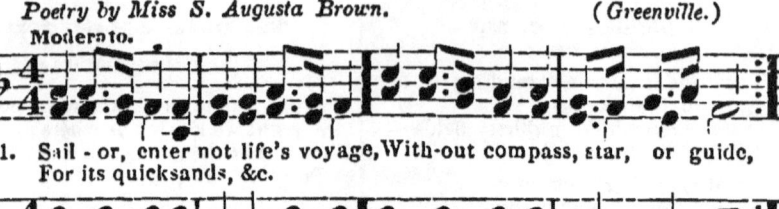

Smooth, serenely flow its waters,
 But the sunken rocks are near,
Many a gallant bark hath foundered,
 How wilt thou the danger clear.

See its circling eddies darken,
 Wave on wave of passion rise,
Earth hath here no hand to guide thee,
 Seek thy Pilot from the skies.

Seek to thread thy path of danger,
 He who once in mortal form,
When the tempest raged in fury,
 Trod the wave and stilled the storm.

He shall guide thee o'er the billow,
 Through each changing wave of strife,
Till thy bark is safely anchored,
 On the "crystal sea of life."

Divine Life-boat. 8s & 7s. S. A. B.

Sailor on the trackless ocean,
 Rife with perils is thy way,
From the billow's wide commotion,
 Thy frail bark thine only stay.

For the tempest art thou ready?
 Is thy life boat at thy side?
Will it float on Death's dark waters?
 Bear thee safe o'er Jordan's tide?

Will it land thee at thy haven?
 Is its course for Canaan's shore,
Where in peace thy voyage ended,
 Thou shalt dwell forevermore?

If so, then in thy blest passage,
 Wreck or storm thou need not fear,
With the heavenly life-boat near thee,
 Safely for thy heaven steer.

OCEAN MELODIES. 119

Mercy's Call. 8s & 7s. J. H. B.

Hardy seamen, listen gladly,
 To the gospel's glorious sound,
When the billow's raging madly,
 Fiercely beat and howl around.
Go, survey with admiration,
 Wand'rers on the raging main,
Where Jehovah, in Creation,
 Makes his wondrous power known.
Oft his voice makes mighty ocean,
 Bidding tempest's din to roar;
Then, amid the wild commotion,
 Mercy e'er from heaven implore.
E'er sustained by gracious power,
 Borne along the treach'rous wave,
Bow, O, bow in danger's hour,
 And protection fervent crave.

The Precious Bible. 8s & 7s.
BY REV. WM. M. JONES.

Holy Bible, blessed treasure,
 Way of truth and path of peace;
Lamp of God to endless pleasure,
 Guiding souls to future bliss.
Hope of freedom and redemption,
 Ark of safety it will prove;
Word of grace and free salvation,
 Full of promised joys above.
Book of warning and of threat'ning,
 With Jehovah's promise sure;
Balm of life and ever saving,
 For all sin a sovereign cure.
Holy wisdom, light unfolding!
 Life from God in Jesus' name;
Saving sinners, grace proclaiming,
 Triumphs thro' the Saviour's reign.

Missionaries Encouraged. 8s & 7s.
BY N. COLVER.

Christian Heralds, like your Saviour
 Go among the sons of wo:
Go to those of sad behavior,—
 Go where streams of death do flow.
Go to those who sigh in blindness,
 Poor and wretched, halt and lame,
Tell them of a Saviour's kindness,
 Sound abroad his wondrous name.
Go to Burmah's sons and daughters,
 Tell them of a Saviour's blood,
Pour abroad those healing waters,
 Gushing from the throne of God.
Go where sickly winds are blowing,
 Scorching suns and poisoned air;
Tears of anguish ever flowing,
 Bitter death and dark despair.
You shall see in that blest morning,
 When your Lord returns to reign,
Precious gems his crown adorning,
 Plucked by you from caves of sin.

The promised Rest.—Heb. iv. 1. 8s & 7s.

Sinners, hear the mighty Saviour;
 Love and pity fill his breast,
Now, in accents sweet, he calls you;
 Come and taste the promised rest.
Though in sorrow now ye labor,
 Weary souls with sin opprest,
Jesus bids you come and welcome—
 Come and taste the promised rest.
Though your sins be red like crimson,
 And ten thousand foes infest,
He is mighty to deliver;
 Come and taste the promised rest.

120. THE TRUTH SHALL TRIUMPH. 11s.

Words by P. Stowe. (Portuguese Hymn.)

1. The truths of the Bible, shall spread o'er the earth, All nations shall know the Lamb's riches and worth: His name shall awaken great joy and delight, While truth from above, While truth from above, While truth from above, is diffusing his light.

2. How cheering the prospect to all who now love, The truth and the Saviour, who came from above; He toil'd to impress truth's bright image abroad, That all might obey, That all might obey, That all might obey their just sovereign and Lord.

We hail that bright epoch the prophet once saw;
When nation with nation shall not be at war;
But peace, love and rapture shall thrill every soul,
While anthems of gladness o'er earth and sea roll.

Let Truth be our buckler, and we may impart
The balm that will gladden, and heal the sad heart;
A hope that will triumph o'er death and the grave,
And rest with Truth's victors, a *well done* receive.

OCEAN MELODIES.

Evening Hymn. 11s.

See daylight is fading o'er earth and o'er ocean,
 The sun has gone down on the far distant sea;
O now, in the hush of life's fitful commotion,
 We lift our tired spirits, blest Saviour, to Thee.

Full oft wast Thou found afar on the mountain,
 As eventide spread her dark wing o'er the wave—
Thou Son of the Highest, and Life's endless fountain,
 Be with us, we pray Thee, to bless and to save.

And oft as the tumult of life's heaving billow
 Shall toss our frail bark, driving wild o'er night's deep,
Let thy healing wing be stretched over our pillow,
 And guard us from evil though Death watch our sleep.

To God, our great Father, whose throne is in Heaven.
 Who dwells with the lowly and contrite in heart—
To the Son and the Spirit all glory be given
 One God ever blessed and holy Thou art.

Pity the Seaman. 11s.

O think on the Sailor toss'd on the billow!
 Afar from the home of his childhood and youth;
No mother to watch o'er his sleep-broken pillow,
 No father to counsel, no sister to soothe.

Ah! little know ye who are peacefully sleeping
 On home's downy pillow, unwaken'd and warm,
The woes of the seaman, his dreary watch keeping,
 Amid all the terrors of midnight and storm.

Oh say! shall the man thus to banishment driven,
 From all that entwines round the bosom below,
Be sternly shut out from communion with heaven,
 And end his sad life in a mansion of woe?

Pour, pour on his pathway of tempest and gloom,
 The radiant light of the Gospel of peace;
And Bethlehem's star shall his passage illume
 To the haven where darkness and tempest shall cease.

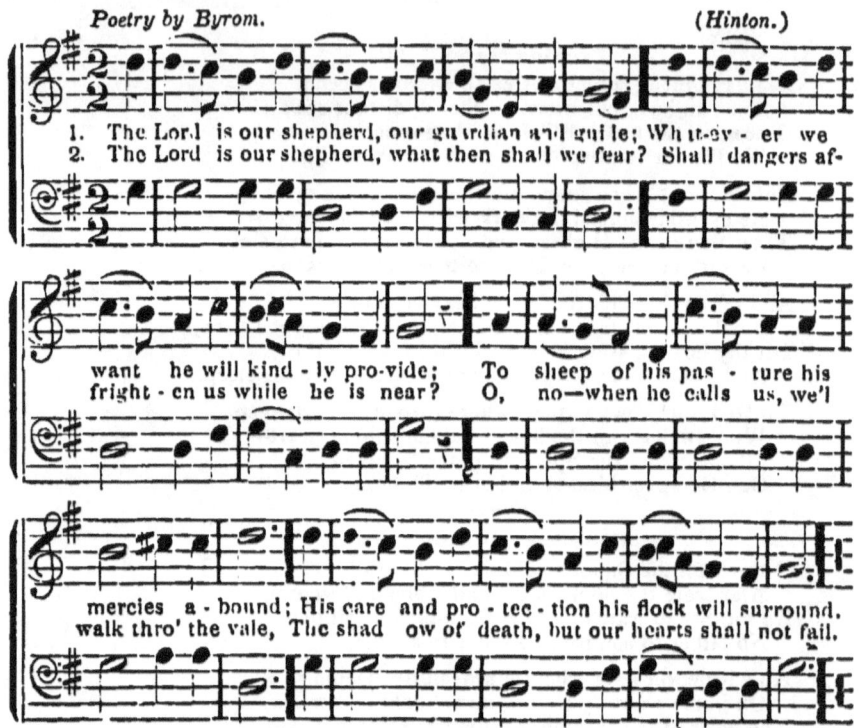

Afraid by ourselves to pursue the dark way,
Thy rod and thy staff be our comfort and stay:
We know, by thy guidance, when once it is past,
To life and to glory it brings us at last.

The Lord is become our salvation and song;
His blessings have followed us all our life long;—
His name will we praise from the heart, with our breath,
Be joyful through life, and resigned in our death.

OCEAN MELODIES.

Rest in Heaven. 11s.   P. 8.

How sweet is that home where the weary shall rest;
No toil, no temptations are known by the blest;
A bright bow of glory will shine o'er their way,
And saints with the angels will chant a sweet lay.

There shall be no night in that blessed abode;
For all shall behold the bright image of God;
His light will illume and cheer every soul,
While age after age shall unceasingly roll.

No sorrow will enter to sadden the heart,
No words will embitter the soul with a smart;
Sweet thoughts and kind words will be spoken above;
While the *Throne of the Holy* is glowing with love.

Let rays from sweet home my pathway now light,
And give me fresh courage to "fight the good fight,"
To finish my course, and receive a bright crown,
And dwell with my Saviour and rest in my Home.

The Cross is my Anchor. 11s.

THE CROSS IS MY ANCHOR,—though wave follow wave,
Though frail be my vessel, this anchor shall save,
Let faith in full vigor now trust in the Lord;
Midst dangers I rest in his life-giving word.

THE CROSS IS MY ANCHOR,—'tis steady and sure,
Within the veil holding all storms I endure;
My Saviour has entered a priest on His throne,
I trust in His promise, and in Him alone.

THE CROSS IS MY ANCHOR.—All storms shall soon cease,
My vessel, though frail, reach the haven of peace:
No shipwreck or storm need I ever more fear,
When danger's extreme, then my Saviour is near.

THE CROSS IS MY ANCHOR,—I now hear His voice,
"Fear not, it is I," now trust and rejoice;
The last storm now low'ring, may speedily come,
I'll trust in His mercy and soon reach my home.

GOD GLORIOUS. 10s & 11s.

Poetry by Grant. (*Lyons.*)

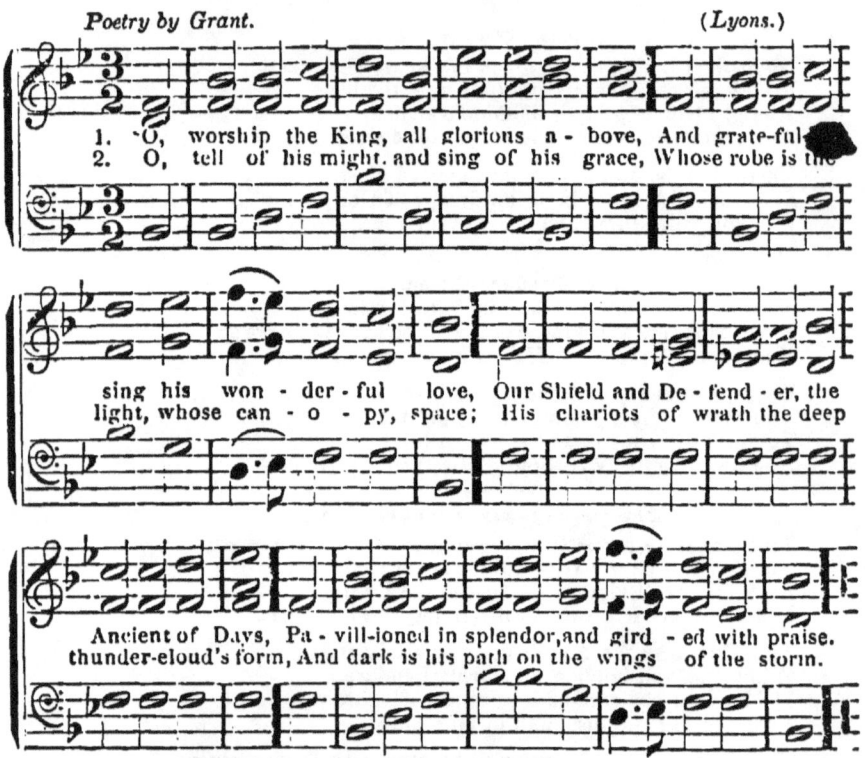

1. O, worship the King, all glorious a-bove, And grate-ful-ly sing his won-der-ful love, Our Shield and De-fend-er, the Ancient of Days, Pa-vill-ioned in splendor, and gird-ed with praise.
2. O, tell of his might, and sing of his grace, Whose robe is the light, whose can-o-py, space; His chariots of wrath the deep thunder-cloud's form, And dark is his path on the wings of the storm.

Frail children of dust, and feeble as frail,
In thee do we trust, nor find thee to fail;
Thy mercies how tender! how firm to the end!
Our Maker, Defender, Redeemer, and Friend.

Father Almighty, how faithful thy love!
While angels delight to hymn thee above,
The humbler creation, though feeble their lays,
With true adoration shall lisp to thy praise.

OCEAN MELODIES.   125

God's Servants should praise Him. 10s & 11s.

Ye servants of God your Master proclaim,
And publish abroad his wonderful name;
The name all-victorious of Jesus extol;
His kingdom is glorious; he rules over all.

God ruleth on high, almighty to save;
And still he is nigh; his presence we have;
The great congregation his triumph shall sing,
Ascribing salvation to Jesus our King.

"Salvation to God, who sits on the throne,"
Let all cry aloud, and honor the Son:
The praises of Jesus the angels proclaim,
Fall down on their faces and worship the Lamb.

Then let us adore and give him his right,—
All glory and power, and wisdom and might,
All honor and blessing with angels above,
And thanks never ceasing, for infinite love.

The Believer's Voyage. H. M.
CHRISTIAN HYMNS.

Jesus, at thy command,
  I launch into the deep;
And leave my native land,
  Where sin lulls all asleep.
For thee I would the world resign,
And sail to heaven with thee and thine.

Thou art my pilot wise;
  My compass is thy word;
My soul each storm defies,
  While I have such a Lord!
I trust thy faithfulness and power
To save me in the trying hour.

Though rocks and quicksands deep
  Through all my passage lie,
Yet Christ will safely keep
  And guide me with his eye;
My anchor hope shall firm abide,
And every boist'rous storm outride.

Come, Holy Ghost, and blow
  A prosp'rous gale of grace:
Waft me from all below,
  To heaven, my destined place.
Then in full sail my port I'll find
And leave the world and sin behind.

Seaman's Prayer. L. M.

Beset with snares on every hand,
In life's uncertain path I stand;
Saviour divine! diffuse thy light,
To guide my doubtful footsteps right

Then let the wildest storms arise;
Let tempests mingle earth and skies,
No fatal shipwreck shall I fear,
But all my treasures with me bear.

If thou, my Jesus, still art nigh,
Cheerful I live, and cheerful die;
Secure, when mortal comforts flee,
To find ten thousand worlds in thee.

Deliverance in a Storm. C. M.

Our little bark, on boist'rous seas,
  By cruel tempest tossed,
Without one cheerful beam of hope,
  Expecting to be lost,—
We to the Lord, in humble prayer,
  Breathed out our sad distress;
Though feeble, yet with contrite hearts,
  We begged return of peace.

The stormy winds did cease to blow,
  The waves no more did roll;
And soon again a placid sea
  Spoke comfort to each soul.

O, may our grateful, trembling hearts,
  Sweet hallelujahs sing,
To Him who hath our lives preserved,
  Our Saviour and our King.

Reapers of the Sea. L. M. H. 8 C.

Seamen! there's noble work for you;
  Your mission is to plough the sea,
The seed of gospel grace to sow,
  And reap for immortality.

"Thy bread upon the waters cast,"
  It shall be fruitful on the wave,
Return to thee a sweet repast,
  And many famished shipmates save.

How rich the harvest of the deep!
  Its sheaves are souls of priceless cost,
These would the Saviour have you reap,
  And gather quickly, ere they're lost.

No matter then what storms should come,
  E'en tho' thy sheaves were 'cast away,'
The mounting wave would bear them home,
  For winds and waves thy Lord obey.

Jesus precious to them that believe. C. M.   DODDRIDGE.

Jesus, I love thy charming name,
  'Tis music to my ear,
Fain would I sound it out so loud
  That earth and heaven might hear.

Yes, thou art precious to my soul,
  My transport and my trust:
Jewels to thee are gaudy toys,
  And gold is sordid dust.

Thy grace shall dwell upon my heart,
  And shed its fragrance there,—
The noblest balm of all its wounds,
  The cordial of its care.

I'll speak the honors of thy name
  With my last laboring breath,
And, dying, clasp thee in my arms,
  The antidote of death.

Desiring a heavenly Breeze. C. M.

O for a breeze of heavenly love,
  To waft my soul away
To the celestial world above,
  Where pleasures ne'er decay.

Eternal Spirit, deign to be
  My pilot here below,
To guide through life's tempestuous sea,
  Where winds do stormy blow.

From rocks of pride on either hand,
  From quicksands of despair,
O guide me safe to Canaan's land,
  Through every fatal snare.

Anchor me in that port above,
  On that celestial shore,
Where dashing billows never move,
  Where tempests never roar.

Success of the Gospel. 7s & 6s.
S. F. SMITH.

The morning light is breaking;
  The darkness disappears,
The sons of earth are waking
  To penitential tears:
Each breeze that sweeps the ocean,
  Brings tidings from afar,
Of nations in commotion,
  Prepared for Zion's war.

Rich dews of grace come o'er us,
  In many a gentle shower,
And brighter scenes before us
  Are opening every hour:
Each cry, to heaven going,
  Abundant answers brings,
And heavenly gales are blowing,
  With peace upon their wings.

See heathen nations bending
  Before the God we love,
And thousand hearts ascending
  In gratitude above;
While sinners, now confessing,
  The gospel call obey,
And seek the Saviour's blessing,—
  A nation in a day.

Blest river of salvation,
  Pursue thy onward way;
Flow thou to every nation,
  Nor in thy richness stay:
Stay not till all the lowly,
  Triumphant reach their home;
Stay not till all the holy,
  Proclaim, "The Lord is come."

The Christian Pilgrimage. 7s & 6s.
(Peculiar.) CENNICK.

Rise, my soul, and stretch thy wings;
  Thy better portion trace;
Rise from all terrestrial things,
  Towards heaven, thy native place:
Sun, and moon, and stars, decay;
  Time shall soon this earth remove;
Rise, my soul, and haste away
  To seats prepared above.

Rivers to the ocean run,
  Nor stay in all their course,
Fire, ascending, seeks the sun;
  Both speed them to their source:
So a soul that's born of God
  Pants to view his glorious face,
Upward tends to his abode,
  To rest in his embrace.

Cease, ye pilgrims, cease to mourn,
  Press onward to the prize;
Soon our Saviour will return,
  Triumphant in the skies:
Yet a season, and you know
  Happy entrance will be given,
All our sorrows left below,
  And earth exchanged for heaven.

Doxology. 7s & 6s.

To thee be praise forever,
  Thou glorious King of kings,
Thy wondrous love and favor
  Each ransomed spirit sings.
We'll celebrate thy glory,
  With all thy saints above,
And shout the joyful story
  Of thy redeeming love.

Deliverance in a Storm. C. M.

Our little bark, on boist'rous seas,
　By cruel tempest tossed,
Without one cheerful beam of hope,
　Expecting to be lost,—
We to the Lord, in humble prayer,
　Breathed out our sad distress;
Though feeble, yet with contrite hearts,
　We begged return of peace.
The stormy winds did cease to blow,
　The waves no more did roll;
And soon again a placid sea
　Spoke comfort to each soul.
O, may our grateful, trembling hearts,
　Sweet hallelujahs sing,
To Him who hath our lives preserved,
　Our Saviour and our King.

Reapers of the Sea. L. M. H. 8 C.

Seamen! there's noble work for you;
　Your mission is to plough the sea,
The seed of gospel grace to sow,
　And reap for immortality.
"Thy bread upon the waters cast,"
　It shall be fruitful on the wave,
Return to thee a sweet repast,
　And many famished shipmates save.
How rich the harvest of the deep!
　Its sheaves are souls of priceless cost,
These would the Saviour have you reap,
　And gather quickly, ere they're lost.
No matter then what storms should come,
　E'en tho' thy sheaves were 'cast away,'
The mounting wave would bear them home,
　For winds and waves thy Lord obey.

Jesus precious to them that believe. C. M.   DODDRIDGE.

Jesus, I love thy charming name,
　'Tis music to my ear,
Fain would I sound it out so loud
　That earth and heaven might hear.
Yes, thou art precious to my soul,
　My transport and my trust:
Jewels to thee are gaudy toys,
　And gold is sordid dust.
Thy grace shall dwell upon my heart,
　And shed its fragrance there,—
The noblest balm of all its wounds,
　The cordial of its care.
I'll speak the honors of thy name
　With my last laboring breath,
And, dying, clasp thee in my arms,
　The antidote of death.

Desiring a heavenly Breeze. C. M.

O for a breeze of heavenly love,
　To waft my soul away
To the celestial world above,
　Where pleasures ne'er decay.
Eternal Spirit, deign to be
　My pilot here below,
To guide through life's tempestuous sea,
　Where winds do stormy blow.
From rocks of pride on either hand,
　From quicksands of despair,
O guide me safe to Canaan's land,
　Through every fatal snare.
Anchor me in that port above,
　On that celestial shore,
Where dashing billows never move,
　Where tempests never roar.

Success of the Gospel. 7s & 6s.
S. F. SMITH.

The morning light is breaking;
 The darkness disappears,
The sons of earth are waking
 To penitential tears :
Each breeze that sweeps the ocean,
 Brings tidings from afar,
Of nations in commotion,
 Prepared for Zion's war.

Rich dews of grace come o'er us,
 In many a gentle shower,
And brighter scenes before us
 Are opening every hour :
Each cry, to heaven going,
 Abundant answers brings,
And heavenly gales are blowing,
 With peace upon their wings.

See heathen nations bending
 Before the God we love,
And thousand hearts ascending
 In gratitude above ;
While sinners, now confessing,
 The gospel call obey,
And seek the Saviour's blessing,—
 A nation in a day.

Blest river of salvation,
 Pursue thy onward way ;
Flow thou to every nation,
 Nor in thy richness stay :
Stay not till all the lowly,
 Triumphant reach their home ;
Stay not till all the holy,
 Proclaim, " The Lord is come."

The Christian Pilgrimage. 7s & 6s.
(Peculiar.) CENNICK.

Rise, my soul, and stretch thy wings ;
 Thy better portion trace ;
Rise from all terrestrial things,
 Towards heaven, thy native place :
Sun, and moon, and stars, decay ;
 Time shall soon this earth remove ;
Rise, my soul, and haste away
 To seats prepared above.

Rivers to the ocean run,
 Nor stay in all their course,
Fire, ascending, seeks the sun ;
 Both speed them to their source :
So a soul that's born of God
 Pants to view his glorious face,
Upward tends to his abode,
 To rest in his embrace.

Cease, ye pilgrims, cease to mourn,
 Press onward to the prize ;
Soon our Saviour will return,
 Triumphant in the skies :
Yet a season, and you know
 Happy entrance will be given,
All our sorrows left below,
 And earth exchanged for heaven.

Doxology. 7s & 6s.

To thee be praise forever,
 Thou glorious King of kings,
Thy wondrous love and favor
 Each ransomed spirit sings.
We'll celebrate thy glory,
 With all thy saints above,
And shout the joyful story
 Of thy redeeming love.

Praise to God. C. M.

Ye Christian Seamen, praise the Lord,
　To you the work belongs;
For God invites you by his word
　To raise your gospel songs
Rejoice in his redeeming love,
　His wondrous mercy tell,
How Christ descended from above
　To save your souls from hell.

Let the sweet praises of his name
　Resound from pole to pole;
To every shore his grace proclaim
　As far as billows roll.

At every time, in every place,
　The glorious theme pursue;
And long to praise him face to face,
　In anthems ever new.

Remember the Sailor. C. M.

Pray for the Sailor—pray for him
　While tossing on the deep,
That harmlessly the raging storm
　May round his vessel sweep.

When clouds o'erhang the wintry sky,
　And howls the tempest loud,
Pray that the angry billows may
　Not be the sailor's shroud.

Pray for his safety and return,
　Some humble cot to cheer,
Where hearts with pain and anguish burn
　In every storm's career.

Pray for the sailor—that his soul,
　When all his toils are o'er,
In heaven be safely moored at last,
　To live for evermore.

Hope in God. C. M.
BY MRS. L. H. SIGOURNEY.

Appear for my defence, my God,
　And let thy shield be spread
Around the sailor's lonely heart,
　And unprotected head.

Let not my hope in thee be crossed,
　Who have no help beside,
Nor on the winds my prayer be 'ost,
　Thou Everlasting Guide.

Uphold me in temptation's field,
　Where I am called to go,
Nor let my feeble spirit yield
　To earthly sin and woe.

For though the wildest storms may rise
　And darkness rule the sphere,
The hope that anchors in the skies
　Hath nought to do with fear.

The Bible the Light of the World.
C. M.　　COWPER.

What glory gilds the sacred page!
　Majestic, like the sun,
It gives a light to every age;
　It gives, but borrows none.

The power that gave it still supplies
　The gracious light and heat:
Its truths upon the nations rise;
　They rise, but never set.

Let everlasting thanks be thine
　For such a bright display,
As makes a world of darkness shine
　With beams of heavenly day.

My soul rejoices to pursue
　The steps of Him I love,
Till glory breaks upon my view
　In brighter worlds above.

OCEAN MELODIES. 13]

Confidence in atoning Blood. C. M.

O Lord, when billows o'er me rise,
 When deep cries out to deep,
When angry clouds obscure the skies,
 My soul in safety keep.

Thy promise has in troubles past
 My staff of succor been;
Support me now, while trials last,
 Nor leave me in my sin.

No sacrifice my soul can plead,
 But that rich offering paid,
When Christ on Calvary deigned to bleed,
 And full atonement made.

Forever here I rest my cause;
 In faith I make this plea:
Christ hath obeyed thy righteous laws;
 Christ hath expired for me.

The Lost Found. C. M.
NEEDHAM.

O, how divine, how sweet the joy,
 When but one sinner turns,
And, with an humble, broken heart,
 His sins and errors mourns!

Pleased with the news, the saints below
 In songs their tongues employ;
Beyond the skies the tidings go,
 And heaven is filled with joy.

Well pleased the Father sees and hears
 The conscious sinner's moan,
Jesus receives him in his arms,
 And claims him for his own.

Nor angels can their joys contain,
 But kindle with new fire;
"The sinner lost is found," they sing,
 And strike the sounding lyre.

Prayer. C. M. MONTGOMERY.

Prayer is the soul's sincere desire,
 Unuttered or expressed,
The motion of a hidden fire,
 That trembles in the breast.

Prayer is the burden of a sigh,
 The falling of a tear,
The upward glancing of an eye,
 When none but God is near.

Prayer is the simplest form of speech
 That infant lips can try;
Prayer, the sublimest strains that reach
 The majesty on high.

Prayer is the Christian's vital breath,
 The Christian's native air,
His watchword at the gates of death;
 He enters heaven with prayer.

Devotion. C. M. BEDDOME.

Prayer is the breath of God in man,
 Returning whence it came;
Love is the sacred fire within,
 And prayer the rising flame,

It gives the burdened spirit ease,
 And soothes the troubled breast;
Yields comfort to the mourners here,
 And to the weary rest.

When God inclines the heart to pray,
 He hath an ear to hear;
To him there's music in a groan,
 And beauty in a tear.

The humble suppliant cannot fail
 To have his wants supplied
Since He for sinners intercedes,
 Who once for sinners died

Invitation to Christ. L. M.
BY REV. J. NEWTON BROWN.

Come, sinner! at our Lord's command,
We would persuade thee now to come;
O, shrink not back, but yield thy hand,
And, wanderer! we will lead thee home.

O, linger not! thou lost one, come,
And give each sinful pleasure o'er;
Is not thy guilt a countless sum?
Why wilt thou, lingerer! make it more?

Hast thou no pity on thy soul,
Whose deep defilement thou hast seen?
Come where the streams of mercy roll;
O, wash! and be forever clean!

For thee a Saviour's heart hath bled;
To give thee peace, He bore thy pain;
O, stay not till thy day is fled;
O, crucify Him not again!

Christ upon the Cross. L. M.
STENNETT.

"'Tis finished!"—so the Saviour cried,
And meekly bowed his head and died:
'Tis finished!—yes, the race is run,
The battle fought, the victory won.

'Tis finished!—this his dying groan
Shall sins of deepest hue atone,
And millions be redeemed from death
By Jesus' last, expiring breath.

'Tis finished!—Heaven is reconciled,
And all the powers of darkness spoiled;
Peace, love, and happiness, again
Return, and dwell with sinful men.

'Tis finished!—let the joyful sound
Be heard thro' all the nations round:
'Tis finished!—let the triumph rise,
And swell the chorus of the skies.

Not ashamed of Christ. L. M.
GRIGG.

Jesus, and shall it ever be—
A mortal man ashamed of thee!
Ashamed of thee, whom angels praise,
Whose glories shine thro' endless days!

Ashamed of Jesus!—that dear Friend
On whom my hopes of heaven depend!
No!—when I blush, be this my shame,
That I no more revere his name.

Ashamed of Jesus!—yes, I may,
When I've no guilt to wash away,
No tear to wipe, no good to crave,
No fears to quell, no soul to save.

Till then—nor is my boasting vain—
Till then, I boast a Saviour slain;
And, O, may this my glory be,—
That Christ is not ashamed of me.

Enjoyment of Christ's Love. L. M.
C. WESLEY.

Jesus, thy boundless love to me
No thought can reach, no tongue declare,
Unite my thankful heart to thee,
And reign without a rival there.

Thy love, how cheering is its ray!
All pain before its presence flies;
Care, anguish, sorrow, melt away
Where'er its healing beams arise.

O, let thy love my soul enflame,
And to thy service sweetly bind;
Transfuse it through my inmost frame,
And mould me wholly to thy mind.

Thy love, in sufferings, be my peace;
Thy love, in weakness, make me strong;
And, when the storms of life shall cease,
Thy love shall be in heaven my song.

OCEAN MELODIES. 133

The Christian's Prospect. L. M.

What sinners value I resign;
Lord, 'tis enough that thou art mine;
I shall behold thy blissful face,
And stand complete in righteousness.

This life's a dream—an empty show;
But that bright world to which I go,
Hath joys substantial and sincere:
When shall I wake, and find me there?

O glorious hour! O blest abode!
I shall be near and like my God,
And flesh and sin no more control
The sacred pleasures of my soul.

My flesh shall slumber in the ground
Till the last trumpet's joyful sound,
Then burst the chains, with glad surprise
And in my Saviour's image rise.

The better Land. L. M.

There is a land mine eye hath seen,
　In visions of enraptured thought,
So bright that all which spreads between
　Is with its radiant glory fraught.

A land upon whose blissful shore
　There rests no shadow, falls no stain;
There, those who meet shall part no more,
　And those long parted meet again.

Its skies are not like earthly skies,
　With varying hues of shade and light;
It hath no need of suns to rise,
　To dissipate the gloom of night.

There sweeps no desolating wind
　Across that calm, serene abode;
The wanderer there a home may find
　Within the Paradise of God.

The Physician of the Soul. L. M.
　　　　　　　STEELE.

Deep are the wounds which sin has made
Where shall the sinner find a cure?
In vain, alas! is Nature's aid;
The work exceeds her utmost power.

But can no sovereign balm be found?
And is no kind physician nigh,
To ease the pain, and heal the wound
Ere life and hope forever fly?

There is a great Physician near;
Look up, O fainting soul, and live;
See, in his heavenly smiles appear
Such help as nature cannot give.

See, in the Saviour's dying blood,
Life, health, and bliss, abundant flow:
'Tis only that dear, sacred flood
Can ease thy pain, and heal thy woe.

Heaven alone unfading. L. M.

How vain is all beneath the skies!
　How transient every earthly bliss!
How slender all the fondest ties
　That bind us to a world like this!

The evening cloud, the morning dew,
　The withering grass, the fading flower
Of earthly hopes are emblems true—
　The glory of a passing hour.

But though earth's fairest blossoms die,
　And all beneath the skies is vain,
There is a brighter world on high,
　Beyond the reach of care and pain.

Then let the hope of joys to come,
　Dispel our cares, and chase our fears;
If God be ours, we're travelling home,
　Though passing through a vale of tears.

The Righteous Blest. S. M.
WATTS.

The man is ever blest
 Who shuns the sinner's ways,
Among their councils never stands,
 Nor takes the scorner's place,—
But makes the law of God
 His study and delight,
Amidst the labors of the day,
 And watches of the night.

He, like a tree, shall thrive,
 With waters near the root;
Fresh as the leaf his name shall live,
 His works are heavenly fruit.
Not so th' ungodly race;
 They no such blessings find:
Their hopes shall flee like empty chaff
 Before the driving wind.

Blessings sought in Prayer. S. M.
NEWTON.

Behold the throne of grace!
 The promise calls me near;
There Jesus shows a smiling face,
 And waits to answer prayer.
Thine image, Lord, bestow,
 Thy presence and thy love;
I ask to serve thee here below,
 And reign with thee above.

Teach me to live by faith;
 Conform my will to thine;
Let me victorious be in death,
 And then in glory shine.
If thou these blessings give,
 And wilt my portion be,
All worldly joys I'll cheerful leave,
 And find my heaven in thee.

Ingratitude deplored. S. M.
WATTS.

Is this the kind return?
 Are these the thanks we owe?
Thus to abuse eternal love,
 Whence all our blessings flow?
To what a stubborn frame
 Has sin reduced our mind!
What strange, rebellious wretches **we**!
 And God as strangely kind!

Turn, turn us, mighty God,
 And mould our souls afresh;
Break, sovereign grace, these hearts of [stone,
 And give us hearts of flesh.
Let past ingratitude
 Provoke our weeping eyes;
And hourly, as new mercies fall,
 Let hourly thanks arise.

Prayer for Deliverance. S. M.
RIPPON'S COL.

Like Israel, Lord, am I;
 My soul is at a stand;
A sea before, a host behind,
 And rocks on either hand.
O Lord, I cry to thee,
 And would thy word obey;
Bid me advance; and, through **the sea**
 Create a new-made way.

The time of greatest straits,
 Thy chosen time has been
To manifest thy power is great,
 And make thy glory seen.
O, send deliverance down;
 Display the arm divine;
So shall the praise be all **thy own,**
 And I be doubly thine.

OCEAN MELODIES.

Rest for the weary Soul. S. M.
MONTGOMERY.

O, where shall rest be found —
  Rest for the weary soul?
'Twere vain the ocean depths to sound,
  Or pierce to either pole.

The world can never give
  The bliss for which we sigh:
'Tis not the whole of life to live,
  Nor all of death to die.

Beyond this vale of tears,
  There is a life above,
Unmeasured by the flight of years;
  And all that life is love.

There is a death whose pang
  Outlasts the fleeting breath:
O, what eternal terrors hang
  Around the second death!

Lord God of truth and grace,
  Teach us that death to shun,
Lest we be banished from thy face,
  And evermore undone.

Christ's Compassion. S. M.
BEDDOME.

Did Christ o'er sinners weep,
  And shall our cheeks be dry?
Let floods of penitential grief
  Burst forth from every eye.

The Son of God in tears
  The wondering angels see;
Be thou astonished, O my soul;
  He shed those tears for thee

He wept that we might weep,
  Each sin demands a tear;
In heaven alone no sin is found,
  And there's no weeping there.

Union and Peace. S. M.
WATTS.

Blest are the sons of peace,
  Whose hearts and hopes are one,
Whose kind designs to serve and please,
  Through all their actions run.

Blest is the pious house
  Where zeal and friendship meet;
Their songs of praise, their mingled vows,
  Make their communion sweet.

From those celestial springs
  Such streams of pleasure flow,
As no increase of riches brings,
  Nor honors can bestow.

Thus, when on Aaron's head,
  They poured the rich perfume,
The oil through all his raiment spread,
  And fragrance filled the room.

Thus, on the heavenly hills,
  The saints are blest above,
Where joy, like morning dew distils,
  And all the air is love.

Joy in the Conversion of Sinners.
S. M.   SWAIN.

Who can forbear to sing,
  Who can refuse to praise,
When Zion's high, celestial King
  His saving power displays?—

When sinners at his feet,
  By mercy conquered, fall?
When grace, and truth, and justice, meet,
  And peace unites them all?

Who can forbear to praise
  Our high, celestial King,
When sovereign, rich, redeeming grace,
  Invites our tongues to sing.

The heroic, yet disconsolate Sailor. L. M.

The heroic sailor who periled his own life, to rescue a man from drowning, at the East Boston Ferry, Nov 29th, 1848. When asked his name, replied, "It's of no consequence, nobody cares a copper for me." This impressive reply, suggested the following lines. P. S.

"No one on earth now cares for me!"
This sad reply, child of the sea;
Will kindle tho'ts and bid them flow,
While musing on thy words of wo.

No one, brave sailor, cares for thee?
Thy path, how gloomy it must be;
Hast thou no one to soothe thy heart,
Or rapture to thy soul impart?

No one, kind sailor, cares for thee?
Behold the Saviour! to Him flee;
He sweetly calls, who is thy friend,
You may upon his love depend.

No one, bold sailor, cares for thee?
Come then, and find true liberty;
Bright angels round the Throne will sing,
O'er thee, an heir of Zion's King.

No friends or kindred cares for thee?
Brave sailor! we will for you plea,
A helping hand to thee extend,
While o'er the sea, and on the land.

What if the world is *cold* to thee? [sea,
And friends prove treach'rous like the
The Lord of glory groaned and bled,
And bowed for *thee*, his sacred head.

Cheer, cheer thy soul with this sweet tho't,
That there is *One*, forgets thee not;
He will each noble deed record,
And faithful souls, in heaven reward.

Sinners Invited to Repentance. L. M
DWIGHT.

While life prolongs its precious light,
Mercy is found, and peace is given:
But soon, ah, soon, approaching night,
Shall blot out every hope of heaven.

While God invites, how blest the day!
How sweet the gospel's charming sound!
Come, sinners, haste, O, haste away,
While yet a pardoning God is found.

Soon, borne on time's most rapid wing,
Shall death command you to the grave,
Before his bar your spirits bring,
And none be found to hear or save.

In that lone land of deep despair,
No Sabbath's heavenly light shall rise,
No God regard your bitter prayer,
No Saviour call you to the skies.

Now God invites; how blest the day!
How sweet the gospel's charming sound!
Come, sinners, haste, O, haste away,
While yet a pardoning God is found.

Sense of Sin. L. M. STEELE.

Jesus demands this heart of mine,
Demands my love, my joy, my care;
But, ah, how dead to things divine,
How cold, my best affections are!

'Tis sin, alas! with dreadful power,
Divides my Saviour from my sight;
O for one happy, shining hour
Of sacred freedom, sweet delight!

Come, gracious Lord; thy love can raise
My captive powers from sin and death,
And fill my heart and life with praise,
And tune my last, expiring breath.

OCEAN MELODIES.

The Tongue. L. M.

All kinds of beasts, and birds, and whales
Are tamed by men, with skilful art;
The serpent brood, whose tongue assails,
With sting and poison, mildly part.

But, O! the tongue of fallen man,
How small, how boasting, and how dire;
A world of sin, whose influence can
All nature's course involve in fire.

Behold, how great and dire a wreck
From storms of passion, float ashore;
Behold, from sin's tempested deck,
A world in flames, and man no more.

Lord, keep my lips, my tongue from guile,
My soul from rage, my words from guilt,
Nor let me thus a world defile,
For which thy sacred blood was spilt.

Let but this wandering sinful bark
Be steered by Christ, and filled with love
His grace can quench each rising spark,
And round the world I'll peaceful rove.

Burden of Guilt. L. M. BEDDOME.

Lord, with a grieved and aching heart,
To thee I look, to thee I cry;
Supply my wants, and ease my smart;
O, hear an humble prisoner's sigh.

Here on my soul the burden lies;
No human power can ease the load;
My numerous sins against me rise,
And far remove me from my God.

Break, break, O Lord, these tyrant chains,
And set the struggling captive free;
Redeem from everlasting pains,
And bring me safe to heaven and thee.

Song of Gratitude and Praise. L. M.
DODDRIDGE.

God of my life, through all my days
I'll tune the grateful notes of praise;
The song shall wake with opening light
And warble to the silent night.

When anxious care would break my rest,
And grief would tear my throbbing breast
The notes of praise, ascending high,
Shall check the murmur and the sigh.

When death o'er nature shall prevail,
And all the powers of language fail,
Joy thro' my swimming eyes shall break
And mean the thanks I cannot speak.

But, O, when that last conflict's o'er,
And I am chained to earth no more,
With what glad accents shall I rise,
To join the music of the skies!

Then shall I learn th' exalted strains
That echo through the heavenly plains,
And emulate with joy unknown,
The glowing seraphs round thy throne.

Heavenly Aspirations. L. M.
WATTS.

Up to the fields where angels lie,
And living waters gently roll,
Fain would my tho'ts ascend on high;
But sin hangs heavy on my soul.

O, might I once mount up and see
The glories of th' eternal skies,
How vain a thing this world would be!
How empty all its fleeting joys!

Great All in All, eternal King,
Let me but view thy lovely face,
And all my powers shall bow and sing
Thine endless grandeur and thy grace

OCEAN MELODIES.

God's Presence makes Death easy.
C. M.   WATTS.

Death cannot make our souls afraid,
  If God be with us there;
We may walk thro' its darkest shade,
  And never yield to fear.

I could renounce my all below,
  If my Redeemer bid;
And run, if I were called to go,
  And die as Moses did.

Might I but climb to Pisgah's top,
  And view the promised land,
My flesh itself would long to drop,
  And welcome the command,

Clasped in my heavenly Father's arms,
  I would forget my breath,
And lose my life among the charms
  Of so divine a death.

Dependance on God. C. M.   J. H. H.

Our God we bow before thy throne,
  And supplicate thy grace;
We would thy sovereign justice own,
  And gladly seek thy face.

Our numerous sins we would confess,
  Our wanderings, Lord, from thee;
We plead our Saviour's righteousness,
  To him for refuge flee.

Tho' fierce the storms that often beat,
  And rude the blasts that roar,
We'll bow before thy mercy-seat,
  Thy guidance to implore.

Our souls will e'er in thee confide,
  A refuge ever near;
As o'er the sea of life we glide,
  May we thy grace revere.

"My Father's at the helm." C M.
An Incident—Spiritually Improved.

'Twas when the seas with horrid roar
  A little bark assail'd,
And pallid fear with awful pow'r,
  O'er each on board prevail'd;

Save one,—the captain's darling child;
  Who fearless view'd the storm,
And, playful, with composure smil'd
  At danger's threat'ning form.

" Why sporting thus ?" a seaman cries,
  " Whilst sorrows overwhelm ?"
" Why yield to grief?" the boy replies;
  " My Father's at the helm!"

Poor doubting soul, from hence be taught
  How groundless is thy fear;
Think what the power of Christ hath wro't,
  And He is ever near.

Then upward look; do not distrust,
  Jesus will guide thee home
To that eternal port of rest,
  Where storms shall never come.
                          J. A. K.

On the Loss of a Child. C. M.

And is thy lovely shadow fled ?
  Yet stop those fruitless tears;
He from a thousand pangs is freed,
  You from ten thousand fears.

Though lost, he's lost to earth alone,
  Above he will be found;
Amidst the stars, and near the throne,
  Which babes like him surround

Look upward, and your child you'll see,
  Fix'd in his blest abode;
What parent would not childless be
  To give a child to GOD ?

OCEAN MELODIES.   139

BY D. RADFORD.
uthless hand to mar
rerish here,
e's brightest star,
s however dear.

l on life's way,
  and decay;
ouch they feel
es o'er them steal.

rker as it bears
fleeting years,
m childhood spares,
bitter tears.

ry clime,
track of time;
s long delayed,
nd sorrow's shade.

n. L. M.
 clasped the child,
 ought it mine;
's joy, forgot
er both were thine.

elfish love,
hy rod,
d from above,
ering heart to God.

om my sight,
tender care;
e the anguish light,
the idol spare.

thy will;
hild's with thee;
hall trust thee still,
God shall see.

The Goodness of God. L. M.
BY REV. J. NEWTON BROWN.

And wilt thou stoop, great God! so low,
  As to behold with pitying eye,
Thy guilty creatures here below,
  Condemned eternally to die?

Why do I ask in doubtful tone,
  When, lo! upon the cross I see
Immanuel bleed, from love alone,
  From pity to a wretch like me!

God in our nature, wondrous sight!
  Endures the curse for man designed;
O, with what ravishing delight
  A scene so glorious fills my mind!

God of immensity! thy love
  Exceeds the grandeur of thy power!
Strike, strike your harps, ye hosts above,
  While saints in sweeter strains adore.

The Greatness of God. L. M.
BY REV J NEWTON BROWN.

O Thou! the high and lofty One,
  Whose dwelling is eternity;
Justice and judgment guard thy throne,
  And prostrate angels worship thee.

Dark and unsearchable thy ways,
  To man mysterious and obscure!
Beyond the reach of mortal gaze,
  The feeblest workings of thy power

E'en in thine acts of Providence,
  Which our unceasing wants supply,
Thy hand, stretched out for our defence,
  Is still concealed from mortal eye.

In vain we stretch our sight to scan
  The mysteries of thy chastening rod,
Awed by that voice which says to man,
  'Be still, and know that I am God!'

The Lord's Supper. L. M.
WATTS.

'Twas on that dark, that doleful night,
When powers of earth and hell arose
Against the Son of God's delight,
And friends betrayed him to his foes.

Before the mournful scene began,
He took the bread, and blest, and brake;
What love through all his actions ran!
What wondrous words of grace he spake!

"This is my body, broke for sin;
Receive and eat the living food;"
Then took the cup, and blessed the wine;
"'Tis the new covenant in my blood."

"Do this," he cried, "till time shall end,
In memory of your dying Friend;
Meet at my table, and record
The love of your departed Lord."

Consecration of the Cross. L. M.
WATTS.

When I survey the wondrous cross,
  On which the Prince of glory died,
My richest gain I count but loss,
  And pour contempt on all my pride.

Forbid it, Lord, that I should boast,
  Save in the death of Christ, my God;
All the vain things that charm me most,
  I sacrifice them to his blood.

See, from his head, his hands, his feet,
  Sorrow and love flow mingled down:
Did e'er such love and sorrow meet,
  Or thorns compose so rich a crown?

Were all the realm of nature mine,
  That were a present far too small;
Love so amazing, so divine,
  Demands my soul, my life, my all.

Remembering Christ. L. M.

O thou, my soul, forget no more
The Friend who all thy sorrows bore;
Let every idol be forgot;
But, O my soul, forget him not.

Renounce thy works and ways, with grief
And fly to this divine relief;
Nor Him forget, who left his throne,
And for thy life gave up his own.

Eternal truth and mercy shine
In him, and he himself is thine:
And canst thou, then, with sin beset,
Such charms, such matchless charms,
  forget!

O, no; till life itself depart,
His name shall cheer and warm my heart;
And, lisping this, from earth I'll rise,
And join the chorus of the skies.

The Memorials of Grace. L. M.
WATTS.

Jesus is gone above the skies,
Where our weak senses reach him not;
And carnal objects court our eyes,
To thrust our Saviour from our thought

He knows what wandering hearts we have,
Apt to forget his lovely face;
And, to refresh our minds, he gave
These kind memorials of his grace.

Let sinful joys be all forgot,
And earth grow less in our esteem,
Christ and his love fill every thought,
And faith and hope be fixed on him.

While he is absent from our sight,
'Tis to prepare our souls a place,
That we may dwell in heavenly light,
And live forever near his face.

OCEAN MELODIES.

Remembering Christ. C. M.
WARDLAW.

Remember thee, redeeming Lord!
 While Memory holds her place,
Can we forget the Prince of life,
 Who saves us by his grace?

The Lord of life, with glory crowned,
 On heaven's exalted throne,
Remembers those for whom, on earth,
 He heaved his dying groan.

His glory now no tongue of man
 Or seraph bright can tell:
Yet 'tis the chief of all his joys
 That souls are saved from hell.

For this he came and dwelt on earth;
 For this his life was given;
For this he fought and vanquished death,
 For this he pleads in heaven.

Join, all ye saints beneath the sky,
 Your grateful praise to give;
Sing loud hosannas to the Lord,
 Who died that you might live.

Home in Heaven. S. M.
MONTGOMERY.

My Father's house on high!
 Home of my soul! how near,
At times, to faith's foreseeing eye
 Thy golden gates appear!

I hear at morn and even,
 At noon and midnight hour,
The choral harmonies of heaven
 Seraphic music pour.

O, then my spirit faints
 To reach the land I love—
The bright inheritance of saints,
 My glorious home above.

The Heavenly Canaan. C. M.
WATTS.

There is a land of pure delight;
 Where saints immortal reign;
Eternal day excludes the night,
 And pleasures banish pain.

There everlasting spring abides,
 And never-fading flowers:
Death, like a narrow sea, divides
 That heavenly land from ours.

Sweet fields, beyond the swelling flood,
 Stand dressed in living green:
So to the Jews fair Canaan stood,
 While Jordan rolled between.

But timorous mortals start and shrink
 To cross this narrow sea,
And linger, trembling, on the brink,
 And fear to launch away.

Could we but climb where Moses stood,
 And view the landscape o'er,—
Not Jordan's stream, nor death's cold flood,
 Should fright us from the shore.

Following Christ. 8s & 7s
DODDRIDGE.

Humble souls, who seek salvation
 Through the Lamb's redeeming blood
Hear the voice of revelation;
 Tread the path that Jesus trod.

Hear the blest Redeemer call you;
 Listen to his heavenly voice;
Dread no ills that can befall you,
 While you make his ways your choice

Plainly here his footsteps tracing,
 Follow him without delay,
Gladly his command embracing;
 Lo! your Captain leads the way.

The Gospel Ship. C. M.
Tune—ARLINGTON.

The gospel ship's a gallant ship,
  In river Time she lies;
For passengers she's waiting now,
  Take passage, and be wise,

While others strike the rocks of wrath,
  And sink to rise no more,
She'll safely pass the straits of death,
  And reach the happy shore.

Her keel is perfect righteousness
  That ever shall endure,
Salvation everlasting is
  Her mighty bulwark sure.

Eternal love's her snow-white sail,
  And truth her noble mast;
She's wafted by the Spirit's gale,
  Nor fears the fiercest blast.

Infinite Wisdom guides her course,
  This is her compass true;
By angels manned, her skilful band,
  A holy, happy crew.

Her chart the living faithful word
  Of Him who cannot lie;
Her blood-stained banner waves aloft,
  That all may it descry.

Her Captain is Immanuel,
  Jehovah's royal Son,
With uncreated glories crowned,
  For Calvary's victories won;

For wisdom, courage, skill, and might,
  There's none can Him excel;
He'll steer his vessel safe to port
  In spite of earth and hell.

Then come into the gospel ship,
  Whoever will, may come:
For thousands, thousands are on board,
  "And even yet there's room."

Come without money, there's no fare;
  No terms can easier be,
Your passage money Jesus paid,
  And you have passage free.

But mark! the starting time's *to-day*,
  And soon that time will fly—
To-day, to-day, we launch away
  Into eternity.

Leave Sodom world without delay,
  Her ruin's near at hand;
Sinners, obey the gospel call,
  And sail for glory's land.
            T. SHEARER.

Still on. C. M.
Tune—DUNDEE.

Still on, still on, still on we sweep,
  The swelling waves among;
The foaming of the restless deep
  Aside is fearless flung.

Still on, still on we fleetly glide,
  At evening and at morn;
Careering on an angry tide,
  And wafted by the storm.

Still on! and yet there seems no change,
  No space as yet seems passed;
To-day the objects in our range,
  Are what they were the last;—

Above, the same pure fields of light;
  Around, the same vast sea;—
Does not this shadow forth the **flight**
  Of an eternity?

OCEAN MELODIES. 143

The Dead Mariner. L. M.
BY C. D. PRENTICE.

The purple gems forever burn
In fadeless beauty round thy urn,
And pure and deep as infant love,
The blue sea rolls its *waves* above.

O'er thee mild eve her beauty flings,
And there the white gull lifts her wings,
And the blue halcyon loved to lave
Her plumage in the deep blue wave.

And there the sea-flower bright and
Is sweetly o'er thy slumber flung. [young
And, like a weeping mourner fair,
The pale flag hangs its tresses there.

And when the wave has sunk to rest,
They then will murmur o'er thy breast;
And the bright victims of the sea,
Perchance will make their home with thee.

Tho' ships and waves wil' o'er thee glide,
Sweet tho'ts are hovering by thy side;
Oft will thy Mother view with tears,
The Eden of departed years.

Burial at Sea. S. M.

Down to unfathomed depths,
　Where hidden fountains flow,
Alone, his dreary bed to find,
　The child of earth must go.

For him no funeral bell
　May weeping friends convene,
Nor dust to kindred dust be laid
　Within the church yard green.

Farewell! one heavy plunge!
　One cleft in ocean's floor!
And then the deaf and sullen surge
　Sweeps on, and all is o'er.

The Mariner's Grave. C. M.
BY C. D. PRENTICE.

Sleep on! sleep on! above thy corse
The winds their Sabbath keep;
The waves are round thee, and thy breast
Heaves with the heaving deep.

Sleep on! no willow o'er thee bends
With melancholy air,
No violet springs, nor dewy rose,
Its soul of love lays bare.

Sleep on! sleep on! the glittering depths
Of Ocean's coral caves,
Are thy bright urn, thy requiem
The music of its waves.

Sleep on! sleep on! the fearful wreck
Of mingling cloud and deep,
May leave its wild and stormy tack
Above thy place of sleep.

Sleep on! thy grave is far away,
But love bewails thee yet;
To thee the heart wrung sigh is breathed,
And lovely eyes are wet.

BY MRS. L. H. SIGOURNEY.

We give thee earnest charge,
　Oh sad, and solemn deep,
Safe in thy cold and strong embrace
　This precious form to keep;

Till at the trumpet's sound,
　Which fills the world with dread,
Thy caverns and the graves of earth
　Shall render up their dead:

Then clothed in glorious light,
　May this our friend arise,
And change thy dark, imprisoning cell,
　For freedom in the skies.

All is Well. 10s & 6, 8s & 6.

What's this that steals, that steals
  upon my frame?
Is it death? Is it death?
That soon will quench, will quench
  this vital flame,
Is it death? Is it death?
If this be death, I soon shall be
From every pain and sorrow free,
I shall the King of glory see;
  All is well, all is well.

Weep not my friends, my friends,
  weep not for me,
  All is well, all is well.
My sins are pardoned, pardoned, I
  am free,
  All is well, all is well;
There's not a cloud that doth arise,
To hide my Saviour from my eyes,
I soon shalt mount the upper skies;
  All is well, all is well.

Hark, hark! my Lord, and Master
  calls with grace;
  All is well, all is well.
I soon shall see, shall see his heavenly
  face,
  All is well, all is well.
Farewell, dear friends, adieu, adieu;
I can no longer stay with you,
My glittering crown appears in view,
  All is well, all is well.

Tune, tune your harps, ye saints in
  glory sing,
  All is well, all is well.
I'll praise, will praise, my Saviour,
  and my King;
  All is well, all is well.
Bright angels are from glory come,
They're round my bed, they're in
  my room,
They wait to waft my spirit home.
  All is well, all is well.

Not Yet. C. M.   L. E. L.

"Not yet! the flowers are in my path,
  My sun is in the sky;
Not yet! my heart is full of hope,
  I cannot bear to die.

Not yet! I never knew till now,
  How precious life could be;
Not yet, my heart is full of love;
  I cannot come with thee."

But Love, and Hope, enchanted twain,
  Passed in their falsehood by,—
Death came again—and then he said,
  "I'm ready now to die."

Those blessed who die in the Lord.
C. M.   WATTS.

Hear what the voice from heaven
  For all the pious dead: [proclaims
"Sweet is the savor of their names,
  And soft their sleeping bed.

"They die in Jesus, and are blest;
  How kind their slumbers are!
From suffering and from sin released,
  They're freed from every snare.

"Far from this world of toil and strife,
  They're present with the Lord;
The labors of their mortal life
  End in a large reward."

The Bible suited to our Wants. C. M.

Father of mercies, in thy word
What endless glory shines?
Forever be thy name adored,
For these celestial lines.

'Tis here the tree of knowledge grows,
And yields a free repast;
Here purer sweets than nature knows
Invite the longing taste.

'Tis here the Saviour's welcome voice
Spreads heavenly peace around,
And life, and everlasting joys,
Attend the blissful sound.

O, may these heavenly pages be
My ever-dear delight;
And still new beauties may I see,
And still increasing light.

Divine Instructor, gracious Lord,
Be thou forever near;
Teach me to love thy sacred word,
And view my Saviour here. *Watts.*

The Sinner invited and Warned. 8, 7 & 4.

Hear, O sinner! Mercy hails you:
Now with sweetest voice she calls;
Bids you haste to seek the Saviour,
Ere the hand of justice falls;
 Trust in Jesus;
'Tis the voice of Mercy calls.

Haste, O sinner, to the Saviour;
Seek his mercy while you may;
Soon the day of grace is over;
Soon your life will pass away:
 Haste to Jesus;
You must perish if you stay. *Reed.*

Glad Tidings. 8s, 7s & 6.

Sinners, will you scorn the message
Sent in mercy from above?
Every sentence, O, how tender!
Every line is full of love:
 Listen to it;
Every line is full of love.

Hear the heralds of the gospel
News from Zion's King proclaim:
"Pardon to each rebel sinner;
Free forgiveness in his name:"
 How important!
"Free forgiveness in his name."

Tempted souls, they bring you succor;
Fearful hearts, they quell your fears;
And, with news of consolation,
Chase away the falling tears;
 Tender heralds!
Chase away the falling tears.

Who hath our report believed?
Who received the joyful word?
Who embraced the news of pardon
Offered to you by the Lord?
 Can you slight it?
Offered to you by the Lord?

O ye angels hovering round us,
Waiting spirits, speed your way;
Haste ye to the court of heaven;
Tidings bear without delay,
 Rebel sinners
Glad the message will obey.

Our only Hope. C. M.

Go, speak of Jesus' dying love,
Ye messengers of God;
Go, bid the wandering sailors prove,
Redemption through his blood.

OCEAN MELODIES.

Our Guide. L. M.

Come, gracious spirit, heaven'y Dove,
With light and comfort from above;
Be thou our Guardian th u our Guide;
O'er every thought and step preside.

To us the light of truth disp'ay,
And make us know and choose thy way;
Plant holy fear in every heart
That we from God may ne'er depart.

Lead us to holiness—the road
Which we must take to dwell with God;
Lead us to Christ—the living way;
Nor let us from his pastures stray;

Lead us to God—our final rest,—
To be with him forever b'est;
Lead us to heaven its bliss to share—
Fulness of joy forever there.

Teachings of the Spirit. L. M.

Come, blessed Spirit, Source of 'ight.
Whose power and grace are uncon
 fine l.
Dispel the gloomy shades of night,
The thicker darkness of the mind.

To mine illumined eyes disp'ay
The glorious truth thy words reveal;
Cause me to run the heavenly way;
Make me delight to do thy will.

Thine inward teachings make me know
Thy wonders of redeeming love,
The vanity of things below,
And excellence of things above.

While through these dubious paths I
 s'ray,
Spread like the sun thy beams abroad.
O, show the dangers of the way,
And guide my feeble steps to God.

The Spirit entreated not to Depart. L M.

Stay, thou insulted Spirit stay.
Though I have'd ne thee such despite;
Cast not a sinner quite away,
Nor take thine everlas ing flight.

Though I have most unfaithful b en
Of all who e'er thy grace received—
Ten thousand times thy goodness seen,
Ten thousand times thy goodness
 grieved,

Yet, O. the chief of sinners spare,
In honor of my great High Priest:
Nor, in thy righteous anger swear
I shall not see thy people's rest.

My weary soul, O God, re'ease;
Uphold me with thy gracious hand;
O, guide me into perfect peace.
And bring me to the promised land.

The Saviour at the Door. C. M.

Amazing sight! the Saviour stands
And knocks at every door!
Ten thousand blessings in his hands,
To satisfy the poor.

"Behold," he saith, "I bleed and die
To bring you to my rest:
Hear sinners while I'm passing by,
And be forever blest.

"Will you despise my bleeding love,
And choose the way to hell?
Or in the glorious realms above,
With me, forever dwell?

"Say, will you hear my gracious voice,
And have your sins forgiven?
Or will you make that wretched choice,
And bar yourselves from heaven."

The Spirit Enlightening and Renewing.

Eternal Spirit, we confess
And sing the wonders of thy grace;
Thy power conveys our blessings down
From God the Father, and the Son.

Enlightened by thine heavenly ray,
Our shades and darkness turn to day;
Thine inward teachings make us know
Our danger and our refuge too.

Thy power and glory work within,
And break the chains of reigning sin;
Our wild, impetuous lusts subdue,
And form our wretched hearts anew.

The troubled conscience knows thy voice;
Thy cheering words awake our joys;
Thy words allay the stormy wind,
And calm the surges of the mind.

Sovereignty of the Spirit. C. M.

The blessed Spirit, like the wind,
Blows when and where he please:
How happy are the men who feel
The soul-enlivening breeze!

He moulds the carnal mind afresh,
Subdues the power of sin,
Transforms the heart of stone to flesh,
And plants his grace within.

He sheds abroad the Father's love,
Applies redeeming blood,
Bids both our guilt and fear remove,
And brings us home to God.

Lord, fill each dear benighted soul
With light, and life, and joy;
None can thy mighty power control,
Or shall thy work destroy.

The Holy Spirit the Comforter. 8, 6 & 4.

Our blest Redeemer, ere he breathed
His tender, last farewell,
A Guide, a Comforter, bequeathed
With us to dwell.

He came in tongues of living flame,
To teach, convince, subdue;
All powerful as the wind he came,
As viewless too.

He came sweet influence to impart,
A gracious, willing guest,
While he can find one humble heart,
Wherein to rest.

He breathes that gentle voice we hear,
Soft as the breeze of even,
That checks each fault, that calms each fear
And speaks of heaven.

And every virtue we possess,
And every victory won,
And every thought of holiness,
Are his alone.

The Spirit's Power. C. M.

Come, Holy Spirit, from above,
With thy celestial fire,
Come, and with flames of zeal and love
Our hearts and tongues inspire.

The Spirit, by his heavenly breath,
New life creates within;
He quickens sinners from the death
Of trespasses and sin.

The things of Christ the Spirit takes,
And to our hearts reveals;
Our bodies he his temple makes,
And our redemption seals.

Excellency of the Scriptures. C. M.

Let all the heathen writers join
 To form one perfect book;
Great God, if once compared with thine,
 How mean their writings look!

Not the most perfect rules they gave
 Could show one sin forgiven,
Nor lead a step beyond the grave;
 But thine conducts to heaven.

I've seen an end of what we call
 Perfection here below—
How short the powers of nature fall,
 And can no further go.

Yet men would fain be just with God,
 By works their hands have wrought;
But thy commands exceeding broad,
 Extend to every thought.

In vain we boast perfection here,
 While sin defiles our frame,
And sinks our virtues down so far,
 They scarce deserve the name.

Our faith, and love and every grace,
 Fall far below thy word;
But perfect truth and righteousness
 Dwell only with the Lord.

Offered Peace. 7s.

Weeping sinners, dry your tears;
Jesus on the throne appears,
Mercy comes with balmy wing,
Bids you his salvation sing.

Peace he brings you by his death,
Peace he speaks with every breath;
Can you slight such heavenly charms?
Flee, O flee to Jesus' arms.

The Riches of God's Word. C. M.

Let worldly men, from shore to shore,
 Their chosen good pursue;
Thy word, O Lord, we value more
 Than treasures of Peru.

Here mines of knowledge, love, and joy,
 Are open'd to our sight;
The purest gold without alloy,
 And gems divinely bright.

The counsels of redeeming grace
 These sacred leaves unfold;
And here the Saviour's lovely face
 Our raptured eyes behold.

Here light descending from above,
 Directs our doubtful feet;
Here promises of heavenly love
 Our ardent wishes meet.

Our numerous griefs are here redressed,
 And all our wants supplied;
Nought we can ask to make us blest
 Is in this book denied. *Stennett.*

Regeneration of the Spirit. C. M.

Not all the outward forms on earth,
 Nor rites that God has given,
Nor will of man, nor blood, nor birth,
 Can raise a soul to heaven.

The sovereign will of God alone
 Creates us heirs of grace,
Born in the image of his Son,
 A new, peculiar race.

The Spirit, like some heavenly wind,
 Breathes on the sons of flesh,
Creates anew the carnal mind,
 And forms the man afresh.

Our quicken'd souls awake and rise
 From their long sleep of death;
On heavenly things we fix our eyes,
 And praise employs our breath.

OCEAN MELODIES. 149

The Mercy Seat. L. M.

From every stormy wind that blows,
From every swelling tide of woes,
There is a calm, a sure retreat:
'Tis found before the mercy-seat.

There is a place where Jesus sheds
The oil of gladness on our heads—
A place of all on earth most sweet;
It is the blood bought mercy-seat.

There is a scene where spirits blend,
Where friend holds fellowship with
  friend;
Though sundered far by faith they meet
Around one common mercy-seat.

There, there, on eagle wings we soar,
And sin and sense molest no more,
And Heaven comes down our souls to
  greet,
And glory crowns the mercy-seat.

It is I; Be not Afraid. L. M.

When power divine in mortal form,
Hushed with a word the raging storm,
In soothing accents, Jesus said,
"Lo, it is I; be not afraid."

So when in silence nature sleeps,
And his lone watch the mourner keeps,
One thought shall every pang remove—
Trust, feeble man, thy Maker's love.

God calms the tumult and the storm;
He rules the seraph and the worm;
No creature is by Him forgot
Of those who know or know him not.

And when the last dread hour shall
  come,
When trembling Nature waits her doom,
This voice shall wake the pious dead—
"Lo, it is I; be not afraid."

Dependence upon Christ. L. M.

Buried in shadows of the night
We lie, till Christ restores the light—
Till he bids ends to heal the blind,
And chase the darkness of the mind.

Our guilty souls are drowned in tears,
Till his atoning blood appears;
Then we awake from deep distress,
And sing the Lord our Righteousness.

Jesus beholds where Satan reigns
And binds his slaves in heavy chains;
He sets the prisoners free and breaks
The iron bondage from our necks.

Poor helpless worms in Thee possess
Grace, wisdom, power, and righteous-
  ness;
Thou art our mighty All, and we
Give our whole selves, O Lord, to thee.
Watts.

The Road to Life and to Death. L. M.

Broad is the road that leads to death,
And thousands walk together there;
But wisdom shows a narrow path,
With here and there a traveller.

"Deny thyself and take thy cross,"
Is the Redeemer's great command:
Nature must count her gold but dross,
If she would gain this heavenly land.

The fearful soul that tires and faints,
And walks the ways of God no more,
Is but esteemed almost a saint,
And makes his own destruction sure.

Lord, let not all my hopes be vain;
Create my heart entirely new—
Which hypocrites could ne'er attain,
Which false apostates never knew.
Watts.

Rest for the weary Penitent. L. M.

Come, weary souls with sin distressed,
Come, and accept the promised rest;
The Saviour's gracious call obey,
And cast your gloomy fears away.

Oppressed with sin, a painful load,
O come and spread your woes abroad;
Divine compassion, mighty love,
Will all the painful load remove.

Here mercy's boundless ocean flows,
To cleanse your guilt and heal your woes;
Pardon, and life and endless peace;
How rich the gift! how free the grace!

Lord, we accept, with thankful heart,
The hope thy gracious words impart;
We come with trembling, yet rejoice,
And bless the kind inviting voice.

Dear Saviour let thy wondrous love
Confirm our faith, our fears remove;
O, sweetly influence every breast,
And guide us to eternal rest. *Steele.*

Yet there is Room. C. M.

Come, sinner, to the gospel feast;
O, come without delay;
For there is room in Jesus' breast
For all who will obey.

There's room in God's eternal love
To save thy precious soul;
Room in the Spirit's grace above
To heal and make thee whole.

There's room within the church, redeemed
With blood of Christ divine;
Room in the white-robed throng convened,
For that dear soul of thine.

There's room in heaven among the choir
And harps and crowns of gold
And glorious palms of victory there,
And joys that ne'er we're told.

There's room around thy Father's board
For thee and thousands more;
O, come and welcome to the Lord;
Yea, come this very hour.

Pardon Penitently Implored. L. M.

Show pity, Lord; O Lord, forgive;
Let a repenting rebel live;
Are not thy mercies large and free?
May not a sinner trust in thee?

My crimes though great cannot surpass
The power and glory of thy grace;
Great God, thy nature hath no bound;
So let thy pardoning love be found.

O, wash my soul from every sin,
And make my guilty conscience clean,
Here, on my heart, the burden lies,
And past offences pain my eyes.

My lips, with shame, my sins confess,
Against thy law, against thy grace;
Lord, should thy judgment grow severe,
I am condemned, but thou art clear.

Should sudden vengeance seize my breath,
I must pronounce thee just in death;
And if my soul were sent to hell,
Thy righteous law approves it well.

Yet save a trembling sinner, Lord,
Whose hope, still hovering round thy word,
Would light on some sweet promise there,
Some sure support against despair.

OCEAN MELODIES. 151

Christ's Example. L. M.

Our Saviour bowed beneath the wave,
And meekly sought a watery grave:
Come see the sacred path he trod—
A path well pleasing to our God.

His voice we hear, his footsteps trace,
And thither come to seek his face,
To do his will, to feel his love,
And join our songs with songs above.

Hosanna to the Lamb divine!
Let endless glories round him shine;
High o'er the heavens, forever reign,
O Lamb of God, for sinners slain.

Sufficiency of the Atonement. C. M.

There is a fountain fil'ed with blood,
Drawn from Immanuel's veins,
And sinners plunged beneath that flood
Lose all their guilty stains.

The dying thief rejoiced to see
That fountain in his day;
O may I there, though vile as he,
Wash all my sins away.

Thou dying Lamb, thy precious blood
Shall never lose its power,
Till all the ransomed church of God
Are saved, to sin no more.

E'er since, by faith, I saw the stream
Thy flowing wounds supply,
Redeeming love has been my theme,
And shall be till I die.

And when this feeble, fa'tering tongue
Lies silent in the grave,
Then, in a nobler, sweeter song,
I'll sing thy power to save. *Cowper.*

Baptism an Emblem. L. M.

Do we not know that solemn word,
That we are buried with the Lord?
Baptiz'd into his death; and then
Put off the body of our sin?

Our souls receive diviner breath,
Raised from corruption, guilt and death,
So from the grave did Christ arise,
And lives to God above the skies.

No more let sin or Satan reign
Within our mortal flesh again;
The various lusts we served before
Shall have dominion now no more.

Glorying in the Cross. 8s & 7s.

In the cross of Christ I glory,
Towering o'er the wrecks of time;
All the light of sacred story
Gathers round its head sublime.

When the woes of life o'ertake me,
Hopes deceive, and fears annoy,
Never shall the cross forsake me;
Lo! it glows with peace and joy.

When the sun of bliss is beaming
Light and love up in my way,
From the cross the radiance streaming
Adds new lustre to the day.

Bane and blessing, pain and pleasure,
By the cross are sanctified;
Peace is there that knows no measure,
Joys that through all time abide.

In the cross of Christ I glory,
Towering o'er the wrecks of time;
All the light of sacred story
Gathers round its head sublime. *Bowring.*

The Baptism of Christ. S. M.

Down to the sacred wave
 The Lord of life was led;
And he who came our souls to save
 In Jordan bowed his head.

He taught the solemn way;
 He fixed the holy rite,
He bade his ransomed ones obey,
 And keep the path of life.

Blest Saviour, we will tread
 In thy appointed way;
Let glory o'er these scenes be shed,
 And smile on us to-day.   *S. F. Smith.*

Let go The Anchor. 8s & 7s.

"Land ahead!"—its fruits are waving,
 On the hills of fadeless green;
And the living waters laving
 Shores where heavenly forms are seen.
Eden's breezes o'er it sigh,
Billows kiss its strand and die.

Onward bark!—"The cape I'm rounding."
See the blessed wave their hands!
Hear the harps of God resounding
 From the bright immortal bands,
Rocks and storms I'll fear no more,
When on that inviting shore.

"Let the anchor go"—I'm riding
 On this calm and silvery bay;
Seaward fast the tide is gliding,
 Shores in sunlight stretch away.
Strike the colors, furl the sail!
I am safe within the vail!

Christian Profession. 8s. 7s. & 4.

Gracious Saviour, we ad re thee;
 Purchased by thy precious blood;
We present ourselves before thee,
 Now to walk the narrow road:
Saviour guide us—
 Guide us to our heavenly home.

Thou didst mark our path of duty;
 Thou wast laid beneath the wave;
Thou didst rise in glorious beauty
 From the semblance of the grave;
May we follow
 In the same delightful way.

Songs of Heaven. 8s.

Ye angels, who stand round the throne,
 And view my Immanuel's face,
In rapturous songs make him known;
 O, tune your soft harps to his praise.

Ye saints, who stand nearer than they,
 And cast your bright crowns at his feet,
His grace and his glory display,
 And all his rich mercy repeat.

He snatched you from hell and the grave;
 He ransomed from death and despair;
For you he is mighty to save,
 And faithful to bring you safe there.

O, when will the moment appear,
 When I shall unite in your song?
I'm weary of lingering here:
 For I to your Saviour belong.

I'm fettered and chained here in clay;
 I struggle and pant to be free;
I long to be soaring away,
 My God and my Saviour to see.

Delay Not. 11s.

Delay not, delay not; O sinner, draw
  near;
The waters of life are now flowing
  for thee.
No price is demanded: the Saviour is
  here;
Redemption is purchased, salvation
  is free.

Delay not, delay not; why longer abuse
The love and compassion of Jesus, thy
  God?
A fountain is opened; how canst thou
  refuse
To wash and be cleansed in his par-
  doning blood?

Delay not, delay not, O sinner, to come,
  For mercy still lingers, and calls
    thee to-day,
  Her voice is not heard in the shades of
    the tomb;
  Her message, unheeded, will soon
    pass away.

Delay not, delay not; the Spirit of grace,
  Long grieved and resisted, may take
    his sad flight,
  And leave thee in darkness to finish
    thy race,
  To sink in the gloom of eternity's
    night.

Sacred Songs.

Delay not, delay not; the hour is at
  hand;
The earth shall dissolve, and the
  heavens shall fade;
The dead, small and great, in the judg-
  ment shall stand
What helper, then, sinner, shall lend
  thee his aid?

Termination of the Christian Warfare. 8s & 7s.

When we pass through yonder river,
  When we reach the farther shore,
There's an end of war forever;
  We shall see our foes no more:
All our conflicts then shall cease,
  Followed by eternal peace.

After warfare, rest is pleasant:
  O, how sweet the prospect is!
Though we toil and strive at present,
  Let us not repine at this:
Toil, and pain, and conflict, past,
  All endear repose at last.

When we gain the heavenly regions,
  When we touch the heavenly shore—
Blessed thought!—no hostile legions
  Can alarm or trouble more:
Far beyond the reach of foes,
  We shall dwell in sweet repose.

O, that hope! how bright, how glorious!
  'Tis his people's blest reward;
In the Saviour's strength victorious,
  They at length behold their Lord:
In his kingdom they shall rest,
  In his love be fully blest.   *Kelly.*

Star of Peace. 8s 7s & 4.

Star of peace, to wan lovers weary,
  Bright the beams that smile on me;
Cheer the pil t s vision dreary.
    Far, far at sea.

Star of hope, gleam on the billow,
  Bless the soul that sighs for thee;
Bless the sailor's lonely pillow,
    Far, far at sea.

Star of faith, when winds are mocking
  All his toil, he flies to thee:
Save him, on the billows rocking,
    Far, far at sea.

Star divine, O safely guide him,
  Bring the wanderer home to thee:
Sore temptations long have tried him,
    Far, far at sea.

Star of hope, gleam on the billow,
  Bless the soul that sighs for thee:
Bless the sailors' lonely pillow,
    Far, far at sea.

Just as Thou Art. 8s & 6s.

Just as thou art—without one trace
Of love, or joy, or inward grace,
Or meetness for the heavenly place,
    O, guilty sinner, come.

Thy sins I bore on Calvary's tree:
The stripes thy due were laid on me,
That peace and pardon might be free—
    O wretched sinner, come.

Burdened with guilt, wouldst thou be
    blest?
Trust not the world: it gives no rest:
I bring relief to hearts opprest—
    O weary, sinner come.

Come, leave thy burden at the cross;
Count all thy gains but empty dross:
My grace repays all earthly loss—
    O needy sinner, come.

Come hither bring thy boding fears,
Thy aching heart, thy bursting tears;
'Tis mercy's voice salutes thine ears;
    O trembling sinner, come.

"The Spirit and the bride say, Come,"
Rejoicing saints re-echo, Come:
Who faints, who thirsts, who will may
    come:
    Thy Saviour bids thee come.

Heaven Anticipated. 8s & 6s.

There is an hour of peaceful rest
  To mourning wanderers given;
There is a joy for souls distressed,
A balm for every wounded breast;
  'Tis found alone in heaven.

There is a home for weary souls,
  By sins and sorrows driven,
When tossed on life's tempestuous
    shoals,
Where storms arise, and ocean rolls,
  And all is drear—'tis heaven.

There faith lifts up the tearless eye,
  The heart no longer riven,—
And views the tempest passing by,
Sees evening shadows quickly fly,
  And all serene in heaven.

There fragrant flowers immortal bloom,
  And joys supreme are given;
There rays divine disperse the gloom;
Beyond the dark and narrow tomb
  Appears the dawn of heaven.

"On the Cross." 11s & 8s.

Behold, behold the Lamb of God—
　On the cross;
For us he shed his precious blood—
　On the Cross:
Oh hear his all important cry,
"Eli, Lama, Sabachthani!"
Draw near and see your Saviour die—
　On the Cross.

Behold his arms extended wide—
　On the Cross!
Behold his bleeding hands and side—
　On the Cross;
The sun withholds his rays of light,
The heavens are clothed in shades of
　　night.
While Jesus doth with devils fight—
　On the Cross.

Come, sinners see him lifted up—
　On the Cross;
He drinks for you the bitter cup—
　On the Cross;
The rocks do rend, the mountains quake
While Jesus doth atonement make,
While Jesus suffers for our sake—
　On the Cross.

And now the mighty deed is done—
　On the Cross;
The battle's fought, the victory's won—
　On the Cross;
To heaven he turned his languid eyes,
'Tis finish'd now, the Conqueror cries,
Then bows his sacred head and dies—
　On the Cross.

Where'er I go, I'll tell the story—
　Of the cross;
In nothing else my soul shall glory—
　Save the Cross;
Yea, this my constant theme shall be,
Through time and in eternity,
That Jesus tasted death for me—
　On the cross.

Subdued by the Cross. C. M.

In evil long I took delight,
　Unawed by shame or fear,
Till a new object struck my sight,
　And stopped my wild career.

I saw one hanging on a tree,
　In agonies and blood
He fixed his languid eyes on me,
　As near his cross I stood.

O, never, till my latest breath,
　Shall I forget that look;
It seemed to charge me with his **death**,
　Though not a word he spoke.

My conscience felt and owned the guilt;
　It plunged me in despair:
I saw my sins his blood had spilt,
　And helped to nail him there.

A second look he gave, which said,
"I freely all forgive;
This blood is for thy ransom paid;
　I die that thou may'st live."

Thus, while his death my sin displays
　In all its darkest hue,
Such is the mystery of grace,
　It seals my pardon too.

OCEAN MELODIES.

The Mission Ship. 10s.

"Look toward the sea," where crested
  bi lows rise.
Look to the Heavens, where the storm-
  sprite flies,
Above, below one dark and threat'ning
  cloud,
Wraps the rough ocean, in its gloomy
  shroud.
Deep in the midst the mission ship
  appears,
'Spite of the blast, her onward course
  she steers.
Guided in safety by a power above,
She bears glad tidings of a Saviour's
  love.
From earliest days the seamen's skillful
  hand,
Has borne the Sacred Book from land
  to land,
Causing the hearts of millions to rejoice
In the sweet sound of a Redeemer's
  voice.
Continue, ever thus, brave generous
  hearts,
To spread the gospel in remotest parts,
Light the dark heathen in his cheerless
  way,
And teach the unbeliever how to pray.

Universal Adoration. 8s & 7s.

Hark! the notes of angels singing,
  "Glory, glory to the Lamb!"
All in heaven their tribute bringing,
  Raising high the Saviour's name.
Ye for whom his life is given,
  Sacred themes to you belong;
Come, assist the choir of heaven;
  Join the everlasting song.

Fill'ed with holy emulation,
  Let us vie with those above:
Sweet the theme — a free salvation!
  Fruit of everlasting love.

Endless life in him possessing,
  Let us praise his precious name;
Glory honor, power and blessing,
  Be forever to the Lamb.

Save, Lord, or we Perish. 12s.

When thro' the torn sail the wild
  tempest is streaming,
When o'er the dark wave the red light-
  ning is gleaming,
Nor hope lends a ray, the poor seaman
  to cherish,
We fly to our maker,—"Save, Lord, or
  we perish."

O Jesus, once rocked on the breast of
  the billow,
Aroused by the shriek of despair from
  thy pillow,—
Now seated in glory, the mariner
  cherish,
Who cries in his anguish, "Save, Lord,
  or we perish."

And, O. when the whirlwind of passion
  is raging,
When sin in our hearts its sad warfare
  is waging,
Then send down thy grace, thy redeem-
  ed to cherish:
Rebuke the destroyer,—"Save, Lord,
  or we perish."

TOUCHING AND BEAUTIFUL LINES.

The New England Diadem gives its readers the following beautiful stanzas, which were suggested by hearing read an extract of a letter from Captain Chase, giving an account of the sickness and death of his brother-in-law, Mr. Brown Owen, who died on his passage to California. We have but seldom met anything so painfully interesting in every line, and it will be read with "teary eyes" by many who have lost brothers, fathers, husbands or sons, upon their way to, or after having reached the land of Gold and Graves:—

Greenville.

Farewell Request. 8s & 7s.

Closer, nearer, brother, nearer,
 For my limbs are growing co'd,
And thy presence seemeth dearer,
 When thy arms around me fold;
I am dying, brother, dying,
 Soon ye'll miss me in your berth,
For my form will soon be lying,
 'Neath the ocean's briny surf.

Hearken to me, brother, hearken,
 I have something I would say,
Ere the veil my vision darken,
 And I go from hence away;
I am going, surely going,
 But my hope in God is strong,
I am willing brother, knowing
 That he doeth nothing wrong.

Tell my father when you greet him,
 That in death I prayed for him,
Prayed that I may one day meet him,
 In a world that's free from sin;
Tell my mother, (God assist her
 Now that she is growing old,)
That I would gladly have kissed her,
 When my lips grew pale and cold.

Listen, brother, catch each whisper,
 'Tis my wife I'd speak of now

Tell, oh tell her how I missed her,
 When the fever burned my brow;
Tell her, brother, closely listen,
 Don't forget a single word,
That in death my eyes did glisten,
 With the tears her memory stirred.

Tell her she must kiss my children,
 Like the kiss I last impressed,
Hold them as when last I held them,
 Folded closely to my breast;
Give them early to their Maker,
 Putting all her trust in God,
And He never will forsake her,
 For He said so in His Word.

O, my children! Heaven bless them!
 They were all my life to me,
Would I could once more caress them,
 Ere I sink beneath the sea;
'Twas for them I crossed the ocean,
 What my hopes were I'll not tell,
But I have gained an orphan's portion,
 Yet He doeth all things well.

Tell my sisters I remember
 Every kindly parting word,
And my heart has been kept tender,
 By the thoughts their mem'ry stirred;
Tell them I near reached the haven
 Where I sought the "precious dust,"
But I have gained a port called Heaven,
 Where the gold will never rust.

Urge them to secure an entrance.
 For they'll find their brother there;
Faith in Jesus and repentance
 Will secure for each a share.—
Hark! I hear my Saviour speaking,
 'Tis, I know his voice so well,
When I am gone, oh don't be weeping,
 Brother here's my last farewell.

"The following is from among the earliest of our poetical reminiscences, fresh and green as it was gathered, more than forty years ago. It is full of evangelical piety, and the poetry in it is of that rich, old aspiring soul-reaching kind, which has passed away with the strong hearts that framed it."

An old Nautical Hymn. 6s & 5s.

Ye brave sons of the main,
  Ye that sail o'er the flood!
Whose sins big as mountains,
  Have reached up to God!
Remember, the short voyage
  Of life soon will end;
Then come brother sailors,
  Make Jesus your friend!

Look back on your life,
  See your wake marked with sin;
Look ahead see what torments
  You'll soon founder in;
The hard rocks of death
  Will soon beat out your keel,
Then your vessel and cargo
  Will all sink to hell.

Lay by your old compass,
  'Twill do you no good;
It ne'er will direct you
  The right way to God!
Desert the black colors,
  Come under the red—
Where Jesus is Captain,
  To conquest he led!

See the Standard unfurled—
  See it wave through the air—
And volunteers coming
  From far off and near.
Now's the time, brother sailors,
  No longer delay;
Embark now with Jesus,
  Good wages he'll pay.

The bounty he'll give you
  When the voyage you begin;
He'll purge your transgressions,
  And cleanse you from sin,
Good usage he'll give.
  As you sail on the way;
And shortly you'll anchor,
  In heaven's broad bay!

In the harbor of glory
  For ever to ride,
Free from quicksands and danger
  And sin's rapid tide;
Waves of death cease to roll,
  And the tempest to roar,
And the hoarse breath of Boreas
  Dismast you no more!

Your storm beaten garments
  No longer you'll wear,
But in robes of bright glory
  With Jesus appear;
A crown on your head,
  That would dazzle the sun;
And from glory to glory
  Eternally run.

Habitual Devotion. C. M.

While thee I seek, protecting Power,
  Be my vain wish stilled;
And may this consecrated hour
  With better hopes be filled.

Thy love the power of thought bestow'd;
  To thee my thoughts would soar;
Thy mercy o'er my life has flowed;
  That mercy I adore.

In each event of life how clear
  Thy ruling hand I see!
Each blessing to my soul more dear,
  Because conferred by thee.

In every joy that crowns my days,
  In every pain I bear.
My heart shall find delight in praise,
  Or seek relief in prayer.

When gladness wings my favored hour,
  Thy love my thoughts shall fill;
Resigned when storms of sorrow lower,
  My soul shall meet thy will.

My life1 eve, without a tear,
  The gathering storm shall see;
My steadfast heart shall know no fear;
  That heart shall rest on thee.

Christ's Humiliation and Triumph.
H. M.

Come, ye who love the Lord,
  And feel his quickening power,
Unite, with one accord,
  His goodness to adore:
To heaven and earth aloud proclaim
Your great Redeemer's glorious name.

He left his throne above,
  His glory laid aside,
Came down on wings of love,
  And wept and bled and died:
The pangs he bore what tongue can tell,
To save our souls from death and hell?

He burst the grave; he rose
  Victorious from the dead;
And at once his vanquish'd foes
  In glorious triumph led:
Up through the heavens the Conqueror rode,
Triumphant, to the throne of God.

Soon he again will come—
  His chariot will not stay—
To take his children home—
  To realms of endless day:
There shall we see him face to face,
And sing the triumphs of his grace.

Coronation of the King of Kings.
8s, 7s & 4s.

Look ye saints; the sight is glorious;
  See the Man of sorrows now;
From the fight returned victorious,
  Every knee to him shall bow:
    Crown him, crown him;
Crowns become the Victor's brow.

Crown the Saviour, angels crown him;
  Rich the trophies Jesus brings;
In the seat of power enthrone him,
  While the heavenly concave rings:
    Crown him, crown him;
Crown the Saviour King of kings.

Sinners in derision crowned him,
  Mocking thus the Saviour's claim;
Saints and angels crowd around him,
  Own his title, praise his name:
    Crown him, crown him;
Spread abroad the Victor's fame.

Hark! those bursts of acclamation!
  Hark! those soul, triumphant chords!
Jesus takes the highest station;
  O, what joy the sight affords!
    Crown him, crown him,
King of kings, and Lord of lords.

OCEAN MELODIES.

A Plea for the Sailor. H. M.

Tune, Lenox.

A cry fills all the air!
Christian! it calls on thee!
Help for the mariner
Whose home is on the sea!
Ye rich! ye poor! it cries to you!
Salvation for the Sailor too!

He hath a noble heart—
Free as the mountain wave;
But oh! your aid impart'
He hath a soul to save!
In all you give will God delight,
The rich man's gold—the widow's mite.

When roars the stormy blast,
And billows mount on high,
When, from the rocking mast
The yards and canvass fly—
Though hope depart, if God be there,
The sailor's heart shall feel no fear,

While we, secure from harm,
On downy pillows sleep,
The Sailor feels the storm—
Toss'd on the raging deep:
His home the sea—the wave he rides—
His heart still brave—whate'er betides.

Ye dwellers on the land,
Beneath your peaceful shade,
Stretch forth the willing hand,
And give the Sailor aid:
Joyful to learn the way to heaven,
He will not spurn the blessing given.

And when religion's voice
Is heard o'er all the sea,
Then shall heaven rejoice,
And earth keep jubilee!
When land and sea, in loud accord,
Shout hallelujahs to the Lord!

All Hands Ahoy! S. M.

The wicked labor much
Beneath corruption's weight:
Yet still at every port they touch,
They swell their guilty freight.

By winds and waves pursued,
They groan beneath their woes;
And yet, in every latitude,
The criminal cargo grows.

As thus their sins enlarge,
Conviction swells the load,
Until they gladly would discharge
Their lading overboard.

But though they have the will,
And labor to be best,
They lack the precious power still
To grasp the promised rest.

But Jesus sees their grief,
And smiles, and bids them come;
The Gospel sails to their relief,
And tows the exiles home.

He pities their complaints,
And takes them home to rest;
And makes his weather-beaten saint
With him forever blest.

The following Hymns are respectfully dedicated to Rev. William Jenks, D. D., by Phineas S. Owe. These hymns were sung at the Baptist Bethel, the Sabbath Dr. Jenk officiated, and related some thrilling incidents of his early efforts to save the mariner.

8s & 7s. *Tune, Greenville.*

Author of the mighty ocean,
 We our voices now would blend
In a song with true devotion,
 Praise Thee! for th' sailor's friend.

When no Bethel flag was waving,
 And for seamen few could weep,
Then a man of God's anointing
 Rous'd the church from her long sleep.

Soon that Star of glory shining,
 Sheds its splendors o'er the deep;
And the prodigals returning,
 Jesus folds them as his sheep.

Joyfully the news is spreading,
 Seamen bow before the Lord;
And the heart of Zion gladdening,
 Sailors herald the blest word.

Now a bow of heavenly radiance,
 Spans the Sailor's pathless way;
And a moral joyful cadence,
 Cheers his soul from day to day.

Seamen love thee for thy kindness;
 In their hearts thy name's enshrin'd;
Thou hast toil'd to cure their blindness,
 That they might behold their Friend.

Watchman, tell us of the morning,
 When beneath that stately dome,°
You proclaimed in language glowing,
 Free salvation — and sweet home.

Most who heard thy voice melodious
 Wooing sailors to the Lord,
Rest from toil, and are victorious,
 Through the Lamb's atoning blood.

May this be a blessed hour;
 Let each heart rejoice to hear,
What a glorious ark and tower,
 Now for mariners appear.

Saviour! hasten that prediction,
 When the men who plough the sea,
All rejoice in thy salvation,
 Saved by grace bestowed by Thee.

*Dr. Jenks nearly forty years ago, was the first clergyman who preached the gospel to seamen in the city of Boston. Miss Mary Webb, a beloved member of Dr. Baldwin's Church, made the first Bethel Flag for Dr. Jenks, and it was unfurled by him on the dome of Central Wharf; and many sailors assembled beneath its folds to listen to the "glorious gospel of the blessed God."

L. M. *Tune, Effingham.*

Spirit of love and light descend;
 Seal on each heart truth so divine;
Gird us with armour to defend
 Thy word, and in its precepts shine.

The Bread of Life, we cast abroad,
 Around the globe it wings its way;
A voice o'er ocean's sound is heard,
 Teaching the sailor how to pray.

Long have you stood on Zion's hill,
 A champion for the truth of God;
Thy works and labors long shall thrill,
 All who admire the precious Word.

When Gabr'l's trump shall wake the dead,
 And sound o'er land and sparkling sea,
A band will rise from Ocean's bed,
 To deck thy crown eternally.

O, may we share with you that home,
 Where all the weary soldiers rest;
When victors shall possess a crown
 Purchas'd by Christ—the ever blest.

OCEAN MELODIES.

The following hymn dedicated to the crew of the United States Steamer Merrimac on her leaving Charlestown Navy Yard, is respectfully inscribed to all brave men on leaving port in the Navy and Merchant services.

Dedicated to the Outward Bound of all Nations.

BY PHINEAS STOWE.

8s. & 7s. *Tune, Bounding Billows.*

Saviour, o'er the restless ocean
 May the gospel banner wave,
And beneath its folds of beauty
 Cheer the sailor—guide the brave.

He beholds thy works and wonders,
 While upon the foaming deep,
And amid its will commotion,
 Safely, Lord, the Sailor keep.

Hasten, Lord, that joyous epoch,
 When each ship that plows the main,
Shall have those who love the Savior,
 And his matchless grace proclaim.

Great Redeemer, save the brave men
 From the inebriate's gloomy path,
Never let the cup of ruin,
 Cloud the mind and fill with wrath.

Noble men, a prosperous voyage:
 Heavenly breezes fill each sail,
Let no angry passions harm you—
 Love divine o'er wrath prevail.

Shun the whirlpool of intemperance,
 Keep the Pledge by prayer and love,
Read the sacred Word with rapture,°
 Message from the realms above.

While upon the sparkling ocean,
 Loved ones, oft for you will pray,
That around your path of danger,
 Bethlehem's star may cheer your way.

O, be faithful to each other,
 Let the star of hope and love,
Shine upon you, and enkindle
 Peace and rapture from above.

O'er the sea in climes of darkness,†
 Care for the immortal soul,
Dread the waves of endless sorrow,
 That will o'er the ruined roll.

Win some priceless soul to Jesus,
 Warn the wicked of his doom,
Tell him of celestial g'ory,—
 He may wear a victor's crown.

May you shine as stars of splendor,
 In the Saviour's diadem,
With a blood-washed band of seamen,
 Who were not "ashamed of Him."

On love's mission you are going,‡
 To the suffering o'er the deep,
May auspicious winds safe waft you,
 Where the brave men sigh and weep.

For your safety humble suppliants,
 Will address the Throne of Grace,
That your pathway o'er the ocean,
 Be a speedy, brilliant race.

Fare-thee-well, shall be our prayer,
 We on earth may meet no more;
But we'll hope to dwell together,
 On that calm and heavenly shore.

---

* Seamen on board the United States Steamship Merrimac and other Government Ships receive a Testament as a memento of their Temperance Pledge.

† The Sailor is the World's Missionary, for or against the Lord Jesus Christ.
"One sinner destroyeth much good.—BIBLE.

‡ The United States Frigate Merrimac was sent on her first cruise to relieve ships that were in a perilous condition in the winter of 1856.

OCEAN MELODIES.

Cast into the Sea. S. M.

Deep in the watery world,
  A poor imprisoned saint,
Beneath the earth's foundations hurled,
  Poured out his sad complaint.

"Thou, Lord hast cast my soul
  Baneath the briny wave,—
All, all thy heavy billows roll,
  High o'er my living grave.

Earth's pond'rous pillars spread
  Their flinty bars around,—
And sea-weeds rumble o'er my head,
  Where plummets never sound.

Yet, here, O, Lord! I will
  Beneath the mountains lay,
And think upon thy temple still,
  And at thy altar pray."

The Lord puts forth his hand,
  And shakes the foaming main;
He drags the monster to the strand,
  And Jonah breathes again.

Just so did Christ explore
  The secret halls of hell,
And drafted the tremendous shore
  Of Death's remotest cell.

He measured every wave;
  He fathomed every part;
And, rising conqueror o'er the grave,
  He gave his Church the chart.

And we are sinking fast,
  Where Jesus sunk before;
But Gabriel's resurrection blast,
  Will roll us all to shore.

Trusting in God. L. M.

We trust forever more,
  O, Jesus Christ, in thee;
The God who saves upon the shore
  Is mighty on the sea.

By thy unerring chart
  We'll navigate our way;
We will not from our course depart,
  Or conscience cast away.

Thy fair, celestial light
  Will cheer us through the day;
We'll keep a bright look out at night,
  Nor cease to watch and pray.

While, drawn with cords of love,
  We'll near the port divine,
Till, anchored with the fleet above
  We'll swell the royal line.

Hell Bound. C. M.

When will rebellious seamen cease
  To fight against their God,
And sue for pardon, grace, and peace,
  Through the atoning blood?

Strike, sailor, strike! no longer dare
  That anger to unfold,
Whose softest touch would sink you far
  In hell's unfathomed hold.

No longer sail in hell's employ,
  Nor 'gainst the Gospel rave:
Your God, though mighty to destroy,
  Is POWERFUL to save,—

And when he hears the suppliant's cries,
  He'll bid the warfare cease—
He'll send salvation from the skies,
  And give the mourner peace.

The Beautiful Land and its Grim Sentry.
Tune, WATCHER. 7s. & 6s.

There is a land immortal—
 The beautiful of lands;
Beside its ancient portal
 A sentry grimly stands:
He only can undo it,
 And open wide the door;
And mortals who pass through it
 Are mortals never more.

That glorious land is Heaven,
 And Death the sentry grim;
The Lord thereof has given
 The opening keys to him:
And ransom'd spirits sighing
 And sorrowful for sin,
Pass through the gate in dying,
 And freely enter in.

Tho' dark and drear the passage,
 That leadeth to the gate,
Yet grace attends the message
 To souls that watch and wait.
And at the time appointed,
 A messenger comes down,
And guides the Lord's annointed
 From cross to glory's crown.

Their sighs are lost in singing,
 They're blessed in their tears;
Their journey heavenward winging,
 They leave on earth their fears,
Death like an angel seeming,
 " We welcome thee!" they cry;
Their face with glory gleaming,
 'Tis life for them to die.

Soulwreck. L. M.

Deceitful is the breeze,
 And placid is the swell;
Strong is the current, smooth the seas,
 That lead to death and hell.

We need not crowd our sail,
 Nor labor to go wrong;
The wind and current will not fail
 To drive our barks along.

But when we shape our course
 For heaven's delightful shores,
We then begin to feel the force
 Of wind and water foes.

Our nature's rapid steam
 Augments its mighty force,
While all the powers of darkness seem
 To stretch athwart our course.

Our stormy passions blow;
 Our fairest prospects frown;
While winds aloft and waves below
 Conspire to bear us down.

But we who do oppose
 The tempest and the tide,
At last shall weather all our foes,
 And every gale outride.

We'll soon the current leave,
 And softer breezes find;
We'll all our stud-sail halyards reeve,
 And scud before the wind.

The service of the Lord
 Will then be our delight,
While Christ himself will come on board,
 And Canaan heave in sight.

The Claims of Seamen.   S. M.
Written for the Ladies' Fair, Exeter, N. H.
by Mrs. Sigourney.

They roam where danger dwells,
　Where blasts impetuous sweep,
Where sleep the dead in watery cells,
　Beneath the faithless deep,
Where tempest threaten loud,
　To whelm the shipwreck'd form,
Show them a sky that hath no cloud,
　A port above the storm.

Beyond the Sabbath-bell,
　Beyond the House of Prayer,—
Where deafening surges madly swell,
　Their trackless course they dare,
Give them the Book Divine,
　Heaven's chart so full and free,
That beacon 'mid the foaming brine
　That pole-star o'er the sea.

Where Satan holds his court,
　Where fierce temptations reign,
From pole to tropic they resort,
　Amid the lawless train:
Wake! — Christian bounty, wake
　To their forgotten claim,
And for the blest Redeemer's sake,
　Instruct them in his name.

Christ our Sheet Anchor.   C. M.

Jesus, our Anchor firm, abides
　Within the heavenly vail;
At which Creation safely rides;
　While Time exhausts its gale.

Though angry devils rage and roar,
　With tempests loud and dark;
Yet Christ, our pilot, will secure
　The weather beaten bark.

And as the tide of time shall swell,
　Death with his active crew,
Will man the rattling windlass well,
　And leave us safely through.

Yes, thro' the pearly gates we'll pass;
　Escape these lower gales,
And, on the eternal sea of glass,
　Spread our immortal sails!

Paul's Faith on the Sea.   L. M.

While o'er the Adriatic main
　The fierce levanter wildly raved,
And sailor saw their labor vain,
　And lost all hope of being saved—

While Paul oppress'd with anxious care,
　Bewailed, as lost, the wretched crew,
And was inclined himself to fear
　The ruthless gale that round him blew—

A lovely angel came to cheer
　And calm the pilgrim's drooping mind;
He bade the captive saint not fear;
　For God himself was in the wind.

"Fear not: the Maker of the seas
　Will bear this wretched crew to land:
And God unchangeably decrees
　That thou at Cæsar's bar must stand."

And can a feeble prisoner's prayers
　Arrest the angry arm of Heaven,
And draw salvation from the skies,
　When hope from ev'ry breast is riven?

The crew with wild amazement stared,
　And owned Jehovah's unseen hand;
While Paul, in irons, guards his guard,
　And leads his pilot safe to land.

Christ the Soul Anchor. L. M.

The Christian sailor fears no ill,
 Tho' calms befall, or storms assail;
His deathless hope is grounded still
 In Christ the anchor in the vail.

When seas are smooth and skies serene,
 And prosperous breezes fill his sail,
He trusts not the deceitful scene;
 His hope is cast within the vail.

And when disastrous clouds arise,
 And earthly prospects sink or fail,
He plants his treasure in the skies,
 And hugs the Anchor of the vail.

And when th' gulf-stream heaves in view
 And strikes the guilty sinner pale,
He boldly shoots the current through,
 To reach his moorings in the vail.

When nature heaves her final blast,
 The pilgrim's courage will not fail;
He'll hold the sov'reign promise fast,
 Of Christ—the Anchor in the vail.

For well the Christian sailor knows
 That hell can never spring a gale,
Which could, with his united foes,
 Remove the Anchor of the vail.

Sea Fight. C. M.

Blest is the man who never faints
 In Virtue's holy cause;
Strong in the righteousness of saints,
 He keeps his Maker's laws.

He never tires in doing well,
 He can not cease to love:
But restless as the ocean's swell,
 His active virtues move.

Salt of the earth, he will retain
 The saving power of grace;
And like the vast salubrious main,
 Preserve our tainted race.

His peace and righteousness abound—
 His river, and his sea—
Till swallowed in the great profound
 Of blest eternity.

Trust in Jesus. 7s.

Saviour, blessed should I be,
Could I always trust in thee;
Trust thy wisdom me to guide,
Trust thy goodness to provide.

Trust thy saving love and power,
Trust thee every day and hour;
Trust thee as the only light
In the darkest hour of night.

Trust in sickness, trust in health,
Trust in poverty and wealth;
Trust in joy and trust in grief,
Trust thy promise for relief.

Trust thy blood to cleanse my soul,
Trust thy grace to make me whole;
Trust thee living, dying too,
Trust thee all my journey through;

Trust thee, till my feet shall be
Planted on the crystal sea;
Trust thee, ever blessed Lamb,
Till I wear the victor's palm.

The Dying Christian to his Soul. P. M.

Vital spark of heavenly flame,
Quit, O, quit this mortal frame:
Trembling, hoping, lingering, flying,
O, the pain, the bliss, of dying!
Cease, fond nature, cease thy strife,
And let me languish into life.

Hark!—they whisper; angels say,
"Sister spirit, come away:"
What is this absorbs me quite?—
Steals my senses, shuts my sight,
Drowns my spirits, draws my breath?—
Tell me, my soul, can this be death?

The world recedes; it disappears;
Heaven open on my eyes; my ears
With sounds seraphic ring:
Lend, lend your wings! I mount! I fly!
"O Grave, where is thy victory?
O Death, where is thy sting?"

Christ's Love. S. M.

Blest be the tie that binds
  Our hearts in Christian love!
The fellowship of kindred minds
  Is like to that above.

When we are called to part,
  It gives us mutual pain;
But we shall still be joined in heart,
  And hope to meet again.

This glorious hope revives
  Our courage by the way;
While each in expectation lives,
  And longs to see the day.

From sorrow, toil, and pain,
  From sin, we shall be free;
And perfect love and friendship reign
  Through all eternity.

The Gospel Ship. 8s. & 7s.

The gospel ship along is sailing,
  Bound for Canaan's peaceful shore,
All who wish to sail to glory,
  Come with us, both rich and poor.
    Glory, glory, hallelujah,
    All our sailors loudly cry,—
    See the blissful port of glory,
    Open to each faithful eye.

Her sails are filled with heavenly breezes,—
Swiftly wafts the ship along;
All her sailors are rejoicing,—
  Glory bursts from every tongue.
    Glory, glory, &c.

Waft along this noble vessel,
  All ye gales of gospel grace;
Carrying every faithful sailor,
  To his heavenly resting-place.
    Glory, glory, &c.

Come, poor sailors get converted,
  Sail with us o'er life's rough sea,—
Then with us you shall be happy,
  Happy in eternity.
    Glory, glory, hallelujah,
    All our sailors loudly cry,—
    See the blissful port of glory,
    Open to each faithful eye.

OCEAN MELODIES.

The Ocean Tomb. 7s.
Dedicated to the Sailor by Miss M. Ball.
Tune, *Pleyel's Hymn.*

Where are those we lately knew?
 They the strong. the brave, the true?
Where are they? hoarse waves reply,
 They *with us* now deeply lie!

Whispering faith, in tones of love,
 Tells of realms of joy above;
As we stand around their bier,
 As we drop the silent tear.

Weep we for the shipmates gone?
 Weep we for the friends who mourn?
He who wept at Lazarus' tomb,
 He shall dissipate the gloom.

Hear His voice,—"I live; and they
 Who my words of love obey,
Shall to endless life arise"—
 Glorious life, beyond the skies!

Lord, when ocean yields her trust,
 And the earth her sacred dust,
Grant that we, and those we love,
 May with Thee ascend above.

Perfect Peace. C. M.

Out on the crested surge I rode,
 When mighty seas arose,
And challenged with their thunder-cry
 The stormy winds as foes;

Then barks were wrecked, and men
 went down
B neath the billowy brine;
But in that tempest of despair,
 The sunbeam still was mine.

The trust in God — I'll hold it fast,
 In peril and in pain,
Until that glorious Sun arise
 That ne'er shall set again.

And when, by death's grim phantom led,
 I tread the shadowy vale,
Still may that *perfect peace* be mine,
 Though flesh and heart should fail.

Life a Vapor, yet Endless. C. M.
An English Translation of a Chinese Hymn. By Rev. Mr. Shuck.

Like sunlight playing on the hills,
 Or dew drops on the grass,
Or stars that twinkle in the sky,
 So short — man's pleasures last.

Like dreams which in the night we see,
 Like meteors' rapid flight,
To day pursues to-morrow's dawn,
 So quickly passes life.

The Gospel has full real joy,
 Lights up man's dark distress,
While Jesus, glorious Prince of Peace!
 Points out the way of bliss.

No night, no end to Heaven's day,
 Ceaseless, life's river flows;
And all who turn — believe in Christ,
 Have endless life's repose.

Christ the Refuge. C. M.

Come, sailor, fly to Jesus, fly
  For refuge from the storms;
His ears are open to your cry.
  He has ten thousand charms

His winning voice now bids you come
  And taste celestial love;
In his bright home there yet is room,
  And joys for you above.

Come with your load of sin, and call
  Upon his precious name;
Before him humbly, meekly fall,
  With all your guilt and shame.

He will your deathless soul set free
  From bondage unto sin;
You, by his cleansing blood, may be
  A saint, and glory win.
                    S.

Prayer for Mariners.
L. M. [P. S.]

Great God! may seamen brightly shine
Like brilliant stars in every clime,
That nations rapt in darkest night,
May see them shed a radiant light.

Help them to be like Noah's Dove,
Bearing the olive branch of love
O'er the blue deep where e'er they go,
To banish pagan guilt and woe.

May Bethlehem's never varying star,
Transfix their souls where'er they are;
In danger's hour help them to say,
The star of hope shines on my way.

Oh, speed that bright, auspicious day,
When all who plough the bois'erous way
Shall be converted to the Lord,
And speak the pardon bought with blood.

Praise God for his Goodness.
L. M.

O let each soul now praise the Lord
And sound his glorious name abroad;
Come, magnify his precious name,
Who is from year to year the same.

O praise the mighty God of love,
Who gives us blessings from above,
Inspires our souls with holy fear
And crowns with goodness every year.

Bold seamen, praise this gracious God,
His wonderous works proclaim abroad;
Where e'er you rove, let praise be given
To him who guides our souls to heaven.

Begin this hour to speak his praise,
And may the remnant of your days,
Be all devoted, Lord, to thee.
At home, abroad, on land or sea.
                    S.

Sinner's Joys Fleeting.

Earthly pleasures what are they?
Like a flashing meteor's ray;
Quickly earthly joys depart,
Leaving bruised the burdened heart.

Conscience often speaks with power,
In the mirthful, sinful hour;
Calls to mind the solemn vows,
Broken by the wine cup's woes.

Will you madly rush along,
Pleased with earth's enchanting song,
While the soul is still unblest,
Thirsting for substantial rest?

Come to Jesus and you'll find
Balm to heal the troubled mind;
He will teach you how to love,
You in heaven he will receive.   S.

OCEAN MELODIES.

Will You go to Heaven? 7s.

Will you, trembling sinner, go
  To that home of pure delight?
O'er you mercy spreads her bow,
  But it's fading from your sight.

Life is waning, time is short,
  And eternity is near;
Can you o'er life's ocean sport?
  Death and judgment, they are near.

Voices tuned by dying love,
  Call upon you to return;
Angel's harps would ring above,
  If eternal death you'll shun.
                                S.

Signal of Distress.
8s & 7s.

God of mercy, hear the sailor
  While he lifts his prayer to Thee;
From the bosom of the ocean,
  Hear his penitential plea.

From his home and friends and kindred,
  In distress, upon the deep,
Save him, or he soon must perish,
  And in coral caverns sleep.

He is suffering from starvation,
  Thirsting for some cooling stream;
All around is one vast ocean,
  Hope still sheds a feeble gleam.

Send a message to him quickly;
  Save him from a watery grave;
He is freezing, dying slowly;
  On the stormy ocean wave.

Blessed Saviour! there is sorrow
  On the ever restless sea,—
Give the sailor hope's sure anchor,
  And a blest eternity.   S.

Flight of Time.
7s. *Newcomb.*

Time is wafting us along,
  To a world to us unknown,
And time's current, deep and strong,
  Bears us onward to our crown.

Let the year's fly swift away,
  We are marching to our home,
In the glorious King's highway,
  Where no howling tempest come.

Onward, onward! we must go,
  Hark! death's tread is on our path
Coming to release from woe,
  Those who live by love and faith.

Saviour, teach us how to live,
  While upon life's sea we sail;
Homage we to Thee will give,
  By the spirit cheering gale.

When death's waves around us beat,
  And life's fleeting voyage is o'er,
May we all the holy greet,
  On that balmy, heavenly shore.
                                S.

Divine Protection for the Sailor.
8s & 7s.

Saviour, on the raging ocean,
  Cheer the sailor in the storm;
Bid him look to Thee for succor,—
  Shield him by thy mighty arm.

May his hope be like an anchor,
  When the howling tempests beat;
Stay his mind and heart on heaven,
  Lead him to the mercy-seat.

On the storm-lashed deep he suffers, —
Hear his supplicating cry;
Thou art near to cheer the sailor,
And will heed each pensive sigh.

Saviour! Ocean's mighty billows
Are with ease controlled by Thee;
Stay the mad'ning tempest, Saviour,
Calm, O calm, the boist'rous sea.

Let the storms and dangers lead him
To be ready to depart;
Give him grace, and love, and wisdom,
Bid him choose the better part.

Soon life's storms will all be over,
Then his soul must launch away,
Where celestial joys shall cluster,
Or where howling tempests play.

May the sailor find a haven;
Moor him in that rest above,
Give him an abundant entrance,
Where the blood-wash'd sing God's love
      —   S.

I'm a Pilgrim.

I'm a pilgrim, and I'm a stranger,
I can tarry, I can tarry but a night,
Do not detain me, for I am going,
To where the streamlets are ever flowing
I'm a pilgrim, &c.

There the sunbeams are ever shining,
I am longing, I am longing for the sight;
Within a country unknown and dreary,
I've been wandering forlorn and weary.
I'm a pilgrim, &c.

Of that country to which I'm going,
My Redeemer, my Redeemer is the light;
There is no sorrow, or any sighing,
Or any sin, or any dying.

Re-union in Heaven.

6s & 5s.

When shall we meet again? —
Meet ne'er to sever?
When will Peace wreathe her chain,
Round us forever?
Our hearts will ne'er repose
Safe from each blast that blows
In this dark vale of woes —
Never — no, never!

When shall love freely flow
Pure as life's river?
When shall sweet friendship glow,
Changeless forever?
Where joys celestial thrill,
Where bliss each heart shall fill,
And fears of parting chill
Never — no, never!

Up to that world of light
Take us, dear Saviour;
May we all there unite,
Happy forever:
Where kindred spirits dwell,
There may our music swell,
And time our joys dispel
Never — no, never!

Soon shall we meet again —
Meet ne'er to sever;
Soon will Peace wreathe her chain,
Round us forever:
Our hearts will then repose
Secure from worldly woes;
Our songs of praise shall close
Never — no, never!

I'm Weary.
11s.

I'm weary of sighing. O fain would I rest
In the far distant land of the pure and
    the blest,
Where sin can no longer her blandish-
    ments spread;
And tears and temptations forever are
    fled.

I'm weary of hoping where the hope is
    untrue,
As fair but as fleeting as morning's
    bright dew;
I long for the land whose blest promise
    alone,
Is changeless and sure as eternity's
    throne.

I'm weary of sighing o'er sorrows of earth
O'er joys glowing visions that fade at
    their birth,
O'er the pangs of the lov'd which we
    cannot assuage,
O'er the blightings of youth, and the
    weakness of age.

I'm weary of loving what passes away
The sweetest, the dearest also may not
    stay;
I long for the land where those part-
    ings are o'er,
And death and the tomb can divide
    hearts no more.

I'm weary, my Saviour, of grieving thy
    love,
O, when shall I rest in thy presence
    above;
I'm weary, but O, never let me repine,
While thy word, and thy love, and thy
    promise are mine.

I Would Not Live Alway.
11s.

I would not live alway; I ask not to
    stay,
Where storm after storm rises dark o'er
    the way;
The few lurid moments that dawn on
    us here,
Are enough for life's woes, full enough
    for its cheer.

I would not live alway, no—welcome
    the tomb,
Since Jesus hath lain there, I dread not
    its gloom;
There, sweet be my rest, till he bid me
    arise,
To hail him in triumph descending the
    skies.

O! who would live alway, away from
    his God;
Away from yon heaven, that blissful
    abode,
Where rivers of pleasure flow o'er the
    bright plains?
And the noontide of glory eternally
    reigns?

Where the saints of all ages in har-
    mony meet,
Their Saviour and brethren transported
    to greet;
While the anthems of rapture unceas-
    ingly roll,
And the smile of the Lord is the feast
    of the soul.

OCEAN MELODIES.

Will You Go?
8s.

We're travelling home to Heaven above,
 Will you go? Will you go?
To sing the Saviour's dying love,
 Will you go? Will you go?
Millions have reached that blest abode,
Anointed kings and priests to God,
And millions more are on the road,
 Will you go? Will you go?

We're going to see the bleeding Lamb,
In rapturous strains to praise his name;
The crown of life we there shall wear,
The conqueror's palms our hands shall
 bear,
And all the joys of heaven we'll share,
 Will you go? &c.

We're going to join the heavenly choir,
To raise our voice, and tune the lyre;
There saints and angels gladly sing
Hosanna to their God and King,
And make the heavenly arches ring.
 Will you go? &c.

Ye weary, heavy laden, come,
In the blest house there still is room;
The Lord is waiting to receive,
If thou wilt on him now believe.
He'll give thy troubled conscience ease.
 Will you go? &c.

The way to heaven is free for all,
For Jew and Gentile, great and small,
Make up your mind, give God your heart,
With every sin and idol part,
And now for glory make a start.
 Will you go? &c.

The way to heaven is straight and
 plain—
Repent, believe, be born again;
The Saviour cries aloud to thee.
"Take up thy cross and follow me,
And thou shalt my salvation see."
 Will you go? &c.

O, could I hear some sinner say,
 I will go! I will go!
I'll start this moment, clear the way,
 Let me go! Let me go!
My old companions, fare you well,
I will not go with you to hell.
I mean with Jesus Christ to dwell,
 Let us go! Let us go!

Parting Hymn.
7s.

When shall we all meet again?
When shall we all meet again?
Oft shall glowing hope expire,
Oft shall wearied love retire,
Oft shall death and sorrow reign,
Ere we all shall meet again.

Though in distant lands we sigh,
Parched beneath a hostile sky:
Though the deep between us roll,
Friendship shall unite our soul,
And in fancies wide domain,
There may we all meet again.

When the dreams of life are fled;
When its wasted lamps are dead,
And in cold oblivion's shade,
Beauty, wealth and fame are laid,
Where immortal spirits reign,
There shall we all meet again.

OCEAN MELODIES.

Missionaries' Farewell. C. M.

Kindred, and friends, and native land,
 How shall we say, "Farewell?"
How,—when our swelling sails expand
 How will our bosoms swell!

Yes, nature, all thy soft delights
 And tender ties we know;
But love more strong than death unites
 To Him that bids us go.

Thus, when, our every passion moved,
 The gushing tear-drop starts,
The cause of Jesus more beloved,
 Shall glow within our hearts.

The sighs we breathe for precious souls,
 Where he is yet unknown,
Might waft us to the distant poles,
 Or to the burning zone.

With warm desire our bosoms swell,
 Our glowing powers expand;
"Farewell," then we can say, "farewell,
 Our friends, our native land."

Prayer for the Enlargement of the Church. C. M.

Shine, mighty God, on Zion shine,
 With beams of heavenly grace;
Reveal thy power through every land,
 And show thy smiling face.

When shall thy name from shore to shore
 Sound through the earth abroad,
And distant nations know and love
 Their Saviour and their God?

Sing to the Lord, ye distant lands;
 Sing loud, with joyful voice:
Let every tongue exalt his praise,
 And every heart rejoice.

My Native Land, Adieu. 8s. & 7s.

By Mrs. Sigourney.

Native land!—in summer smiling,—
 Hill and valley, grove and stream;
Home!—whose nameless charms beguiling,
 Peaceful nursed our infant dream;
Haunts! to which our childhood hasted,
 Where the earliest wild-flowers grew;
Church! where Christ's free grace we tasted,—
 Grav'd on memory's page,—*Adieu.*

Mother!—who has watched our pillow,
 In thy tender, sleepless love,
Lo! we dare the crested billow,—
 Mother! put thy trust above.
Father!—from thy guidance turning,
 O'er the deep our way we take,—
Keep the prayerful incense burning
 On thine altar, for our sake.

Brothers!—Sisters!— more than ever
 Are our fond affections twin'd,
As that hallowed bond we sever,
 Which the hand of Nature joined.
But the cry of Burmah's anguish
 Through our inmost hearts doth sound,
Countless souls in misery languish,—
 We would fly to heal their wound.

Burmah! we would sooth thy weeping;
 Take us to thy sultry breast,
Where thy sainted dust is sleeping,
 Let us share a kindred rest.
Friends! this span of life is fleeting—
 Hark! the harps of angels swell—
Think of that eternal meeting,
 Where no voice shall say—*Farewell.*

OCEAN MELODIES.

Missionaries Charged.

8s & 7s.

Onward, onward, men of heaven;
Bear the gospel banner high;
Rest not till its light is given —
Star of every pagan sky:
Send it where the pilgrim stranger
Faints beneath the torrid ray;
Bid the hardy forest-ranger
Hail it, ere he fades away.

Where the Arctic Ocean thunders,
Where the tropics fiercely glow,
Broadly spread its page of wonders,
Brightly bid its radiance flow:
India marks its lustre stealing;
Shivering Greenland loves its rays;
Afric, 'mid her deserts kneeling,
Lifts the untaught strain of praise.

Rude in speech, or wild in feature,
Dark in spirit, though they be,
Show that light to every creature—
Prince or vassal, bond or free;
Lo! they haste to every nation;
Host on host the ranks supply;
Onward! Christ is your salvation,
And your death is victory.

God Trieth the Righteous. 7s.

In the furnace God doth prove
All who taste redeeming love;
He upholds them by his grace.
He's their rock and hiding place.

When the waves of sorrow roll,
He their madness will control,
Safely bring them to the shore,
Where the billows dash no more.

Jesus never will forsake
Those who love to wear his yoke;
He will cheer them in distress.
He's their life and righteousness.

Trials, they prepare his sheep
To abide and humbly keep,
In the shepherd's glorious way,
Leading to eternal day. S.

Parting Hymn.

By THOMAS HARDLY, one of the crew of the
C. S Frigate Independence, on her return from
Leghorn, July 1. 852.

C. M.

Ye chosen few of Christ our King,
Partakers of his love,
We part, perhaps, to meet no more,
Until we meet above.

Oh! may we ne'er forget the day
When Jesus took us in,
And with his own atoning blood
He cleansed us from our sin.

And may we ever watchful be
O'er our deceitful hearts,
And put our trust in Him alone,
Who grace to us imparts.

That grace to conquer every sin,
And climb the rugged mount,
To shun the path of sin and death,
And plunge beneath the fount;

Where rescued sou's forever drink
Sweet endless pleasures in,
And with the Angels of the Lord
Eternal praises sing.

Then let us here renew our vows,
While parting hands we give,
To meet around the Throne of God,
And with Him forever live.

OCEAN MELODIES

Dedicated to sick and disabled Seamen in the U. S. Marine Hospital, Chelsea, by PHINEAS STOWE, Pastor of 1st Baptist Mariners' Church, Boston.

L. M. TUNE—*Hamburg.*

God of the boundless, pathless deep,
Behold with pity from above.
The sailor, far from childhood's home,
And o'er him spread thy bow of love.

No mother's magic voice is heard
To cheer his troubled, aching heart,
Dark waves of sorrow madly roll,
No kindred near joy to impart.

Is hope thine anchor, firm and sure,
And cast within the glorious vail?
Is Jesus thy great Captain now,
To cheer thee in this trying gale?

Around thy bed, and in thy room,
His dying love perfumes the air,
He calls upon thee now to turn
And offer up the contrite prayer.

He knows thy sorrows and can heal
Thy wounded heart, with precious balm,
Purchased by his most sacred blood,
That will all tumult quickly calm.

Though far from home your lot is cast,
Still He is always near thy side:
He walked upon the sparkling sea,
And o'er the billow oft did ride.

He is a kind and faithful friend.
He cares for you—he died to save
Thy soul from sinking in the deep,
While woe's dark billows foam and rave.

Oft have you heard his mighty voice
In thunder's peal and ocean's roar,
And asked him your frail bark to save,
And o'er your path bright visions pour.

The solemn vow you oft have made,
To live for him who made the sea!
Now is the time to pay that vow,
And to him for salvation flee.

He now will listen to your prayer,
And grant you pardon from above,
O'er your dark path his bow will spread,
And thrill your soul with joy and love.

The strong, the weak, the sick and all
Must have the great Physician's skill
To cure the leprosy within,—
And take away the love of sin.

Thy body earthly skill may heal,
But thy lost soul must ever wail
In the dark prison of despair.
If health Divine you do not share.

Go not, bold seaman, from this home,
Upon God's boundless deep to roam,
Regardless of the grace of God,
The purchase of a Saviour's blood.

Now you may have salvation free,
And share that glorious liberty
That fills the soul with rapture here,
And robs the grave of gloom and fear.

Delay not to secure this prize,
Held up by him who loves the wise,
A crown of glory awaits the just,
Who put in Jesus all their trust.

Then when the voyage of life is o'er,
You'll rest from toil on that bright shore
Where sickness, sorrow ne'er shall come,
To mar thy joys in that sweet home.

Decision of Character.
BY P. STOW.
"Burn the Ships."

" Dr. Judson's constancy of purpose, which never flagged, nor sought retreat nor change, and in the consciousness of its indomitable strength, led him, on reaching the shores of Burmah, in his own significant language to " Burn the Ships."

TUNE—BOUNDING BILLOWS. 8s & 7s.

" Burn the Ships, I'm safely landed,
In this clime of gloom and wo;
I would toil amid its darkness
And the seed of glory sow.

" Burn the Ships, my heart is throbbing
To unfold Christ's banner here;
I would not return, but wander
O'er this land with tidings dear.

" Burn the Ships, my soul is kindling
With a love that's firm on high,
To diffuse abroad a radiance,
Cheer the desolate who sigh.

" Burn the Ships, I now am moored
In a dark and angry sea;
Yet above the sky is brilliant,
And bright bethlehem's Star I see.

" Burn the Ships, who would not toil
In a field so full of thorns,
With his Master's bow around me,
What are life's tempestuous storms?

" Burn the Ships, do not decoy me
From the land I love so well;
Jesus died to save the heathen,
I would his glad tidings tell.

" Burn the Ships, I would remember
His command to spread abroad
News of that redemption purchased
By the suffering, dying Lord.

" Burn the Ships, the heathen calls me,
I would listen to their moan;

Rapt they are in sable garments,
Hark! they wail and sigh and groan.

" Burn the Ships, I here must suffer
In the prison night and day:
While the heathen's rage and fury
Urge me on in heaven's highway.

" Burn the Ships, here I would linger
Till my Master calls me home;
Then with sheaves for him I've gather'd
Bow around his radiant Throne."

The Aged Christian Soldier.
BY P. STOW.

TUNE—SICILY. 8s & 7s.

Band of soldiers of Immanuel!
Marching on to victory,
O'er you waves a crimson banner
Of the Lamb of Calvary.

Long have you been in his army,
And achieved by strength divine,
Jewels for your matchless leader,
That will ever glow and shine.

Some who joined with you the battle,
And were valiant in the fight,
Have the conqueror's song re-echoed,
Where no foe will them affright.

On the moral field of conquest,
You still linger to defend,
His great name and rising glory,
And his triumph shall extend.

Soon your warfare will be over,
And your master will say come,
Rest from conflict faithful soldiers
In the victor's tearless home.

That will be a glorious gathering,
When the warriors meet above;
And with palms of bloodless victory
Chant the song of boundless love.

The Stranger's Welcome.
BY P. STOW.

"Be not forgetful to entertain strangers," is a divine command. May such resort to the Mariner's Bethel to receive spiritual food. It is a "house for all nations." The following lines are dedicated to the lonely stranger.

TUNE—LET THY KINGDOM. 8, 7s & 4.

Welcome, stranger, to the Bethel,
Join with us in song and prayer;
Here enjoy life's richest blessing,
And with us each pleasure share,
   You are welcome,
Here dismiss the goading care.

Far away from home and kindred,
Desolate and lone you feel,
And the tear of love and sorrow
Down your cheeks does often steal;
   Lonely stranger,
Wounded spirits God can heal.

Though like Jacob, you have wander'd,
Far from native clime and home,
Still bright angels on the ladder,
Sweetly say, "come, stranger, come;"
   Enter heaven
Now by faith, and journey home.

If you are to peace a stranger,
In God's household all are one,
Strangers, foreigners are welcome
To the banquet of his Son.
   For your ransom
Thorny was his earthly crown.

He invites all nations to him,
All may taste the fount of love;
And enjoy the smiles of heaven,
While on sea or land you rove;
   Mercy calls you,
Gently woes the Holy Dove.

In that port of peerless glory,
No one will be stranger there—
All will speak the native language,
"Babel's" curse will not appear;
   All the nations
Who love God, shall glory share.

"Faith's Silver Thread."
BY MISS M. D. BALFOUR.

A little girl when dying, was told by her mother that all along through the dark valley there ran a silver shining thread, which, if she would grasp and hold firmly, would bear her safely across the cold river, and, at length, land her upon the opposite shore of life and glory.

TUNE—ZION. 8, 7s & 4.

When thy trembling feet are pressing,
   Jordan's cold and swelling stream,
Yield thee not to fears distressing,
   Death is not the foe we deem.
     Cherished daughter!
Light from heaven shall on thee beam.

Catch that silver thread and shining,
   Which thy struggling faith discerns;
Let it now, thy heart entwining,
   Hold thee while the conflict turns.
     Dying daughter!
How my spirit o'er thee yearns!

From a mother's fond embracing,
   Early thou art called away;
Still that little thread be tracing,
   Till it leads to endless day.
     Oh! my daughter!
Can I here consent to stay?

Yes, my God, thy time abiding,
   I beneath the cross will spend;
Ever in Thy grace confiding,
   Watching always to the end.
     Thus, my daughter!
Where thou'rt gone, my steps shall tend.

OCEAN MELODIES.

The Sacred Hour.
BY DR. T. FLETCHER OAKES.
Tune—Eltham. 7s.

Dear to me the sacred hour,
  Cheer'd by JESUS' guardian love,
Then I seek thine aid and power,
  Asking blessings from above:
Then I lift the tearful eye,
  Mourn my cold reserve to see,
Then resolve from sin to fly,
  And commune, oh GOD! with thee.

Oft, I from the mercy-seat,
  Feel a glorious radiance fall,
When I kneel in silence sweet,
  Pray to thee, unseen by all.
Then a boon I fondly claim,
  JESUS, grant the pure desire;
That I may exalt thy name,
  Live in thee—in thee expire.

When my heart, oppress'd and filled,
  Crush'd with sadness, doubt and gloom;
And when dark despair has chill'd
  All that's bright beyond the tomb,
Then he heals my broken heart,
  Freely at the shrine of prayer;
Bids presumptuous doubts depart,
  Turns away my sad despair.

Then my heart with hope he fills,
  Decks my soul in heavenly bloom;
Then my doubts he sweetly stills,
  Breaks the terror of the tomb!
Sweetly, then, my ardent heart,
  Full of heavenly hope again;
Feels the bliss his smiles impart,
  Gently through each bursting vein.

JESUS, may thy look, so sweet,
  Ever on me deign to shine;
And thy love forever beat
  In this conscious heart of mine;
Ever let me feel thee nigh,
  While my life to me is given;—
Soothe my last convulsive sigh,
  Be my bliss and theme in Heaven.

The Mariner Saved.
BY REV. NATH'L COLVER.
TUNE—AMERICA. 6 & 4.

Great God! in safety keep
The sailor on the deep—
  In dread dismay,
When skill avails no more,
And storms around him pour,
And angry billows roar,
  Thy power display.

O, let thy mighty voice
Be heard above the noise
  Of wind and storm,
In accents sweet and clear,
"Dismiss thy trembling fear,
'Tis I, myself, am near
  To shield from harm."

Great God! the sailor save,
When, from the rolling wave,
  He seeks the land.
Where pleasure spreads her sail,
And passion blows a gale,
Where soon, his dying wail,
  His voyage may end.

O! let thy grace divine,
Upon the sailor shine,
  With saving power.
With cable strong and fast,
With hope, his anchor, cast
Beyond the stormy blast,
  His bark secure.

Doxology. 8, 7, & 4.

Glory be to God the Father,
  Glory to th' eternal Son;
Sound aloud the Spirit's praises;
  Join the elders round the throne;
    Hallelujah,
Hail the glorious Three in One.

OCEAN MELODIES.

The Lent Jewel Above. S. M.
HYMN OF REMEMBRANCE,
Dedicated to Bereaved Parents.
BY P. STOW.
TUNE—BOYLSTON.

Death loves a shining mark;
  He blights the fairest flower,
And spreads his sable mantle o'er
  Life's sweet, domestic bower.

The tenderest ties are riven,
  By his relentless grasp;
Affection's tear stays not his arm,
  The child of love he'll clasp.

Our Father bids death come,
  And dash the idol down,
To plume our souls with grace divine,
  That we may deck his crown.

Thy words and smiles will live
  Embalmed in memory's book;
Oft shall we muse, and oft behold
  Each sweet, enchanting look.

And would we call thee back,
  From those bright bowers above?
Where the rapt soul will ever lave
  In that pure fount of love?

God lent that darling child
  To parents fond and dear;
Then called the JEWEL home again,
  Sparkling more bright and clear.

In heaven we hope to greet
  The loved one gone before;
With thee and countless millions bow,
  And all God's ways adore.

The Sea hath Spoken. S. M.
Hymn,
In the loss of the captain, officers and crew of the ship Hanover, of Bath. She was wrecked in a terrific gale at the mouth of the majestic Kennebec, November 5th, 1849.
BY REV E. H. GRAY.

A wail comes o'er the breeze,
  A low and moaning sound
And still it's heard above the seas
  That wildly dash around.

It was the piercing cry
  Of seamen homeward bound—
When 'mid the white foam dashing high,
  A *home* in the deep they found.

"Oh God! we die," they say,—
  "In sight of friends and home;
Our winding sheet the ocean's spray,
  Our bed the ocean's foam!"

The waves shall roll for them
  A mournful, solemn dirge;
The low winds chant their requiem,
  And rock them with the surge.

God of the storm and sea!
  Oh condescend to hear
The orphan's cry, the widow's plea
  And dry the mourner's tear.

How Softly on the Bruised Heart
BY S. D. STUART, ESQ.
TUNE—WOODLAND. C. M.

How softly on the bruised heart
  A word of kindness falls,
And from the dry and parched soul
  The moistening tear-drop calls;
O, if they knew, who walk the earth
  Mid sorrow, grief and pain—
The power a word of kindness hath,
  'T were paradise again.

The weakest and the poorest may
  This simple pittance give,
And bid delight, to withered hearts
  Return again and live;
O, what is life if love be lost?
  If man's unkind to man—
Or what the heav'n that waits beyond
  This brief and mortal span.

As stars upon the tranquil sea
  In mimic glory shine,
So words of kindness, in the heart
  Reflect their source divine;
O, then, be kind, whoe'er thou art
  That breathest mortal breath,
And it shall lighten all thy life,
  And sweeten even death.

OCEAN MELODIES. 181

The Dying Girl's Appeal.

Stay, father, stay, the night is wild,
O leave not now your dying child;
I feel the icy hand of death,
And shorter, shorter grows my breath,
    O, father, leave me not

Stay, father, stay, my mother's gone,
And thou and I art left alone;
And from her star-lit home on high,
She'll weep that I alone should die;
    O, father, leave me not.

Stay, father, stay; O leave this night
The mad'ning bowl, whose withering blight,
Has cast so dark a shade around
The home where joy alone was found.
    O, father, leave me not.

Stay, father, stay, once more I ask,
O, count it not a heavy task,
To stay with me till life shall end,
My last, my only living friend.
    O, father leave me not.

Cling to the Mighty One.
Tune—"Happy Land."

Cling to the Mighty One,	Ps. lxxxix 19.
Cling in thy grief;	Heb. xii, 11.
Cling to the Holy One,	Rev. iii, 7.
He gives relief;	Ps. cxlvi, 9.
Cling to the Gracious One,	Ps. cxvi, 5.
Cling in thy pain;	Ps. lv, 4.
Cling to the Faithful One,	1 Thess. v, 24.
He will sustain;	Ps. xxviii, 8.
Cling to the Living One,	Heb. vii, 25.
Cling in thy woe;	Ps. lxxxvi, 7.
Cling to the Loving One,	1 John iv, 16.
Through all below;	Rom. viii, 38, 39.
Cling to the Pardoning One,	Isaiah vi, 7.
He speaketh peace;	John xiv, 27.
Cling to the Healing One,	Exodus xv, 26.
Anguish shall cease;	Ps cxlvii. 3.
Cling to the Bleeding One,	1 John i, 7.
Cling to his side;	John xx, 27.
Cling to the Risen One,	Rom. vi, 9.
In him abide;	John xv, 4.
Cling to the Coming One,	Rev. xxii, 20.
Hope shall arise;	Titus ii, 13.
Cling to the Reigning One,	Ps. xcvii. 1.
Joy lights thine eyes.	Ps. xvi, 11.

Cold Water Army Pledge.

Tune—"Haste thee, winter."

We, Cold Water girls and boys,
Freely renounce the treacherous joys,
Of Brandy, Whiskey, Rum and Gin,
The serpents' lure to death and sin.

Wine, Beer and Cider, we detest,
And thus we'll make our parents blest;
So here we pledge perpetual hate,
To all that can intoxicate.

The Temperance Horn.

Merrily the temperance horn
  Is sounding o'er the silver lake,
Cheerily at early dawn
  Its swelling notes bid echo wake.
Temperance for thee, thee only,
  These sounds are ever sweet to me;
Each haunt of pleasure lonely,
  Is found, when 'tis unblest by thee.

Sound, sound, sound, sound the merry,
  merry temperance horn,
At close of eve, and morning's early
  dawn.

Cheerfully, my harp I bring,
  And wake a wilder, sweeter strain,
Joyously my songs I sing,
  And bid the inebriate smile again.
  Temperance, etc.

Cheerily our footsteps stray,
  Nor wait to think of danger near;
Merrily at close of day,
  We breathe the sweetest music here.
  Temperance, etc.

182. PRAY, SAILOR, PRAY. L. M.

Words by J. H. H. (*Devotion.*)

1. When launched up-on the bri-ny tide, You o'er its am-ple bosom glide; From home and kindred far a-way, From home and kindred far away, Then look above,—" pray sai-lor pray."

When tossed on ocean's broad domain,
The sport of danger, toil and pain,—
As borne along thy watery way,
   Then pause awhile,—" pray sailor pray."

When troubled depths disparted yawn,
And death's embrace is round thee drawn;—
When th' ransomed soul would leave its clay,
   O gladly soar,—" pray sailor pray."

Praise God for a Converted Crew.

Three seamen, the Steward and Cabin Boy of the Brig PACIFIC, Captain HARDY, were converted while on a sea-voyage, and on their return home, May 10, 1857, were baptized by PHINEAS STOWE, Pastor of the 1st Baptist Mariners' Church, Boston. The Captain and Mate of the Pacific are members of this Church, and have sailed together a number of voyages, having daily prayers when on shipboard. The Pacific is truly a floating Bethel.

TUNE—*Greenville.* 8s & 7s.

Saviour, on the mighty ocean,
  Thou hast met the sailor there;
Heard his deep and bitter pleadings,
  Watched each penitential tear.

No bright star illumes the sailor,
  Waves of sin in madness roll;
All on board are weeping freely,
  Anguish fills each gloomy soul.

But thy pardoning love, blest Saviour,
  Banishes their gloomy fears;
Speaking peace, the sea is tranquil—
  Joy divine to them appears.

Now they bow with joy and rapture,
  Low before the mercy seat;
Praising Christ, who died to save them,
  From the world where storms shall beat

Saviour help them to be watchful
  While upon the sea of time;
Fix their eye on Thee, their Captain,
  Cheer and guide in every clime.

May the Port of heavenly glory
  Fill our minds with peace and love,
Plume our souls with wings of power,
  Holy Spirit, Heavenly Dove!

Life's short voyage soon is over,
  Soon we'll round the Cape of Death;
But with Jesus for our Pilot
  We may shout with dying breath.

May we meet on heavenly highlands,
  Where no howling tempest come,
Where the good of every nation
  Meet in one celestial Home;

There to bow before the Saviour
  And to worship at his Throne,
Praising Him who died on Calvary
  Our transgressions to atone.

May we strike our golden lyres
  With the blood-washed happy throng,
Singing praises to Immanuel,
  Chanting heaven's immortal song.

S.

"Thy Kingdom Come."

Matt. vi. 10.   C. M.

Thy kingdom come! Almighty Lord,
  Amongst our fallen race;
Soon may all people hear thy word
  And know thy saving grace.

Thy kingdom come! with power divine,
  Reign thou from sea to sea:
All creatures and all souls are thine;
  Let all men worship Thee.

Thy kingdom come! with truth and peace
  And wisdom from above;
Let war and strife and error cease,
  And all men live in love.

Thy kingdom come! with blessings more
  Than earth has ever known,
When men their Maker shall adore
  And their Redeemer own.

Then shall all lands be filled with joy,
  Saved from the curse of sin,
Thy praise all hearts and tongues employ,
  And heaven on earth begin.

184. THE CONVERTED SAILOR.

Words by J. H. H. (*Hosanna.*)

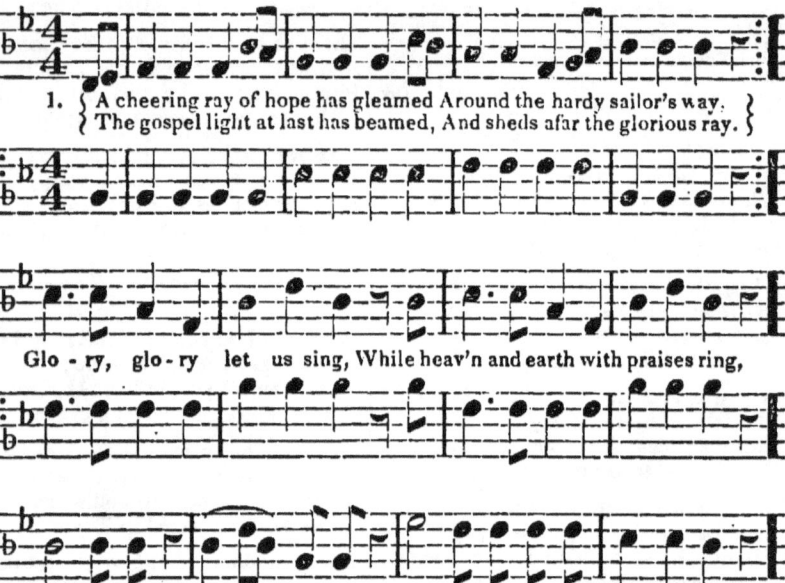

1. A cheering ray of hope has gleamed Around the hardy sailor's way.
The gospel light at last has beamed, And sheds afar the glorious ray.

Glo-ry, glo-ry let us sing, While heav'n and earth with praises ring,

Ho-san-na! ho-san-na. Ho-san-na to the Lamb of God.

Allegretto.

Glo-ry, glo-ry let us sing While heaven and earth with paises ring,

OCEAN MELODIES.

Ho-san-na! ho-san-na! Ho-san-na to the Lamb of God.

On ocean's heaving billows borne,
  The Christian seaman bows in prayer;-
Submissive kneels before the throne,
  And joys to meet his Savior there.
    Glory, glory, &c.

Though winds may howl and tempests beat,
  And lightnings glare, and surges roar,—
He calmly bows at Jesus' feet,
  Nor fears in danger's darkest hour
    Glory, glory, &c.

O let loud songs of praise ascend
  To our exalted, mighty King;
Let heaven and earth in union blend,—
  And every tongue in chorus sing,
    Glory, glory, &c

THE ANGEL OF THE WATERS. C. M.

Words by Mrs. Sigourney. (*The Mellow Horn.*)

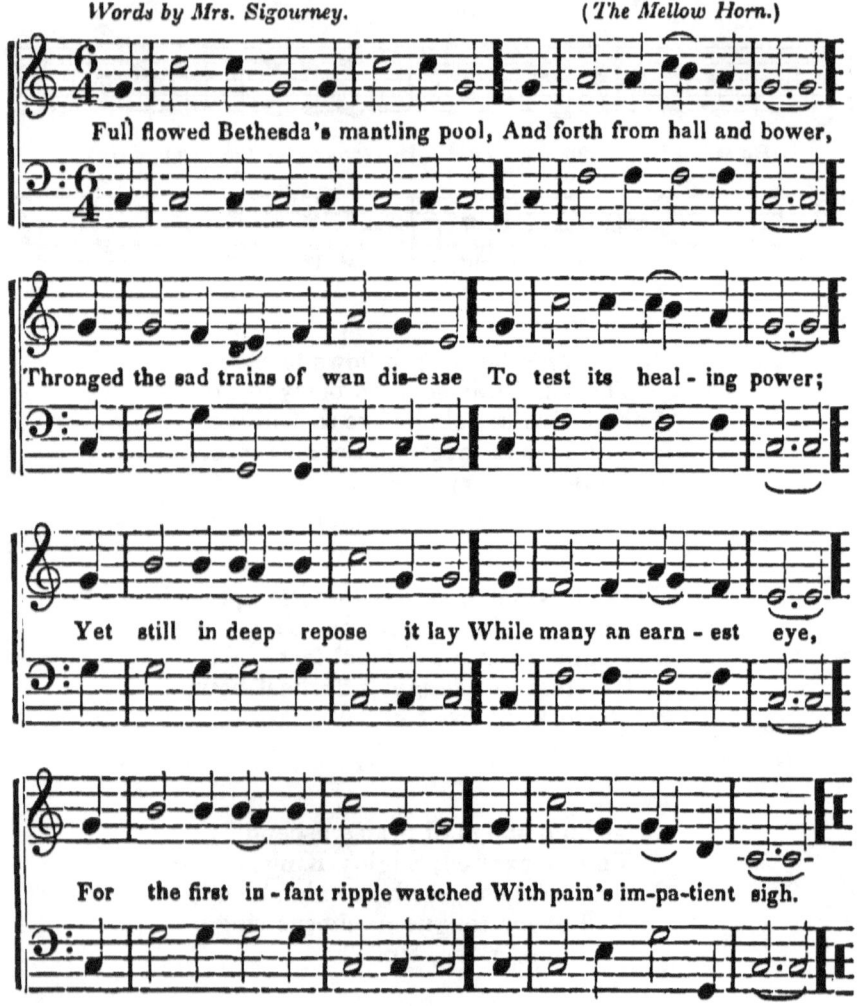

Oh! if the fever of the mind,
  The palsy of the brain,
Should smite us, Father, till we find,
  All earthly helpers vain,—
Send forth thine angel to the stream,
  That holy health can give,
And bid him stir its blessed wave,
  That we may bathe and live

Still, for the ocean's suffering sons,
  Who oft in darkness pine,—
Incite our pity and our prayers,
  And wake a zeal divine,
Till we their poverty enrich
  With heaven's eternal gem,—
And what the angel did for us,
  Delighted do for them.

God's Protection.
BY J. H. H.

O'er raging waves, thou mighty God,
  When rolling thunders pealed,
We've seen thy wonders spread abroad,—
  Thy glorious might revealed;
In darkest hour of deep despair,
  When billows towered on high,
Our God in mercy stooped to hear
  The humble sailor's cry.

CHRIST STILLING THE TEMPEST. C. M.

Words by Mrs. Hemans. (*Majesty.*)

1. Fear was with-in the tossing bark, When stormy winds grew loud, And waves came roll-ing high and dark, And the tall masts were bowed; And men stood breathless in their dread, And baffled in their skill; But One was there who rose and said To the wild sea, "Be still." But One was there, &c.

Then slumber settled on the deep,
    And silence on the blast;
As when the righteous falls asleep;—
    When death's fierce throes are past.
Thou that didst rule the angry hour,
    And tame the tempest's mood—
O send thy Spirit forth in power,
    O'er our dark souls to brood.

Christ revealeth the gospel.
BY N. COLVER.

God of the land and rolling flood,
    Throughout thy wide domain,
Thy works proclaim the mighty God,—
    But *not* the Savior's reign;
The raging storm, the heaving flood,
    The sun that shines above,
Proclaim the wise and powerful God,—
    But not a Savior's love.

The gospel only can impart
    The knowledge of thy grace;
No light can reach and cheer the heart
    But from a Savior's face;
O let the sons of ocean be
    Converted to the Lord;
Then shall they bear to realms of death,
    The knowledge of thy word.

OCEAN MELODIES. 191

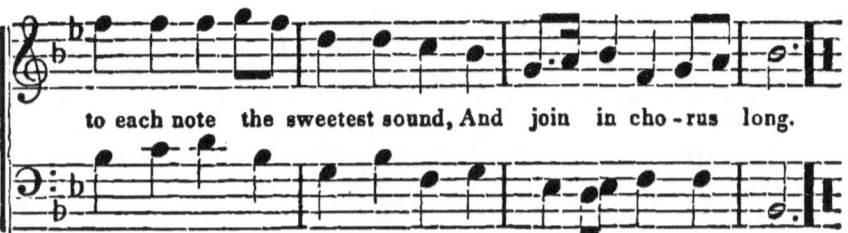

to each note the sweetest sound, And join in cho-rus long.

Ye children of the heavenly King,
   Away with doubts and fears;
Trust in the mighty arm above,
   And dry your falling tears.

He safely brought you on the way,
   When foes could not molest;
He swept the host of Egypt's King,
   That Israel might be blest.

Then from the willows take your harp!
   Which on them hung so long;
With timbrel and melodious voice,
   Join all the happy throng.

Soon will your tasks and marches cease,
   When Shur and Maron lie,
And Canaan, too, will all be left
   For promised lands on high.

OCEAN MELODIES. 193

meet to part no more, When we meet to part no more, On Canaan's happy shore, 'Tis there we'll meet at Je-sus' feet, When we meet to part no more.

Should earth against my soul engage,
 And hellish darts be hurled,
Then I can smile at satan's rage,
 And face a frowning world.
  O that will be, &c,
Let cares, like a wild deluge, come,
 And storms of sorrow fall;
May I but safely reach my home,
 My God, my heaven, my all.
  O that will be, &c.
There shall I bathe my weary soul
 In seas of heavenly rest,
And not a wave of trouble roll
 Across my peaceful breast,
  O that will be, &c.
When we've been there ten thousand years,
 Bright shining as the sun,
We've no less days to sing God's praise,
 Than when we first begun.
  O that will be, &c.

PILOT ON THE DEEP. C. M. (DOUBLE.)

1. Oh! Pi-lot, 'tis a fear-ful night, There's dan-ger on the deep; I'll come and pace the deck with thee, I do not dare to sleep. "Go down," the sai-lor cried, "go down, this is no place for thee; Fear

OCEAN MELODIES.

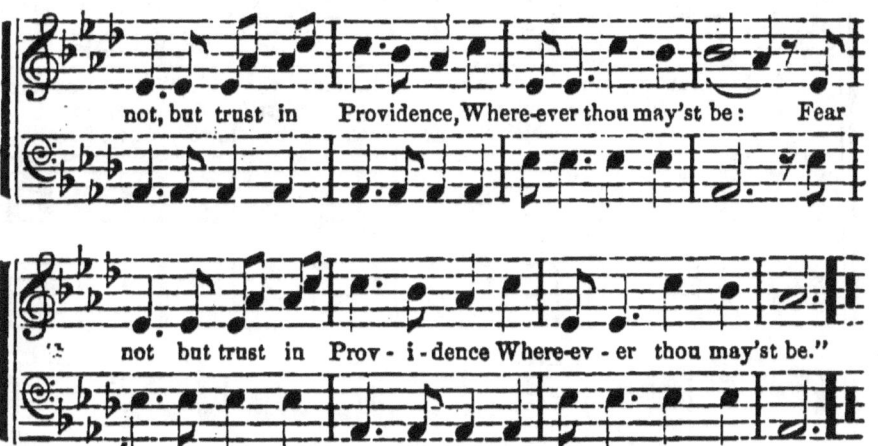

not, but trust in Providence, Where-ever thou may'st be: Fear not but trust in Prov-i-dence Where-ev-er thou may'st be."

Oh, Pilot, dangers often met,
  We all are apt to slight;
And thou hast known these raging waves,
  But to subdue their might.
"It is not apathy," he cried,
  "That gives this strength to me:
Fear not, but trust in Providence,
  Where ever thou may'st be.

On such a night the sea engulfed
  My father's lifeless form;
My only brother's boat went down,
  In just so wild a storm.
And such perhaps may be my fate,
  But still I say to thee,
Fear not, but trust in Providence,
  Where ever thou may'st be."

HOMEWARD BOUND.

1. Out on an o-cean all boundless we ride, We're homeward
Tossed on the waves of a rough restless tide, We're, &c.
Promise of which on us each he be-stowed, We're, &c.

bound, homeward bound. Far from the safe quiet har-bor we've rode,
Seeking our Father's ce-les-tial a-bode.

2 Wildly the storm sweeps us on as it roars, We're, &c.
Look! yonder lie the bright heavenly shores, We're, &c.
Steady, O pilot! stand firm at the wheel,
Steady! we soon shall outweather the gale,
O how we fly 'neath the loud creaking sail, We're, &c.

3 Into the harbor of heaven now we glide, We're, home at last, &c.
Softly we drift on its bright silver tide, We're, &c.
Glory to God! all our dangers are o'er,
We stand secure on the glorified shore,
Glory to God, we will shout evermore, We're, &c.

MELODIES.

Home at last. 10s & 5s.

We live as pilgrims and strangers below,
  We're homeward bound;
Though often tempted, yet onward we go,
  We're homeward bound.
Trials and crosses we cheerfully bear,
Toils and temptations expecting to share,
We hasten forward, content with the fare,
  We're homeward bound.

Earth with its trifles we all have resigned,
  We're homeward bound;
Heaven, with its glories, we shortly shall find,
  We're homeward bound.
Sinful amusements no longer are dear,
O how delusive and vain they appear,
While to our home we are drawing so near,
  We're homeward bound.

We'll go rejoicing in God every day,
  We're homeward bound;
Shout hallelujah along by the way,
  We're homeward bound.
Millions have travelled this pathway before,
Entered their rest, when their labors are o'er;
Soon we shall meet them to part never more,
  We're homeward bound.

We'll tell the world as we journey along,
  We're homeward bound;
Try to persuade them to enter our throng,
  We're homeward bound.
Come, trembling sinner, forlorn and opprest,
Join in our number, O come, and be blest;
Journey with us to the mansions of rest,
  We're homeward bound.

Soon we'll be singing, if faithful we prove,
  We're home at last!
Sounding in triumph in mansions above,
  We're home at last.
Soon as our toils and temptations are o'er,
Up to our home with the blest we shall soar;
O how we'll shout as we enter the door,
  We're home at last.

Longing for Heaven. 7 & 6.

1 O when shall I see Jesus,
  And reign with him above,
And from that flowing fountain,
  Drink everlasting love?
When shall I be delivered
  From this vain world of sin,
And with my blessed Jesus,
  Drink endless pleasure in?

2 But now I am a soldier,
  My Captain's gone before:
He's given me my orders,
  And bid me not give o'er.
If I continue faithful,
  A righteous crown he'll give,
And all his valiant soldiers,
  Eternal life shall have.

3 Through grace I am determined
  To conquer though I die,
And then away to Jesus
  On wings of love I'll fly.
Farewell to sin and sorrow,
  I bid you all adieu;
And O, my friends, prove faithful,
  And on your way pursue.

4 And if you meet with troubles
  And trials on your way,
Then cast your care on Jesus,
  And don't forget to pray;
Gird on your heavenly armor
  Of faith, and hope, and love.
And when the combat's ended
  He'll carry you above.

Power of a Mother's name. 10s.

The following lines were suggested on reading a touching incident related of a convict just entering Sing Sing prison, who seemed to be regardless of the pertinent interrogatories of the kindhearted warden, till the name of his mother fell upon his guilty ears. The name of his parent filled his soul with the deepest emotions of sorrow, and he implored the warden not to 'mention her name in that dreadful place! Do what you may with me, but don't mention *that* name to me!'

There's magic power in a mother's name,
To kindle souls into a glowing flame;
It bids the waves of woe or joy to roll,
In all their might, upon a deathless soul.

Behold, the convict stands, with form erect, [pect,
Gaily attired; who would this youth sus-
That one so brilliant could so tho'tless be,
And plunge himself in crime's dark raging sea?

Buoyant and reckless his replies were made. [played
While in his eyes, and o'er his features
A scornful smile, 'till the kind warden spoke [was broke.
His mother's name: then, then, his heart

His mother's name unlocks the fount of tears;
He calls to mind the sunny months and years, [given,
When on his cheek the kiss of love was
By her whose heart with anguish now is riven.

'My mother's name! O utter not that sound! [surrounds;
Now guilt's dark pal, my brightest hopes
A name too sweet to echo in this place;
Where the mute walls now trumpet my disgrace.

Load me with fetters, let me toil in pain,
But mention not that balmy, precious name, [soul,
Let 'grievous words' fall on my guilty
Soft words molest—and bid dark billows roll.

My mother's name! it brings with vivid power [dower,)
Her slighted counsels, (mother's richest
Bestowed in vain upon her wayward son,
Whose course in folly, has to ruin run.

O that my mind in fetters could be bound,
But this, alas! can never be confined;
It soars above my massive prison walls,
And bids me hear my mother's winning calls.

'Her mellow voice now lingers on my ears,
And oft will make the bitter, scalding tears
In torrents from my youthful eyes to flow,
While musing on my cup of gall and woe.

'Mother, thy name is precious, while it brings [stings;
Remorse of conscience, with its thousand
Tho' dismal clouds around my pathway are, [Star.
Yet on this path there shines one *lovely*

'In angel robes, my mother, you will come,
To cheer my spirit in my gloomy home,
Unlock each gate, and ope each bolted door,
And on my soul the myrrh of love will pour.

'Then breathe her name, kind warden, when you may,
A bow of beauty o'er my mind will play,
Tinged with the rays of mother's tireless love,
That lures my heart to brighter scenes above.   P. S.

OCEAN MELODIES.

The Power of Hope. 10s.

BY P. STOW.

The allusion in the following Poem has been thought pertinent to this "golden age," although ten years have elapsed since it was composed.

Sweet bow of promise! thy propitious
    beam   [theme,
Shines from afar, my bright and lovely
In every age thy sovereign sway confest,
Controls the movement of the human
    breast;
In every clime, thy magic power imparts
A charm to soothe the anguish of our
    hearts,
A light to cheer, an enterprize to dare,
A strength to toil, and fortitude to bear.

Thy power is felt in childhood's sunny
    days,
A ray of beauty round our pathway plays,
Throws its soft light o'er earth's delicious things,   [springs;
And leaves the soul to joy's prolific
The youthful bosom warms beneath its
    ray,   [day;
And hails to-morrow brighter than to-
In future prospects that before him rise,
More dazzling splendors cheer his youthful eyes.

On, on he bounds o'er life's enchanted
    plain,   [in vain.
Nor deems these splendors charm his eye
Manhood is reached, and still the glittering light   sight:
Unfolds strange beauty to his ravished
Hope draws him onward with resistless
    power,
Go seek repose within her loveliest bower;
Then cull the sweets that breathe on
    every side,   [foliage glide.
And quaff the streams that through the

And while he rests him in his fond embrace,
Imbibe fresh vigor for his future race.

  *   *   *   *   *

The hope of wealth prompts myriads to
    endure
All toil, all suffering, *riches* to secure;
That golden goddess at whose shrine
    they bend,
Forgetful of their being's highest end:
Thousands have left New England's
    peaceful shore,   [ore.
And crossed the deep in quest of glittering
Far from their native land and childhood's home,   [roam;
O'er dangerous seas and deadly climes to
Hope still before them like a meteor's
    ray,   [prey.
Lured to the spot where death awaits his

  *   *   *   *   *

If hope so strongly moves the human
    breast,   [point of rest!
How vast its power, when *Heaven*, its
When round the bleeding Saviour's cross
    it clings,
And rising with him, soars with outspread wings;
New-plumed, the soul now eyes the joys
    of Heaven,   [riven;
And calmness fills the heart by sorrow
A holy light irradiates the gloom
That once o'erhung the passage to the
    tomb.

Immortal hope! I see thy hand unfold
Celestial visions to yon Christian's soul;
Even while he grapples with the arm of
    Death,   [breath;
The shout of victory swells his latest
Thine, thine it is to light thy glorious fire,
And triumph when all other hopes expire.

The Burning Ship. L. M. P. S.

The Ship, Thomas P. Cope, of Philadelphia, on her way to Liverpool in 1846, was struck by lightning on the third day from port. She had on board over seventy souls. They were on the burning ship six days and seven gloomy nights, expecting every moment that the flames would devour them. In this perilous condition they were discovered by the ship Emigrant, and all saved except a little girl, 6 years old, the mother was not able to carry both of her children on deck at once, she had but just time to escape with her dear boy. The seamen were in the act of putting on the hatches to prevent the flames from spreading, as she came up the hatchway. It was heart rending to listen to her tale of sorrow.

The noble ship glides swiftly o'er
The pathless sea to a foreign shore;
Her flowing pennons proudly wave,
O'er noble hearts, all true and brave.

But see those clouds, they warring meet,
And battle o'er the mighty deep;
The lightnings flash, and thunders peal,
Vast ocean heaves, and seamen reel.

The brilliant stars, the queen of night,
From periled strangers hide their light,
While forked lightnings o'er them play;
Their lurid glare wraps night in day.

The vivid gleam now speeds its way;
That splendid ship is wrapt in spray;
The shock is o'er, the flames arise—
"The ship's on fire!" the captain cries.

That piercing cry filled hearts with grief.
Where shall they flee to find relief?
The boundless ocean's mighty flood,
Stays not the fire that's sent of God.

Alarm and fear now fill each soul;—
Still tempests roar, and thunders roll,
While flame and smoke ascend around,
And billows dash, and waves resound.

A mother rushes from her berth;
In wild dismay she gasps for breath!
She folds her children in her arms,
To snatch from death their tender forms.

What tongue can tell that mother's wo,
For that dear one that's left below?
Alone she dies, in black despair,
'Mid all a mother's tender care.

All human power and wails were vain
To quench that fire o'er ocean's main;
Amid the gloom of th' raging sea,
The Cope in flames alone must be.

The burning ship still sadly rides;
O'er the blue deep she swiftly glides;
Heeds not the shrieks and wild dismay,
As trembling hearts now weep and pray.

When waning hope had almost died,
The Cope on fire a seaman spied,
Far off upon the foaming deep,
Where heaving billows never sleep.

Behold! the Emigrant draws nigh,
To give relief to those who sigh!
Her generous Captain, noble crew,
The burning ship in haste pursue.

But see! the mighty billows foam,
And rising hopes oft sink in gloom;
An angry sea,—a ship on fire,
Successive wake forebodings dire.

That kind relief is near at hand,
Yet some of this dejected band,
Must linger on the burning Cope,
Till sea subsides and gives fresh hope.

What language can that scene portray,
Of each dark night and cheerless day?
The hours of grief; what tongue can tell,
What hopes one *flash of light* may kill.

OCEAN MELODIES.

Loss of the Atlantic.

The Steamer Atlantic was lost on Thanksgiving day, in 1846 on her way to New York. Capt. Dustan, the intrepid commander, said, "If the Atlantic goes, I go with her." He and many *loved ones* found a watery grave; and her bell by a singular providence, was tolled mournfully by the wind and waves after their spirits had fled.

While others on the happy shore
  Made merry jubilee,
Ye heard the thunder-surges roar,
  Far on the cold night sea.

The darkness of that night's despair,
  The coldness of each breast,
Were deepened by the moonlit air
  Which showed your bed of rest.

No downy couch, no gaudy hall
  Invited you to sleep,
Your bed the rock where billows fall,
  Your chambers in the deep.

How gaily sang the wife afar!
  How would have changed her tone,
If by that evening's rising star
  Her husband's doom were known.

Oh! lips on land wore gladdest guise,
  And hearts throbbed wild with glee,
While pallid cheeks and ghastly eyes
  Found death upon the sea.

And streaming eyes are mourning now,
  That festal's fatal close,
Which bound in blood the kindred brow
  Of some which wore the rose.

And he, the fearless martyr there,
  Who shared his vessel's tomb,
Who may unmoved the tidings bear
  That tell of Dustan's doom?

A seaman's honor his the fame
  Of all that dare to die;
Not strangers may repeat his name.
  And wear a tearless eye.

The shadow of his gloomy death
  May well make manhood weep;
But where can seaman spend his breath,
  More fit than on the deep.

Farewell, brave heart! though drearily,
  Went down my sun at even;
I ask no nobler death for me
  To bear my soul to heaven.

"The sea hath spoken." S. M.

The following hymn was sung at the funeral solemnities in Marblehead, occasioned by the loss of 11 vessels belonging to that town, with sixty-five men and boys, in a single gale in 1846.

God of the Mariner,
  We raise our prayers to thee;
Friend of the fatherless, a voice
  Comes o'er the deep, dark sea:—
Where the wild billows rave
  Far mid the angry deep,
There have they found a watery grave,
  For them we mourn and weep—
Those whom we loved the most,
  Father and brother dear,
Those who were once our joy and boast,
  No more our homes will cheer
Our heavenly Saviour, hear!
  We raise our prayers to thee,
Friend of the poor and destitute,
  God of the mighty Sea.
Thus o'er the waves of grief
  Which in our bosoms swell,
Come with thy sweet relief and love,
  And all our sorrow quell.

'I heard a voice from Heaven.' S. M.

I heard a voice from heaven
  Say, "Blessed is the home
Of those whose trust is in the Lord,
  When sinking to the tomb."

The Holy Spirit spake—
  And I the words repeat—
"Blessed are they,"—for, after toil,
  To mortals rest is sweet.

The War-Ship of Peace. C. M.

The famine in Ireland of 1847, induced the benevolent Americans to send speedy relief to this land of sorrow and death. The United States Ship, Jamestown, Capt. R. B. Forbes, commander, made a remarkable short passage across the ocean; the winds of heaven were auspicious for their work of humanity. The following lines were composed on her arrival in Cork, by SAMUEL LOVER.

Sweet land of song, thy harp doth hang
 Upon the willows now,
While famine's blight and fever's pang
 Stamp misery on thy brow.

Yet, take thy harp and raise thy voice,
 Though faint and low it be,
And let thy sinking heart rejoice
 In friends, still left to thee.

Look out, look out across the sea
 That girds thy emerald shore,
A ship of war is bound for thee,
 But with no warlike store.

Her thunder sleeps,—'tis Mercy's breath
 That wafts her o'er the sea,
She goes not forth to deal out death,
 But bears new life to thee.

Thy wasted hand can scarcely strike
 The chords of grateful praise;
Thy plaintive tone is now unlike
 Thy voice of prouder days.

Yet, even in sorrow, tuneful still
 Let Erin's voice proclaim
In bardic praise on every hill
 Columbia's glorious name.

The Heroic Sailor. S. M.

The circumstances here related, took place during the great fire in the city of New York, on the night of December 16, 1836.

It was a fearful night!
 The fire devouring spread
From roof to roof, from street to street,
 And on their treasures fed.

Hark! 'tis a mother's cry,
 Shrill mid the tumult wild, |home,
As rushing toward her flame-wrapped
 She shrieks, "My child! my child!"

A wanderer from the wave,
 A sailor marked her woe,
And in his feeling bosom woke
 The sympathetic glow.

Quick up the cleaving stairs,
 With daring step he flew,
Though sable clouds of stifling smoke
 Concealed him from their view.

The astonished crowd beheld
 His bold, adventurous part,
And while they for his safety feared,
 Admired his noble heart.

For blazing timbers fell
 To choke his dangerous road,
And the far chamber where he groped
 Like reeking oven glowed.

How loud the exulting shout!
 When from that mass of flame,
Unhurt, unshrinking, undismayed,
 The brave deliverer came.

While in his victor arms
 A smiling infant lay,
Pleased with the flash that round his bed
 Had wound its glittering ray.

The mother's speechless tears,
 Forth like a torrent sped,
Yet ere the throng could learn his name,
 That generous hero fled.

Not for the praise of man
 He wrought this deed of love,
But on a bright, unfading page,
 'Tis registered above.

To the Sailor Boy. L. M.
Tune.—WARD.

The following lines were recently addressed by a lady, to a young friend about to embark for California.

Again thou leavest thy youthful home,
 The home of all life's purest joy—
Upon the treacherous sea to roam,
 A free, defenceless sailor boy.

Thou leavest *her*, whose changeless love
 No time, no distance can destroy,
Whose prayer, sent every hour above,
 Will be, 'God bless my sailor-boy!'

Thou goest from the guardian eye,
 That wearies not in love's employ;
But, there's a Father in the sky,
 That still will watch the sailor-boy.

Not easier love embraceth thee
 In its maternal pride and joy,
Than heaven's wide arms unfold the sea,
 To guard and bless the sailor-boy.

Not easier thy desires expressed
 A father's bounty now enjoy,
Than will thy prayer to heaven confessed,
 A blessing bring the sailor-boy.

When slippery shrouds thy feet shall climb,
 When peril's task thy hands employ;
When ocean is with storms sublime,
 O God, protect the sailor-boy!

When glittering dust attracts thine eye,
 O, turn to gold without alloy—
Search truth's deep mine where riches lie,
 That will reward the sailor-boy.

Let sordid minds and grasping hands,
 The Sacramento's treasures cloy;
There is a stream whose "golden sands"
 Can richer make the sailor-boy.

Go search, and that true wealth obtain
 Which moth and dust do not destroy,
And, till home's welcome rings again,
 God keep and bless the sailor-boy!

The Ballad of the Tempest. 8s & 7s.
Tune.—SICILY.

The following beautiful gem of poetry is taken from a volume of poems, by James T. Fields, just published in Boston. It is the most exquisite ballad we have met for a long while.

We were crowded in the cabin,
 Not a soul would dare to sleep,—
It was midnight on the waters,
 And a storm was on the the deep.

'Tis a fearful thing in winter
 To be shattered in the blast,
And to hear the rattling trumpet
 Thunder, "Cut away the mast!"

So we shuddered there in silence,—
 For the stoutest held his breath,
While the hungry sea was roaring,
 And the breakers talked with death.

As thus we sat in darkness,
 Each one busy in his prayers,—
"We are lost!" the Captain shouted,
 As he staggered down the stairs.

But his little daughter whispered,
 As she took his icy hand,
"Isn't God upon the ocean,
 Just the same as on the land?"

Then we kissed the little maiden,
 And we spoke in better cheer,
And we anchored safe in harbor,
 When the moon was shining clear.

TRIBUTE OF RESPECT
TO CAPTAIN DANIEL TRACY,

On his leaving Boston to take the superintendence of the "Sailor's Home," in Cherry Street, New York, May 1, 1853. By PHINEAS STOWE.

Blessed Saviour! we will praise thee
  For thy free undying love;
Depth it hath no mind can fathom;
  Mercy drew Thee from above,
    Great Redeemer!
May thy grace each bosom move!

We rejoice, that on the waters,
  While from home and kindred dear,
Th' sailor boy's heart was broken
  By the Holy Spirit's power;
    On the ocean.
Light from heaven dispelled his fear.

God hath made him bold and faithful
  To defend the cause of truth,
Shedding light o'er sin's dark ocean,
  Warning giddy, thoughtless youth
    Of those pitfalls
Where are found disease and death.

Go, and kindle, faithful brother,
  Beacon lights in that sweet "Home,"
Send them o'er the deep, dark ocean
  To illume each pagan clime.
    Bid the sailor
Tell how Jesus Christ says "come."

Nobly have you fought that monster;
  One of that illustrious band, *
First to raise the Temperance Standard
  High and fearless around it stand;
    And defend it
On the sparkling sea and land.

We shall miss thee in the Bethel,
  Where we oft have heard thy voice
Warning, urging noble seamen,
  To make Jesus Christ their choice,
    And go forth,
Making all around rejoice.

Long thy name shall be remembered—
  Ocean's sons have blessed the day,
For thy faithful counsels heeded,
  Clouds of sin have passed away;
    Light is shining;
Now they view a glorious day.

Ties of holy love and friendship—
  They can never be dissolved;
We are one in Christ the Righteous
  Toiling for our Well-Beloved;
    He is near us,
And for us he pleads above.

May the blessed Jesus cheer thee—
  Give thee many precious souls
That shall deck thy crown of glory,
  Where no wave of trouble rolls.
    In that ocean,
Endless bliss shall fill our souls.

"Fare-thee-well," shall be our prayer,
  And we hope to meet again
With a noble band of seamen,
  Who have been blood washed from sin,
    In that Bethel,
Where no sin or death shall reign.

* Captain Tracy was one of the first, who formed in Boston, twenty years ago, a Mariner's Temperance Society, called the "Windward Anchor T. S." He has been a bold and able advocate of sobriety from that time till the present.

AFFECTION'S TRIBUTE.
TO LIEUTENANT HENRY ELD, JR.

The following Poem is dedicated to the memory of Lieutenant HENRY ELD, JR., of New Haven, Ct., the much respected and beloved officer of the U. S. Ship-of-the-Line. Ohio. The departed was a member of the United States Exploring Expidition to California and the Southern Ocean, and who first saw the Antarctic Continent, died on his homeward passage, after an absence of three and a half years, and was buried at sea.

A mother's yearning heart of tenderness
Watched for the coming of a home bound sail,
That once again her fervent lips might bless
The child she long had fondly hoped to hail—
That once again her eyes might look upon
  Her long remembered son.

A happy father, too, with joyful pride,
Longed to embrace his gallant boy again,
And counted every hour that slowly died,
Ere yet the 'good ship' came from o'er the main,
And a beloved sister's heart was yearning
  For his long-hoped returning.

Long had he wandered far from scenes he loved,
Amid deep Western wilds his footsteps lay,—
By many a broad and noble stream had roved,
And climbed the rugged mountain's dangerous way,
New features on Columbia's chart to trace
  Of fair Creation's face.

And he had visited the spicy Isles,
Beneath the ardent sun's perpetual eye,
And gathered from their gorgeous beauty, spoils
To deck the pleasant Halls of Memory—
Remembrances of sunny climes, and hours
  Among their forest flowers.

And far across the Southern sea he sped
His careful way, where ne'er before the sail
Of venturous navigator dared to spread
Its waving whiteness to the frosty gale—
And, from afar *his eye was first* to view
  A country broad and new!

Much had he suffered, when the torrid sun
His strength had withered, and oppressed his brain—
And when the freezing blast came shrieking on,
To thwart his passage of the icy main—
And oft he feared the passing hour would sever
  Life's trembling chord forever.

And thrice had weary sickness laid him low
Upon the troubled couch of feverish pain—
And days and nights of anguish measured slow
Their length upon the prostrate sufferer's chain;
Yet oft bright visions to his heart would come
  Of his far happy home.

But once again, with health's returning smile,
The torch of Hope was lighted in his eye—
And nights of gloom, and days of tedious toil,
Were all forgotten, as the hour drew nigh,
That saw him safely spread the homeward sail
  To woo the homeward gale.

Fallacious Hope! ere yet the days were numbered,
That should have borne him to his native land,
The angel Death breathed o'er him as he slumbered,
And on his brow impressed a marble hand—
And lo! that noble spirit from its home of clay
  For aye had passed away.

Far from his home he found an ocean grave,
Proud to engulf him in its billowy bed—
Beneath Equator's deeply heaving wave,
With bitter grief, was plunged the sheated dead
And o'er the waters boomed the solemn gun,
  That told their task was done.

And sadly then the noble ship rolled on
Her homeward course, to tell the tearful tale--
To bear sad tidings of that precious one—
To bring a father's groan, a mother's wail---
And o'er a household's glowing hopes, to spread
  The drapery of the dead!

Oh! fearful hour, that brought to those fond hearts
The gloomy tidings of their blighted hope!
And keenly yet its memory imparts
An anguish that with time shall ever cope ;—
Yet mourn, not faithlessly—an angel stands
To point your tearful eyes to loftier lands!
The Lord hath given,—sorrowing mourner say
  "*Shall He not take away?*"

OCEAN MELODIES.

Death and Burial of Rev. Adoniram Judson, D. D. at Sea.

Almost the last words of this great and good man, were "Bury me, bury me, quick, quick,"— and his voice failed. The author of the following lines has supplied the expression, "In the sea," to the impressive request of the dying Christian. It may, or it may not have been his wish to be buried in the deep. His wide grave however, is emblematical of the vast moral influence he has had in arousing a slumbering world to the subject of foreign missions, in which sublime cause he had devoted over thirty years of untiring toil to promote. He expressed his views freely of the vast importance of converted mariners in the work of evangelizing the world. He was a friend to seamen, and they with others, performed the last sad office of committing his cold remains to the bosom of the "great and wide sea." His last words suggested the lines dedicated to his memory.

BY P. STOW.   11s.

"Bury me, bury me, quick, quick,"—in the sea!
Thy grave will be far from the "Hopia Tree,"
And far from the "Rock,*" where the loved is at rest,
The ocean beneath her, the turf on her breast.

"Bury me, bury me, quick, quick,"—in the sea,
It's the emblem of One who died on the Tree."—
Thy grave it is boundless, and pure like his throne,
And o'er it he mirrors the work he hath done.

"Bury me, bury me, quick, quick," — in the sea!   [thee?
What tomb could be chosen more fitted for
Thou loved the bright sea and o'er it had sailed,
To the land where gross darkness long had prevailed.

The champion has fallen! life's battle is o'er,
He's landed above on the victor's bright shore;
Where death cannot enter, no foe can affright,
In that "mansion prepared," all, all is delight.

Sublime was thy life,—and the wide ocean grave.
Both blending in one, to embalm and engrave
Deep, deep on the heart, thy works in dark climes,
Where the Lamp of Salvation brightly now shines.

The word of Immanuel by thee spread abroad,
Will gladden the gloomy with smiles from the Lord;
Yes, millions shall bow to the might of that power,

"Bury me, bury me, quick, quick," in the sea;
From toil and from sorrow the loved one is free;
Thy anchor is cast in the sea of God's love,
Thy soul on bright pinions is carried above.

Yes, they buried thee quick in the cold blue deep,
At the calm hour of eve, when the winds were asleep,
Around thee were gathered the true and the brave,
And tears of affection were shed o'er thy grave.

The waves that roll over the noble one's form,
The calm breath of summer, and the loud howling storm,
O'er the jewel we've lost, their requiem sung;
Will waft the sad sound to each kindred and tongue.

That cheered thy rapt soul in death's trying hour.

In the deep, dark ocean thy body shall rest;
Till the archangel's trump shall sound its loud blast;
Then, from thy wide tomb thy body shall rise,
With myriads of "Burmese" ascend the bright skies.

How joyous the greeting, when loved ones shall meet
On the banks of deliverance, with melody sweet,
And chant all in union the Lamb's dying love,
In crowning, and saving, the ransomed above.

* Dr. Judson's second wife was buried at St. Helena.

OCEAN MELODIES.

Requiem on the death of a Mariner. 11s.
Tune.—Araby's Daughter.

The following beautiful and appropriate lines were composed by Mr. B. S. HALL, on the death of Mr. GEORGE O. BATES, of Springfield, Mass., who perished at sea, January, 26, 1849. His ship was run into in the night, and most of the crew died from exposure.

O! cold is the night wind, and loud blows the gale,
And the sailor boy's brow mid the tempest is pale;
Yet his heart groweth warm, for his thoughts are afar,
And the home of his childhood beams forth like a star,

The gallant ship plows through her homeward bound path,
But the storm-god hath ROUSED in his fury and wrath,
Her sails catch the winds, and now onward she flies—
"O, fly to my home!" the lone sailor boy cries.

Wo! wo! sailor boy! for the angel of death
Is seen on the storm-cloud, and chill is his breath.
There's danger, poor sailor boy, on the dark sea;
A death-knell is ringing, lone sufferer, for thee.

The home of thy childhood is lonely—oh, there
Thy mother hath knelt in anguish in prayer,
There's weight on her heart — in sorrow she cries,
O, save the poor wanderer, tossed o'er the dark waves.

The voice of her loved one, with terror is wild,
The cold waves are dashing the form of her child—
He is freezing! oh God! his pale brow is now chilled!
The terrors of Death his young heart hath filled.

"My God! must I die, when my home is so near?
My father, my mother, are waiting me there;
Dear home of my childhood — so happy and free,
Where sweet buds and blossoms are blooming for me."

No refuge is near him—and vain are his cries;

No human power meets him, to cheer his sad eyes:
He sits in his anguish all suffering and lone,
And the night winds can only repeat his sad moan.

But hark! there's a voice! sweet and soothing it falls,
A POWER hath been touched that responds to his calls;
A form full of MERCY is walking the wave,
He cometh, poor sufferer, thy spirit to save!

"Thou hast sinned—hast repented—and pardon is given,
And a home brighter far shall be thine now in heaven;
Lay thy head on my bosom—my son thou art free!
No more shall the earth, with its snares compass thee."

The form thou hast cherished lies deep in its grave,
And over its bosom the dark sea doth wave;
They sing his requiem in tones deep and sad,
But the soul of thy loved one is happy and glad.

The iron hath entered thy bosom, and now
In sorrow and anguish of spirit ye bow;
Yet the angel of hope whispers peace unto thee,
Trust — trust in His promise who ruleth the sea.

For the sea by His power shall give up its dead,
And that loved one with joy shall leave his dark bed;
All clad in soft raiment, that dear one shall rise,
The same! 'tis thy lost one; that greets thy glad eyes.

"Come hither, ye blessed — dwell near to my throne.
Thy tears are all vanished, thy sorrows are gone,
Ye shall drink of a fountain that never can dry,"
Then onward! and upward! thy home is on high!

BURIAL SERVICE AT SEA.

In preparing for this solemn duty, let the body of the deceased person be laid on the deck in a coffin or hammock, as the case may be; and when all are orderly assembled around, the person appointed to perform the service may read the following select portions from the Bible.

I am the resurrection and the life, saith the Lord; he that believeth in me, though he were dead yet shall he live. And whosoever liveth and believeth in me, shall never die. *John* xi. 25, 26. As by one man, sin entered into the world, and death by sin; so death passed upon all men, for all have sinned. *Rom.* 5. 12. It is appointed unto men once to die, but after this, the judgment. *Heb.* 9. 27. We must all appear before the judgment-seat of Christ, that every one may receive the things done in his body, according to that he hath done, whether it be good or bad. 2 *Cor.* 5. 10. My days are swifter than a weaver's shuttle, swifter than a post they flee away. They are passed away as the swift ships; as the eagle that hasteth to the prey. *Job.* 7. 6. *Job* 9. 25 26. There is but a step between me and death; Lord, make me to know mine end, and the measure of my days, what it is, that I may know how frail I am. *Ps.* 39. 4. Watch and pray, for ye know not the day nor the hour when the Son of man cometh. Be ye also ready. *Matt.* 25. 13.—24. 44.

This may be followed by a short exhortation, suggested by the feelings of the speaker; or the following may be read.

My dear friends. we see here the end to which we are hastening. Death is what we must all come to at last. Death has come into our little company, and ushered our shipmate and friend into the presence of God, and to the amazing scenes of eternity. It is a solemn thing to exchange worlds. Yet there is no discharge in that war. This is a change we never pass but once. None return to tell us what they have experienced in the other world. All we know of it comes by the testimony of God, in the Bible. There is no opportunity to correct our mistakes. If we are wrong once, we are wrong forever. Let us profit by the admonitions of mortality. Let us lay it to heart that we must die. Soon we shall close the voyage of life, and then launch into the boundless ocean of eternity.

Here a hymn may be sung, or the funeral service begin here. When all hands are ready to launch the body over-board, the Leader may say,

Forasmuch as it hath pleased Almighty God, in his wise providence, to take out of this world the soul of our deceased shipmate and friend, we therefore commit his body to the deep, looking for the resurrection of the body, when the sea shall give up her dead; when the corruptible bodies of those who sleep in Jesus, shall be changed and made like unto his glorious body, according to the mighty working whereby he is able to subdue all things unto himself; and where the wicked also shall awake and come forth to shame and everlasting contempt.

Here launch the body overboard, let it have time to go down, and then all fall on their knees, while the leader makes the following prayer.

O merciful God, the Father of our Lord Jesus Christ, who is the resurrection and the life; in whomsoever believeth, shall live though he die; and whosoever liveth and believeth on him, shall not die eternally; we humbly beseech thee, O Father, to raise us from the death of sin unto the life of righteousness; that when we shall depart this life, we may rest in him; and that at the general resurrection in the last day, we may be found acceptable in thy sight; and receive that blessing which thy well-beloved Son shall then pronounce to all who love and fear thee, saying, Come, ye blessed children of my Father, receive the kingdom prepared for you from the beginning of the world. Grant this, we beseech thee, O merciful Father, through Jesus Christ, our Mediator and Redeemer. *Amen.*

Close the solemn services with remarks, or singing a hymn on the 82, 76, 85, 87, 109, 116th, or 143d page of this Book.

www.ingramcontent.com/pod-product-compliance
Lightning Source LLC
Chambersburg PA
CBHW020904230426
43666CB00008B/1301